Richard Hofmaier
Marketing, Sales and Customer Management (MSC)

Richard Hofmaier

Marketing, Sales and Customer Management (MSC)

───

An Integrated Overall B2B Management Approach

DE GRUYTER
OLDENBOURG

ISBN 978-3-11-041025-9
e-ISBN (PDF) 978-3-11-041026-6
e-ISBN (EPUB) 978-3-11-041255-0

Library of Congress Cataloging-in-Publication Data
A CIP catalog record for this book has been applied for at the Library of Congress.

Bibliographic information published by the Deutsche Nationalbibliothek
The Deutsche Nationalbibliothek lists this publication in the Deutsche
Nationalbibliografie; detailed bibliographic data are available in the Internet
at http://dnb.dnb.de.

© 2015 Walter de Gruyter GmbH, Berlin/Munich/Boston
Cover illustration: Idea: Prof. Dr. Richard Hofmaier / Compiled: Irina Apetrei
Typesetting: Michael Peschke, Berlin
Printing: CPI books GmbH, Leck
♾ Printed on acid free paper
Printed in Germany

www.degruyter.com

Preface

This book introduces a modern and future-oriented marketing approach for national and international small, medium-sized and large enterprises in all business-to-business (B2B) industries, which includes the necessary explicit **integration of marketing, sales and customer management (MSC)**.

The relevant integrative **analysis** and **strategy methods** are presented herein, as well as the derived **programs**, **measures** and **tasks** of an integrated marketing, sales and customer management – integrated in a holistic context and frame of reference. In addition, there is the detailed discussion of operational policies and tools in terms of their specific use, control, feedback and continuous improvement. Thus, a **long-term**, **sustainable** and **successful application** of the identified measures, methods and procedures is possible, which was confirmed and substantiated through a variety of hands-on projects and experiences in various national and international B2B industries. In addition, a variety of tools, checklists and practical implementation aids is presented, which should support and facilitate the application and implementation.

Through such an integrative marketing management, a holistic customer focus can be achieved, and the sustainable success of key marketing, sales and customer management measures can be made possible and supported in terms of concepts, tools and implementation, which is not usually possible just by implementing singular measures.

In terms of content, the themes of this book can be divided into the following main parts. In **Part I**, the **overall approach**, its possibilities and advantages of marketing, sales and customer management integration are presented and clarified. Also, it is explained how to recognize corresponding deficits and how to phase them into an integrated approach and further develop them.

Part II describes the **analyses** that need to be done in order to derive and define an integrated marketing, sales and customer management **strategy (Part III)**. This is followed by derived, strategy-based and operational **programs** and **measures** of product and service management as well as product development and innovation management in **Part IV**. In Part IV, the programs, measures, tools and tasks of an integrated sales management are clarified in terms of its sales tools, the respective sales processes, and its optimization and implementation options.

Based on that, **Part V** will discuss the integrated consideration of a no longer negligible holistic **customer relationship management (CRM)**, which explores customer satisfaction management, customer loyalty, business and interpersonal relationship management, customer retention management as well as additional necessary customer loyalty tools, CRM tool management and corresponding implementation options. **Part VI** then illustrates modern, differentiated and potential-based customer development, and focuses specifically on **key account management (KAM)** with its variety of options and possibilities of developing potential customers and the common benefits.

Finally, in **Part VII**, the relatively new approach of an integrated **Focus Group Management (FGM)** will be discussed, with its additional possibilities of business development with select customers, before last, but not least, the concluding and summarizing concept of an efficient marketing, sales and customer **scorecard management** is discussed, which explicitly allows the holistic control and optimization of integrated programs and methods.

Thus, this book speaks primarily to **experts** and **executives** in the fields of marketing, sales, customer and service management of B2B businesses, but also to **professionals** in the fields of quality management, research and development, project management, procurement, logistics and production, etc., which are integrated in marketing-related topics and areas of responsibility. Due to the condensed practical and implementation-related presentation of each method and their applications and reviews, especially responsible practitioners will find additional tools and implementation guides. However, this book also speaks to **students** of business administration with an emphasis on marketing, sales and customer management, who would like to learn about a conceptually sound, but also practical "guide" for the application of relevant strategies, programs, activities and tasks.

My **special thanks** go to my assistants Astrid Greve-Spencer MBA and Daniela Döser M.Sc. who helped finalizing this book and its textual and graphical illustrations with commitment and motivation.

Table of Contents

Introduction

In this book, an **innovative and sustainable overall marketing, sales and customer management (MSC)** approach is introduced, which has become especially important for national and international business-to-business markets (B2B markets) in recent years and will claim its "position" for **B2B companies** in the near future: the so-called **integrated** marketing, sales and customer management approach (holistic customer orientation).

The individual parts, beginning with the introduction of the holistic frame of reference of this marketing, sales and customer management (MSC) approach or management concept, will first present the necessary B2B **analyses** as well as the derivation of **multi-stage growth potential** (Part I), which generally arise for each B2B company. Part II is building on that by presenting the integrated **strategic** marketing, sales and customer management approach, while the subsequent chapters explain the thus deriving and nowadays relevant integrated MSC **programs and measures**.

These include integrated **product, service and product development management** (Part III), integrated sales, customer acquisition and negotiation management (Part IV), **customer loyalty, customer relations and customer retention management (CRM)** (Part V), integrated **customer development and key account management (KAM)** (Part VI), **focus group management (FGM)**, and integrated marketing, sales and customer **scorecard management** (Part VII).

Implementations of the corresponding tools and tasks and their integrative coordination are particularly taken into consideration. Without such a gradual "**synchronization**" of marketing, sales and customer management, an efficient and effective operation of relevant, modern and sustainable market oriented B2B activities is often not possible today to the necessary extent.

A variety of appropriate practical projects, which are partially referred to here, has clearly shown that both marketing-relevant **measures and tools** as well as sales-specific and customer-specific tools and their **implementation** are only purposeful, sustainably implementable and measurable, trackable and thus effective in the short and long term through a "**triad**".

The hereby presented "integrative framework" also supports the structure and breakdown of the various strategies, programs and tools accordingly. Through the overall context of such a MSC management, as identified in Part I, its areas of **analysis and strategy, measures, individual tools, procedures** and **feedback processes** are clearly visible. First and foremost, the right B2B segmentation, potential and positioning approach are essential, because they form the basis for all marketing activities. The strategy development builds on that, before the essential programs and tools of the integrated marketing, sales and customer management can be derived and defined. The topics of "modern" holistic CRM, i.e. customer satisfaction and loyalty management, customer relations, customer retention, and customer development or key account management, and their implementation steps and scorecard feedback as continuous directive opportunities are relatively new.

I The holistic marketing, sales and customer management approach (B2B)

1 The holistic framework and segmentation approach

This first chapter starts by discussing the holistically integrated marketing, sales and customer management (MSC) approach in the overall context (see Fig. 1). This describes the general approach of MSC management in a B2B business. Through overlapping steps, the approach presents the respective sequence of the corresponding task priorities and processes.

The first step (Ia) is to analyse the initial actual company or **business situation** ("DNA" Analysis), which mainly includes an analysis of its own core competence and strengths and weaknesses. The question to be answered is where the core competencies (today and tomorrow) lie, which contain the general and possibly also technology application-oriented basis for current and future product and/or service-specific strengths. The competencies, individual strengths and development opportunities that are relevant for future plans should be clearly defined, and necessary improvements and "insourcing" measures might need to be derived. The focus is on the analysis and coverage of market-relevant areas of expertise and strengths, and the analysis of relevant weaknesses and risks and their reduction or avoidance.

In a second step (Ib), it is important to carry out the necessary **segmentation**. As there are typically no longer general markets today, but rather specific, ever more divided market, industry, application, product, customer and decision-maker segments, these must be defined precisely in order to enable a specific coverage and the necessary alignment of individual marketing tools. The classic "watering can concept", which uses general and not segment-specific tools and measures, is no longer successful and effective today.

The various possible **segmentation dimensions and levels** are illustrated in Fig. 2. It shows (from the perspective of an electronic component supplier for the automotive market) that the overall automotive market should first be divided into the targeted **industry markets** (e.g., cars), which in turn are to be divided into the individual applicable **industry segments**, which stretch from the so-called micro car (e.g., Smart), to medium-sized cars, SUVs (sport utility vehicle segments), and all the way to luxury cars (e.g., Maybach/S-Class). (In the automotive industry, there can be more than 50 sub-segments today.) The subsequent level contains the so-called **application segments** (application areas such as anti-lock braking (ABS) systems, airbag systems, engine management, transmission management, dashboard systems, seating systems, etc.). The following segmentation levels are the so-called **product group** and **individual product segments** (modules/module groups). This level lays out which products or product groups represent a company in which application areas. (Then at the lowest level are the individual product segments.)

Marketing, Sales & Customer Mgt. (MSC)
Programs, Instruments,
Implementations & Measurements

M & S & C Programs, Tasks and Competencies

M & S & C Processes, Integrations, and Implementations

M & S & C BSC, HRD and Structures / Tools

Segment focused

TARGET
Dimensions
Priorities
Urgencies

Selections Optimization
M & S & C Scorecard

Marketing, Sales & Customer Mgt. (MSC)
Strategy, Targets & Positioning

- Strategic Targets
- Scenarios
- Assumptions
- Business Models
- Strategic Positioning

STRATEGIES

FIT

SWOT

Marketing, Sales & Customer Mgt. (MSC)
Analysis

I. DNA/ Status Analysis & Segmentation
- Ia. "DNA" Analysis / Identity &
- Ib. Segmentation

II. Segment Potential Analysis (SPOT)
- IIa. Quantitative Segment Data / Figures
- IIb. KSF Key Success Factors

III. Segment Positioning Analysis (SPOS)
- IIIa. Competitive Positioning & Differentiation
- IIIb. Value Chain & Positioning & Proposition
- IIIc. Business Model Advantages

[Feedback]

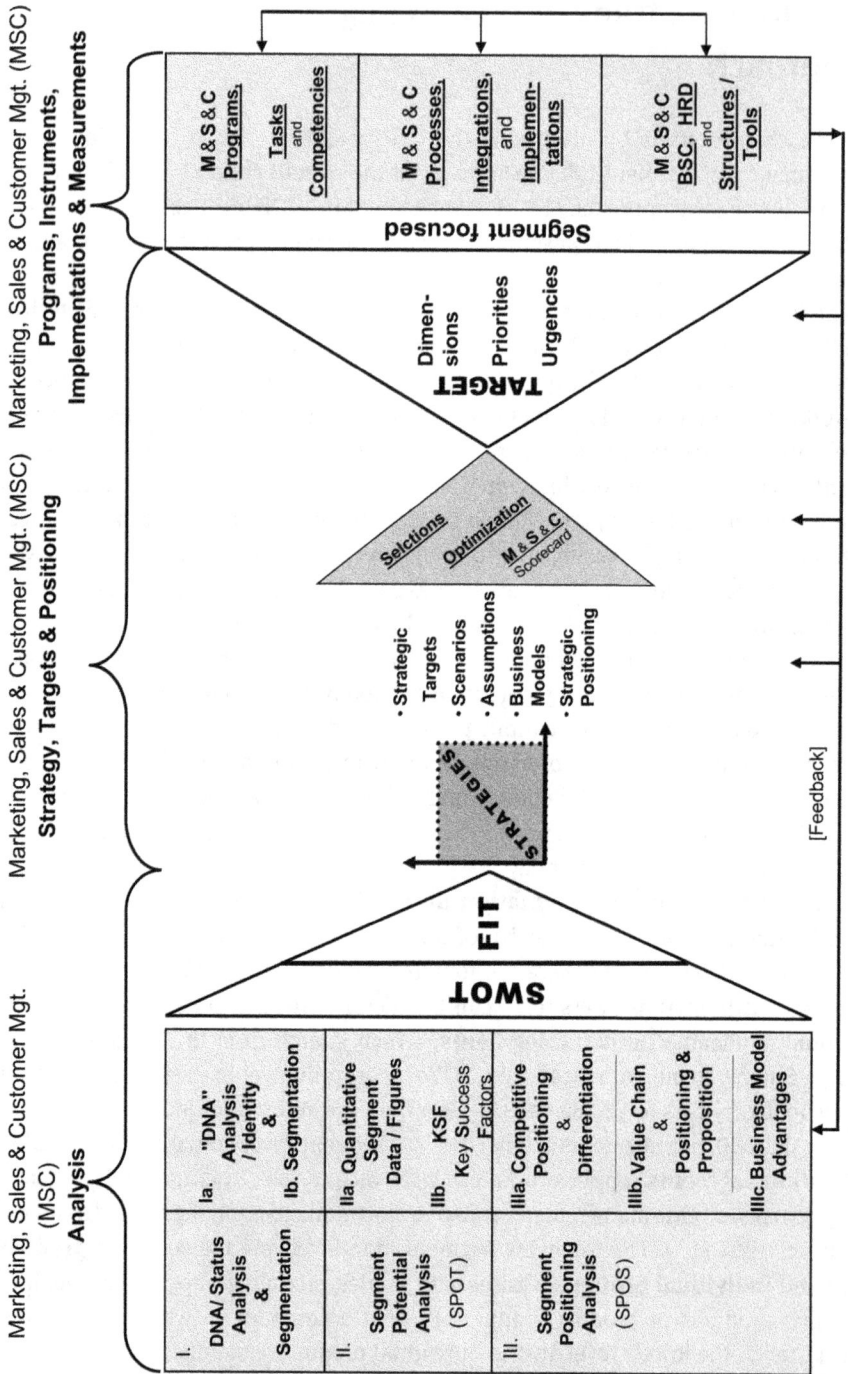

Fig. 1: Framework of a holistic marketing, sales and customer management approach (B2B) (© Prof. Dr. R. Hofmaier).

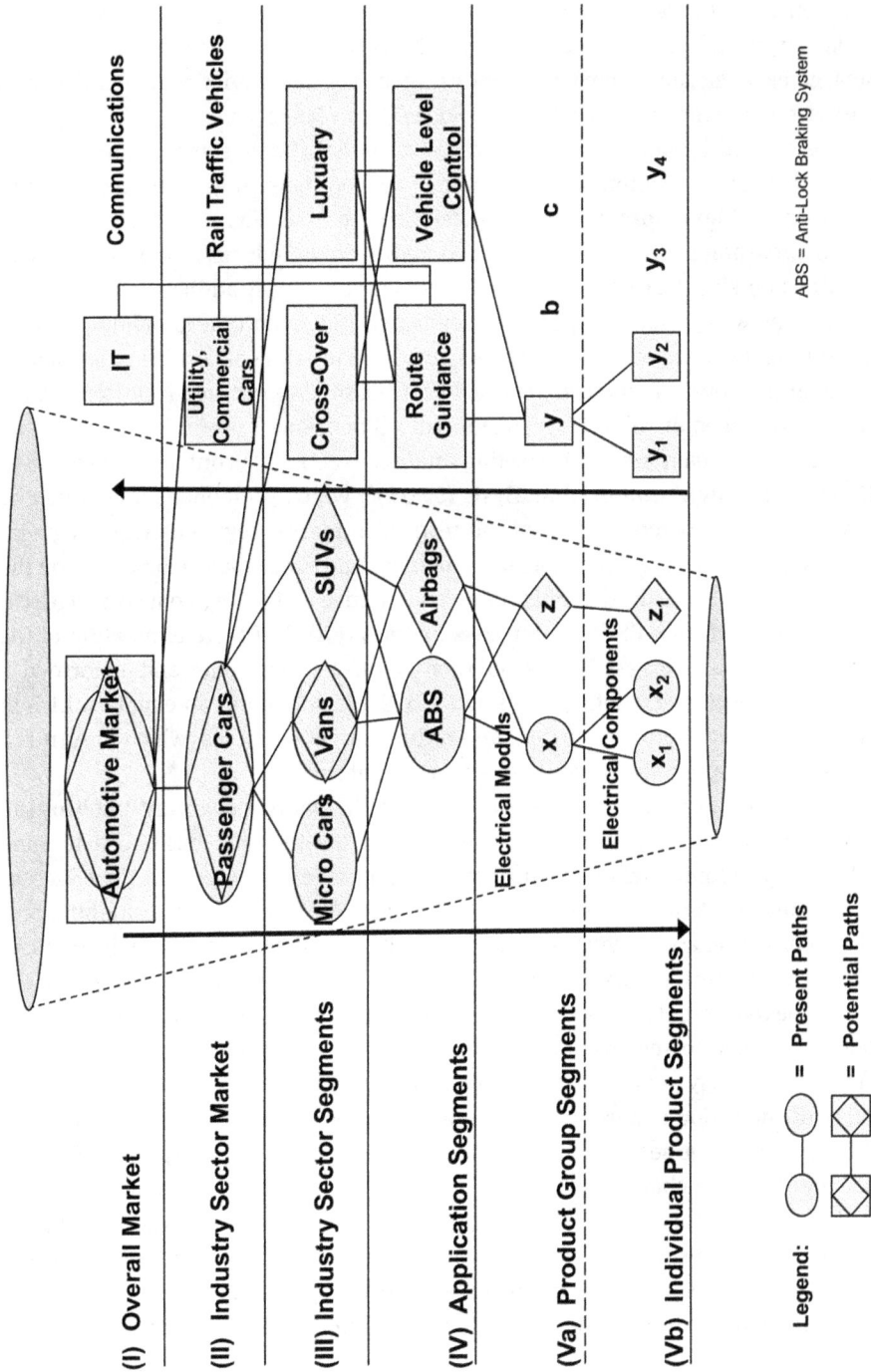

Fig. 2: Stages of systematic market segmentation and possibilities of business development based on "path" potentials (© Prof. Dr. R. Hofmaier).

If one continues the segmentation into the respective client companies (mostly OEMs, system suppliers), the different groups of decision-makers, co-decision-makers, users, gatekeepers, and other target groups can be specifically defined, identified and addressed in the next step (see Part VII: Focus Group Management).

In a second approach, such a (top-down) actual ("is") segmentation can now also lead to the derivation and development of (bottom-up) growth potential and new business **"development paths"** (potential paths) (see Fig. 2). Using the outlined "funnel presentation", modified, extended and/or new products/product groups can be defined outside the existing business funnel for previously addressed actual ("is") segments as well as for new potential segments. It is important to define products for additional (previously not addressed) application segments, industry segments, sectors and/or overall markets. This makes it possible to systematically generate a variable growth potential over several growth "dimensions"!

The second main area of marketing analysis (see Fig. 1) contains the so-called (II) market **segment potential analysis (SPOT)** [1], which is on one hand defined by (a) a quantitative determination of the respective market segments (e.g., segment volumes, potentials, growth, income, occupation, and exogenous factors), and on the other hand by the specific determination of qualitative market segment criteria **(Critical Success Factors = CSF/Key Success Factors = KEF).** The determination of the number of relevant success factors and their manifestations (today and tomorrow) is crucial in determining whether one's own skills and strengths can enable sufficient coverage and penetration of current and future market segments, which in turn is a prerequisite for a sustainable and long-term market success.

The third main area includes the so-called (III) market **segment positioning analysis (SPOS).** Here, sound customer surveys are the man basis to determine individual positioning relative to the competition based on key criteria (Key Success Factors and Key Performance Criteria – KSF/KPC). The actual ("is") positioning provides information about which segments contain critical personal shortfalls that can be resolved swiftly ("early warning system"), and where there are possible surpluses that can be reduced. It is important that the relevant criteria are sufficiently weighted from a customer perspective, in order to take into account the importance of these criteria accordingly (today and tomorrow). Furthermore, a query of these criteria can lead to the detection of new or "developing" **sub-segments** for the near future (e.g., different price-value segments), which would require marketing adaptation. In addition, the (b) value chain positioning and (c) business model positioning allow the development of a competitively differentiating value chain and business model positioning in the corresponding market segments, in order to implement the expansion of value chain coverage for the customer (e.g., cross-/up-selling, see also Part VI) and possibly also the **extension of the business model** approach (e.g., implementation

---

1 For SPOT and SPOS analysis (more below), see also in detail Hofmaier, 1993, pp. 145–172 and Hofmaier, 1996, pp. 32–61.

of additional strategic project management tasks, strategic services or alternative payment for "service use" of the implemented products) that are necessary for future marketing success.

After the overall analysis, including a comparison of the **strengths/weaknesses and opportunities/threats (SWOT)**, the next main step (see Fig. 1) includes the deduction of integrated marketing, sales and customer management **strategies** and their **objectives** and **target positions**. The focus is on macro- and micro-strategic decisions based on different strategic methods, models and procedures. This can be based on various scenarios, optimizations and **scorecard** evaluations of estimates (see Part II).

This strategy context forms the basis for the next main step, namely the priority-based development and detailed specification of relevant marketing, sales and customer **programs** as well as their individual **measures, procedures, implementation** steps, **measuring systems** and **feedback and control processes** (see Part III–VII). Here, it is necessary to simultaneously consider human resource development (HRD), business scorecards (BSC), structures and tools (e.g., CRM tools).

2 The creation of market segment potential (SPOT) and market segment positioning analyses (SPOS)

2.1 The market segment potential analysis (SPOT)

Due to the ever-changing and increasing diversity and heterogeneity especially among the targeted market, application and customer segments for B2B companies, a segment-differentiating marketing analysis, i.e. a **segment potential analysis (SPOT)**, is necessary in order to record the individual actual ("is") and future segments with respect to their quantitative potentials and their segment-specific, key or critical success factors (qualitative potentials).

Such an approach based on potential is recommended because it has proven as ineffective for B2B marketing to plan only bottom-up, i.e., to "project" future values based on past revenues, sales, contribution margins, etc. A more promising approach is to focus on the **potentials of targeted segments** (volume, growth and profit potentials, etc.), i.e. a top-down approach. Only then can (previous and new) market and application opportunities be recognized and addressed early enough and thus be exhausted (capitalization of potential opportunities).

Examples of **criteria to measure the quantitative segment potentials** are:
- segment volume (as item and value units)
- segment potential (as item and value units)
- segment growth

- segment quality (segment-based average income/margin, etc.)
- segment casting (including provider/customer ratios, competition status and behavior, entry/exit barriers)
- exogenous factors (including substitution potential; economic, environmental, political, social, and technological factors and potential influences).

That way, one leaves the narrow basis of a more "preserving" marketing approach (momentum strategy) and focuses on a broader, demand-initiated or stimulating growth approach (potential strategy) that eventually meets demand. This can facilitate above-average growth rates (even in declining or stagnant markets) by using a "strategic leverage effect" (segment focusing of resources based on potential). Therefore, a top-down approach involves the determination of the total segment potential using key figures for segments per SBU (Strategic Business Unit), BC (Business Center), and BU (Business Unit) or product group for today and tomorrow. It is also important to answer the question to what extent existing and new segments must be addressed with current or diversifying products and services (including solution bundling) for growth insurance and added-value optimization.

The next step defines the **"critical success factors" (CSF)** or **"Key Success Factor" (KSF)** (SPOT qualitative analysis) for each segment and places them in a hierarchy based on their importance. Main indicators for the determination of the key success factors (KSFs) in the respective segments can include:

- Criteria for product quality
- Criteria for quality of service
- Criteria for (total) solution competence and quality
- Criteria for innovation skills and quality
- Criteria for the spectrum of product and/or service programs
- Criteria for commanding complexity and expertise of integration/quality
- Criteria for generating new demand and (value-adding, cross-over) covering (new product/business development)
- Criteria for general new business modeling
- Criteria for cross- and up-selling skills
- Criteria for project management skills
- Criteria for sales skills
- Criteria for communication skills and image/brand quality
- Criteria for customer relationship skills
- Criteria for the speed of delivery and delivery flexibility
- Criteria for price-value differentiation competence and its flexibility
- Criteria for client specialization etc.

Both of these steps (quantitative and qualitative SPOT analysis) provide a first **prioritization** of market, application and customer segments that are relevant to the enterprise (as a prerequisite for targeted marketing).

Fig. 3 provides an example to show the importance of the timely analysis of KSF[2] and the design measures that are to be derived. This illustrates the possibilities of **market micro segmentation** and the corresponding segment prioritization. This can in turn lead to a different configuration of marketing, sales and customer management tools. The starting point for the analysis of key success factors (KSFs) is the UK electric motor market in terms of segments A and B (Today; see Fig. 3). The smallest segment unit is characterized by a **homogeneous** shaping of the KSF. For the electric motor market under consideration, there are thus two different segments (A and B). Based on their different KSF-shaping, they each have a **differentiated** marketing approach. Segment A is a so-called **high-value segment**, which has an outstanding product quality as well as high innovation and reputation competence, and which requires matching marketing tools (innovative products, sales and customer management tools of very high quality) today and especially in the future. Only then can the targeted marketing success be achieved today and tomorrow, and there can be more penetration.

Segment / Time Perspective	Today		Tomorrow (next 2-3 years)		
Key Success Factors (KSFs):	Segment A	Segment B	Segment A	Segment B	Segment C
Product Quality	⬬	⬬	⬬	⬬	⬬
Product Innovation	⬬	⬬	⬬	⬬	⬬
Consulting Quality & Experience	⬬	⬬	⬬	⬬	⬬
Reputation	⬬	⬬	⬬	⬬	⬬
Delivery Flexibility	⬬	⬬	⬬	⬬	⬬
Price-Value Ratio	⬬	⬬	⬬	⬬	⬬

Key Success Factors (KSF):

(a) Product Quality
(b) Product Innovation (Lead Sser Driven)
(c) Consulting Quality & Experience
(d) Reputation
(e) Delivery Flexibility
(f) Value-Price-Ratio

Degree of Importance of KSF (Weighting):

⬬ Very High Importance
⬬ High Importance
⬬ Above Average Importance
⬬ Average Importance
⬬ Below Average Importance

Fig. 3: (Detailed) market segmentation based on the analysis of key success factors (KSFs)/critical success factors (CSFs) (© Prof. Dr. R. Hofmaier).

---

2 For KSF analysis, see also Hofmaier, 1999, pp. 130–139 and in detail Kotler / Cox, 1988, pp. 249–251.

On the other hand, for segment B (in Fig. 3), it is necessary to find out whether a **successful positioning** is possible today and how implementable it is in the near future (trend towards standardization). The question now is, if the molding of tomorrow's KSF is already being analysed today, does it make sense economically to offer so-called standardized **low-cost** B products and B-services. However, this only happens when cost savings that are appropriate compared to the relevant competition can be planned and implemented in time (today) based on their own procurement, production and marketing costs. Thus, does it even make sense to include offers in segments B and C in two to three years, or should one rather focus on being an "innovation and quality" provider in other high-value segments besides segment A? Offering and competing in future segments B and C (in the future, segment B will be divided into segments B and C with different KSF-forms) only makes sense if the corporate and marketing-specific factors can be created in time in such a way that relevant costs can be significantly reduced (which could potentially include moving the production abroad), and the necessary price reduction still ensures a sustainable margin. In addition, it is necessary to clarify whether a parallel offering in the low-value or "low price" segment interferes with the quality of positioning (or credibility) in the high-value segment. With such a **"differentiation strategy"**, a so-called two-brand strategy might be required.

All of these questions can be explored, clarified and resolved in time, if segmentation and KSF analyses focusing on the near future are carried out, if the relevant customer surveys are aligned accordingly, and if sufficient time is given for marketing and design simulations as well as alternative preparations. This way, such KSF analyses will include not just answers to the correct segment focus and orientation, but also the preparation and deduction of **segment-differentiated** marketing tools.

2.2 The market positioning analysis (SPOS)

This step builds on the analysis of the initial situation by considering **positioning** in each segment specific to the competitive landscape with relevant business metrics (segment positioning analysis SPOS, see Fig. 4). The question to be addressed here refers to the specific positioning of the SBUs or business units/products in direct comparison to relevant competitors in each segment from a customer perspective based on business, marketing, sales, customer, R&D, and production metrics, etc. The goal is to identify and determine the **realistic** positioning and its improvement opportunities for today and tomorrow (based on given assumptions).

Main **indicators or criteria** of the **segment positioning analysis (SPOS)** include:
- Key metrics of the business positioning (**quantitative** positioning indicators):
    - Segment Share (absolute and relative)
    - database/return
    - shares of wallet (key customer's market share)

- Key metrics of **marketing, sales and customer positioning**:
  - Criteria for product quality
  - Criteria for quality of service
  - Criteria for (overall) solution skills and quality
  - Criteria for innovation competence and quality
  - Criteria for the spectrum of product and/or service programs
  - Criteria for mastering complexity or integration expertise/quality
  - Criteria for generating new demand and (value-creating cross-over) coverage (new product/business development)
  - Criteria for new business modeling
  - Criteria for cross-selling and up-selling skills
  - Criteria for project management skills
  - Criteria for sales skills
  - Criteria for distribution skills
  - Criteria for communication skills and image/brand quality
  - Criteria for customer relationship skills
  - Criteria for speedy delivery and delivery flexibility
  - Criteria for price-value differentiation capability and its flexibility
  - Criteria for client specialization
- Indicators of **R&D positioning**:
  - Technological expertise and quality
  - Product/service development expertise and quality
  - Endogenous and exogenous innovation expertise and quality
  - Patent and licensing expertise
- Data of **production positioning**:
  - Production quality and flexibility
  - Production costs
  - "Virtual" production capabilities

After the **segment weighting and evaluation** through the SPOT analysis, as well as the above segment positioning (SPOS) and the improvements that are necessary in regards to the optimal coverage of the Key Success Factors KSFs) for today and tomorrow (see Fig. 3), further opportunities and risks of the individual segments must now be determined and targeted with the strengths as much as possible. By comparing the strengths and weaknesses to the segment-specific opportunities and threats (SWOT matrix, see Fig. 6 and 7), existing business segments can be penetrated deeper or extended and, if necessary, new ones can be successfully addressed. Furthermore, risks are to be avoided and weaknesses should be decreased as much as possible. (It is not rare to find that your own strengths are not lead by opportunity and marketed proactively enough!)

Based on the **positioning analysis** and its results shown in Fig. 4, it is clear that four **optimization options** are necessary and very important for further marketing, namely the improvement of "physical product performance" among the analyzed products, and the clear improvement of product compatibility, service quality and service range. (If this is not done, there is not only the threat of deteriorating marketing opportunities, but possibly also of being forced out by the competition in the medium term.)

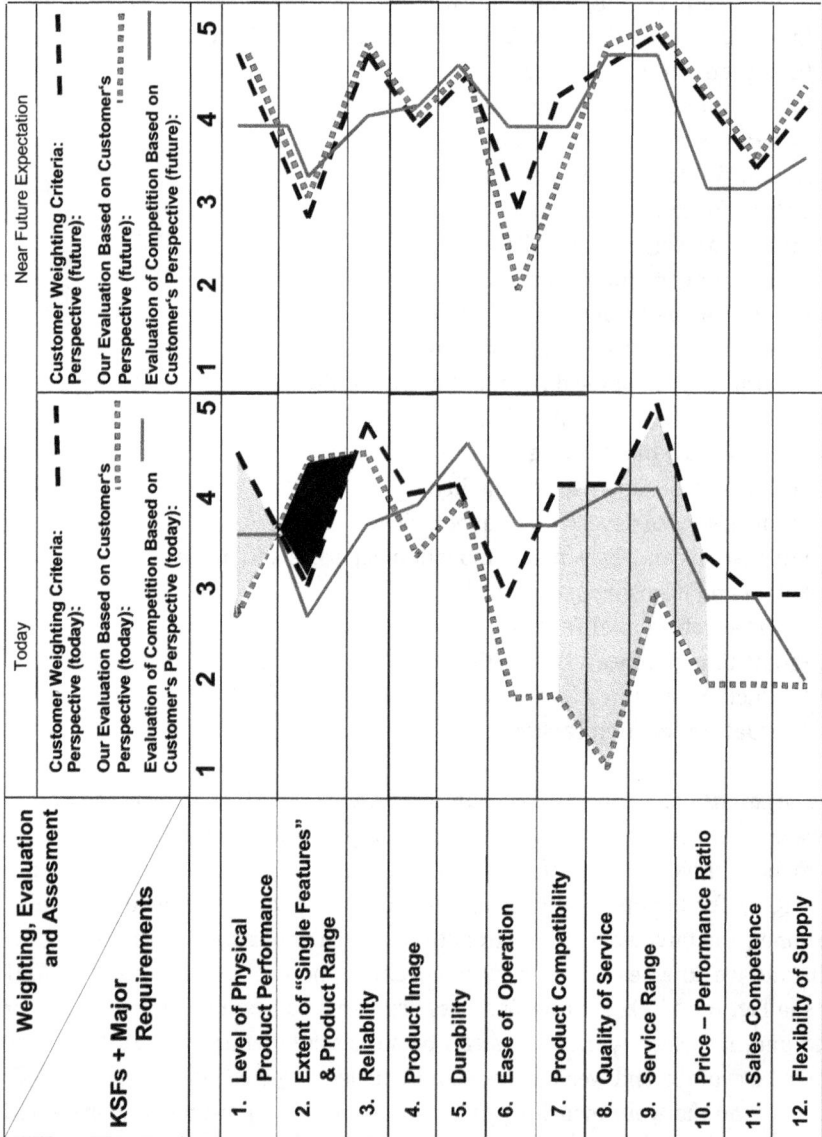

Fig. 4: Segment-based positioning analysis (SPOS) to derive opportunities for improvement (© Prof. Dr. R. Hofmaier).

Conversely, a **surplus** was derived of the number of appropriate specific "features", which can be resolved with a targeted reduction of individual characteristics that are no longer relevant. (If necessary, specialty segments or niches that are still of high quality can be covered through a feature-specific price-value differentiation.) In addition, column 3 in Fig. 4 allows the query of the development of the Key Success Factors (KSFs) and requirements for the near future. This also makes it possible to answer the question whether the queried segments are still homogeneous, or whether they should already be split into different heterogeneous partial segments and be processed with a **corresponding** marketing mix.

3 The derivation of market penetration, market development and growth potentials

In connection with the necessary analyses of marketing and strategy, it is important to develop sustainable and thus long-term **growth opportunities and potentials**. Therefore, the following explains a relevant systematization and development approach, i.e. the so-called "eight-section potential matrix" or **site strategy and business development matrix** for deducting growth potentials and defining site strategies for B2B companies (see Fig. 5).

The "**eight-section potential matrix**"[3] is based on the segmentation levels in Fig. 2 and makes it possible to identify and develop possible **growth potentials** in different steps. Section I (actual **segment penetration**) concerns itself with selling more products and services of the currently offered range of services (for example through participation in growing customer demand and/or by gaining segment shares over the competition) with so-called "push"-marketing steps of previous segments (overall market/industry market/industry segments/application segments/customer and product segments/customer segments) and regions (actual/"is" regions). In contrast, section II **(advanced segment penetration)** contains a mostly qualitative expansion of service offerings (extended or modified performance improvement) for more thorough customer base penetration in existing segments and regions. Growth potential section III **(innovative segment penetration)** refers to an innovative expansion of product/service offerings (demand-based expansion) with respect to a qualitatively enhanced customer base penetration in actual segments and actual regions. Section IV **(expanded/new business segment penetration)** also refers to a correspondingly more intense customer base penetration based on a modified or expanded business model. For example, this can include a combinatorial expansion of integrated product-service offerings, where an expansion of the actual demand is possible thanks to new payment options and service combinations for the base product business (for

---

3 This matrix is based on the fundamental "four-section matrix"; see Ansoff (1966), pp. 132–133.

example, instead of paying the total price when buying equipment, one only has to pay upon the use of service, or there is an option of providing rental options, sale and lease-back options, sharing options, bundling and partial solution options, etc.).

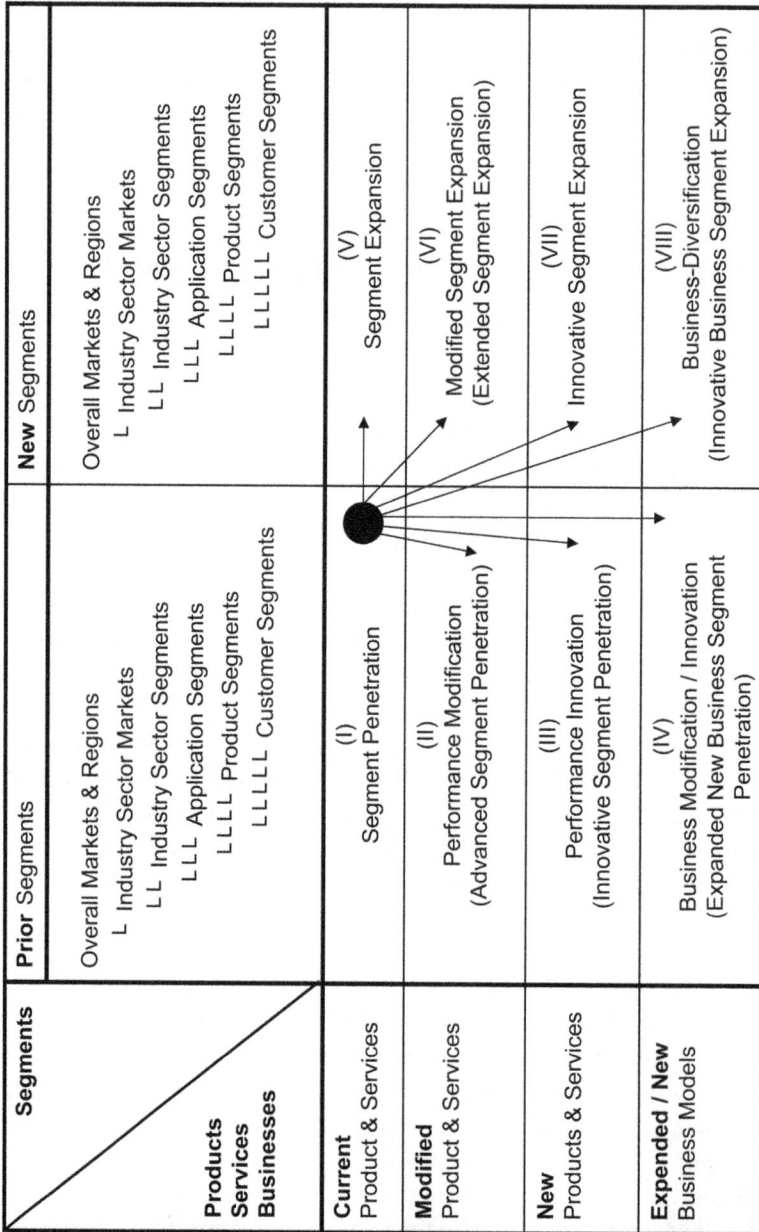

Segments	Prior Segments Overall Markets & Regions L Industry Sector Markets LL Industry Sector Segments LLL Application Segments LLLL Product Segments LLLLL Customer Segments	New Segments Overall Markets & Regions L Industry Sector Markets LL Industry Sector Segments LLL Application Segments LLLL Product Segments LLLLL Customer Segments
Current Product & Services	(I) Segment Penetration	(V) Segment Expansion
Modified Product & Services	(II) Performance Modification (Advanced Segment Penetration)	(VI) Modified Segment Expansion (Extended Segment Expansion)
New Products & Services	(III) Performance Innovation (Innovative Segment Penetration)	(VII) Innovative Segment Expansion
Expended / New Business Models	(IV) Business Modification / Innovation (Expanded New Business Segment Penetration)	(VIII) Business-Diversification (Innovative Business Segment Expansion)

Fig. 5: The "Eight-section potential matrix" or site strategy (business development) matrix (for B2B companies) (© Prof. Dr. R. Hofmaier).

Additional significant growth opportunities now arise from the fact that the present services are not only available in existing regions and countries, but also in additional prioritized regions, as well as not only in the recent customer segments (e.g., large OEMs), but also for newly targeted customer groups (e.g., small OEMs, system suppliers, solution providers) as well as new application areas (electronics modules for additional applications), new industry segments (electronics modules for additional product and model series), new industry markets (electronics modules not just for the car industry, but also for the commercial vehicle industry, rail transportation vehicle industry) and for the new overall markets (electronic modules/solutions for the aerospace industry) (potential section V: **segment expansion**).

A similar four-step segmentation procedure now applies equally to modified services (section VI: **modified segment expansion**), to innovated products and services (section VII: **innovative segment expansion**), and to a corresponding new business model (section VIII: **innovative business expansion and business diversification**). Sufficiently new markets, segments, target applications and regions, etc., can be tapped into especially through modified innovated products and expanded business models, as many innovation examples of industrial mid-sized (especially "hidden champions") and large enterprises show.

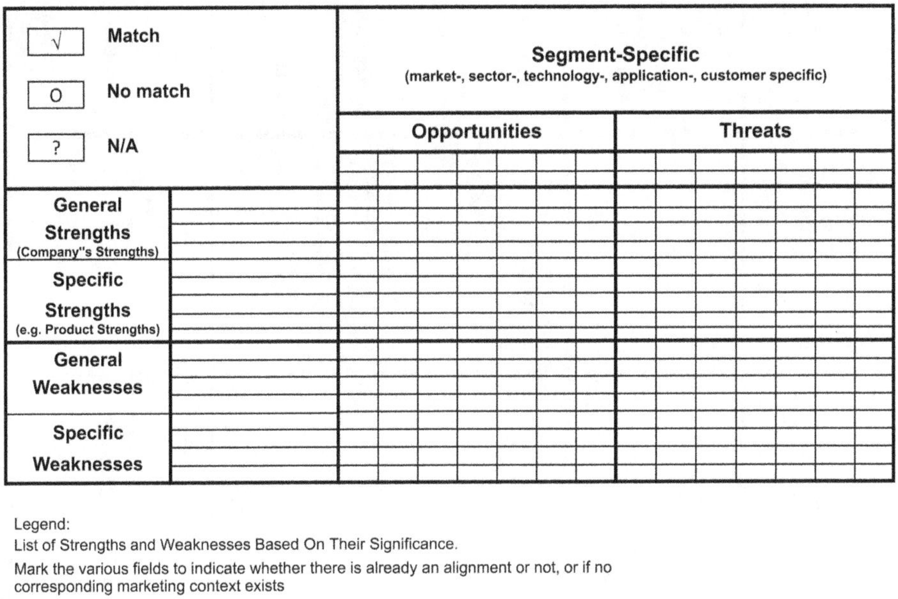

√ Match	Segment-Specific (market-, sector-, technology-, application-, customer specific)		
O No match			
? N/A	**Opportunities**		**Threats**
General Strengths (Company"s Strengths)			
Specific Strengths (e.g. Product Strengths)			
General Weaknesses			
Specific Weaknesses			

Legend:
List of Strengths and Weaknesses Based On Their Significance.
Mark the various fields to indicate whether there is already an alignment or not, or if no corresponding marketing context exists

Fig. 6: SWOT matrix (strengths – weaknesses/opportunities – threats) (© Prof. Dr. R. Hofmaier).

Exogeneous Focus / Endogeneous Focus	Based on: market segment/ sector segment application segment/ product and customer segment	Opportunities	Threats
		• Higher Level of Furnishings for Premium Cars • To-down development in the marketplace • Need-based development and coverage potential for additional Warming and Heating possibilities • Related Technological Developments	• Customer (OEM) & End-User Acceptance • Substituting Technologies • Competitive Threats
Strengths	Based on: Core Competencies and general (company) strengths as well as specific product/ application/ technology/ service srengths • Specific processor expertise • Automotive-based application expertise (heat control, etc.) • Integration expertise • Fundamental technological development expertise potential • Related service/ consulting expertise	**① Opportunities-Strengths (Action) Area** ⇨ Demand Creation of „Heating" Added Values via implementation & Lead User-Based Marketing of these Strengths ⇨ Development of New and Modified Processor Algorithms for Warming/ Heating of additional need-relevant Applications in Premium Cars (e.g. Electronically Controlled Heating for All glass paneling, All Seats, Head Rests, Arm Rests, Gear panels and stick shifts, Integrated Coffee Makers & insulated cups, etc.)	**② Opportunities-Threats Area** → Avoidance of threats or use of Acceptance Strategies ⇨ Timely implementation of Win-Win Projects with Select (Lead) customers and "Pull Research" (Enduser-Oriented, Acceptance-Promoting Market Surveys/ results) • Innovation Leadership (compared to Competition) • Clarification and differentiation of Possible Substitutes
Weaknesses	• Relatively long development times	**③ Weaknesses-Opportunities Area** ⇨ Shortening Development Times via Simultaneous Product Development e.g. through Integrated Lead User-Oriented Product Development	**④ Weaknesses-Threats Area** ⇨ Enforcement of (II-) & (III-) Measures • Timely Win-Win Generation and Lead User-Oriented Product and Application Development

Fig. 7: Example of a SWOT matrix (© Prof. Dr. R. Hofmaier).

The already mentioned **SWOT matrix** (strengths/weaknesses/opportunities/threats)[4] (see Fig. 6 and 7) also presents a supporting method for finding **additional growth options**. It can be configured differently (with a focus on market, technology, application and/or customer opportunities) and can facilitate a derivation of additional business options with appropriately corresponding strengths. This allows for consideration to which extent these strengths can raise the addressed opportunities "to marketing maturity", i.e. how they can be converted into business opportunities (upper left main quadrant), while avoiding the possible risks and reducing weaknesses in the best possible way.

An example of a SWOT matrix could be a manufacturer of different products for industrial markets, who develops and markets LED light pipes for industrial applications in the security sector. An opportunity analysis found that even in the passenger car segment, there are basic need-based configurations for future interior lighting modules. Thanks to commerce level cross-over target group analyses, this need can be specified and targeted with select automotive OEMs and their customer target groups. Based on its own core competencies and strengths, concrete product modifications and applications can now be developed marketed based on lead-users, while avoiding potential risks and minimizing potential problems and weaknesses.

Another example is the completed SWOT matrix in Fig. 7. A provider of processors for heating projects for car interiors has elicited the following market segment opportunities for the future: a higher level of equipment in the premium-car sector and sufficient potential for demand-based development of additional "heating" applications. His core competencies and strengths include first and foremost an appropriate knowhow of product and application development with lead-user-supported consulting. These strengths, coupled with the given market opportunities, can enable lead-user-based demand, pilot and new product application development and thus the equipment of the premium-car sector with its own corresponding products. In addition, risks should be avoided by using personal strengths (e.g., acceptance support), and possible weaknesses should be purposefully decreased for better opportunity utilization (see Fig. 7).

An additional method for **finding** basic business development and product application opportunities is shown in the **segment-performance product matrix** (see Fig. 8.):

The first column lists the existing and eligible products and services for select marketing segments (actual and potential performances or products/services). These are now being defined and assigned to the respective main segments in the following columns (A = industry/branch segment: for example, SUV, B = industry/branch segment Van) and in detail to the respective application and/or product and customer segments (e.g., based on sales, earnings, quantity). Through **appropriate cross comparisons and plausibility checks**, one can now find out a fundamentally deeper

---

4 For the SWOT matrix, see also Meffert, 2012, pp. 237–242.

penetration is possible in some segments (compared to established segment volumes, growth rates, etc.), and whether some segments can be tapped that have so far not been addressed (mostly for historical reasons), but that are winnable in principle (see similar segments). (For example, why shouldn't currently developed application segments for SUVs also be attainable for Vans?)

Market Segment / SBU/Product Group/BU (Services)	Industry Sector Segment A:								Industry Sector Segment B:			Industry Sector Segments A/B:	
	Application Segment A_1			Application Segment A_2			Application Segment A_3			Application Segment B_1		Application Segments $A_1.../B_1...$	
	Customer a_1:	Customer b_1:	Customer c_1:	Customer a_2:	Customer b_2:	Customer c_2:	Customer a_3:	Customer b_3:	Customer c_3:	Customer .../...	Customer .../...	⊠ ...	⊠ ...
Product Group 1:													
Product Group 2:													
Product Group 3:													
Product Group 4:													
Product Group n:													
⊠ 1-n													

Fig. 8: Segment-performance/product (service) matrix (© Prof. Dr. R. Hofmaier).

An additional but often neglected **growth potential** approach can be seen in the **service sector** (see Fig. 9). Based on the **dimensions** of commercial and technical services as well as strategic and operational services, the latter divided into A-, B- and C-services, a systematic classification of actual services can very well recognize and close service "gaps." The examination of a number of B2B companies showed that they offer primarily technical and commercial C-services, but usually few B-services, and hardly any A-services and usually no strategic services. Since **C-services** can be defined as me-too services that are usually "interchangeable" and are also offered by the competition, and that usually cannot be invoiced (or cannot create a margin), but that create expenses that must be paid for, it is certainly useful to further develop and offer more of the **higher-quality service categories.**

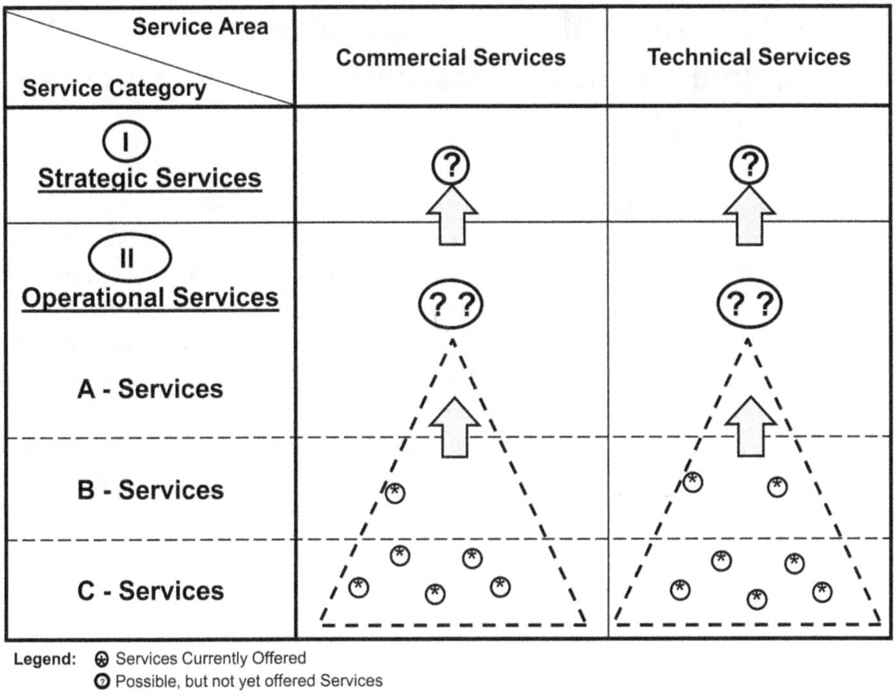

Fig. 9: Service development matrix (for strategic and operational services) (© Prof. Dr. R. Hofmaier).

Thus, **B-services** are characterized – at least indirectly – by being included in the invoice for the main product. **A-services** have multiple advantages: they offer the customer a verifiable added value, which they are willing to pay and which makes an additional margin possible for the provider. In addition, A-services can contribute to an improved competitive differentiation, as the competitor (still) does not offer this service or not in this way (and also improve customer expertise, relationship and allegiance). For example, A-services can be present engineering, testing, pre-development, design, calculation, marketing, special care, and delivery services, etc., for the client.

Furthermore, **strategic services** can often lead to a deepening customer base coverage and penetration through with the chance of a more demand creation for the customer and thus more business development and collaboration with the customer. Strategic services can range from product development services to specific total-cost-of-ownership services, strategic project management services, or a so-called "general contractor community for the customer." Especially the latter allows for an additional and deeper customer understanding, and thus a more ambitious and upgraded customer (demand) development.

4 Manifestations of marketing, sales and customer management-focused marketing models and their integration

For the application and implementation of the integrated marketing approach that is applied in this book, it is generally important to also be aware of how focused the previous marketing approach has been carried out and "lived" within the company in terms of methods and tools, settings and accordingly distinct decision-making skills, etc., and whether or how a technically coordinated as well as methodically integrative approach is necessary and whether or how to gradually implement it. Thus, it is possible to first use specific criteria to define whether your company has indeed **"marketing- and sales-integrated"** B2B management, or whether it is mostly a **sales-dominated** or at least sales-focused company – as is often the case in B2B markets (see Fig. 10). If this is the case, it has been shown that the establishment of a "powerful" marketing plan and its gradual integration up to an equitable and thus inclusive marketing and sales management is very important and helpful for successful marketing management.[5]

Typical sales-dominant marketing management (mostly justified based on tradition) can be identified mainly through comprehensive sales functions and sales staff (compared to marketing), decision-making powers and marketing principles associated with sales, appropriate sales and marketing support in upper or top-level decision-making committees and sales-dominant marketing processes.

Similar guidelines exist for the explicit consideration and integration of a customer management perspective as a third dimension of marketing and sales. In many cases, it is necessary nowadays for B2B businesses to design and implement specific

---

[5] In addition to experience-based evidence of this connection, see also a series of initial related studies, e.g. Haase, 2006 and in detail Hofmaier, 2014/2015.

integrated customer or key account management (see Fig. 11 and 12)[6] in addition to sales and marketing management (see Part VI), since this is not promised solely based on purely sales-dominant marketing management.

If, for example, marketing and/or sales and/or customer management deficiencies are now identified, they can include the following **integration mechanisms** (esp. by FGM/Part VII and see also Fig. 10 and 11: from non-cooperation to **integrated** marketing, sales and customer management (MSC Mgmt)) in addition to a content-themed vote (integrative consideration of marketing, sales and customer management-related topics).

Progressive alignment and **integration can be through** (see Fig. 12):

1. Task- and person-based information, communication and coordination (of marketing, sales and customer management focal points)
2. Shared task decision making, responsibility and empowerment
3. Integrative implementation of such program, method activities and implementation measures (process integration)
4. Organization-based structural and finally
5. Corporate culture-based integration

The **themes and topics** could range from Analysis Tasks to Strategic Program, Operational, Implementation and Potentially Feedback Tasks (step by step for low intensity to fully cooperation and integration); and they can be supported by the Influence Factors like Customer Focus, Role Identity, Individual Competence, Information Management, and Strategic Orientation (see Fig. 11 as a result of empirical studies, Hofmaier 2010/2013 and 2014/2015).

---

6 For such specific integrated key account management, see also Hofmaier, 2012, pp. 6–13.

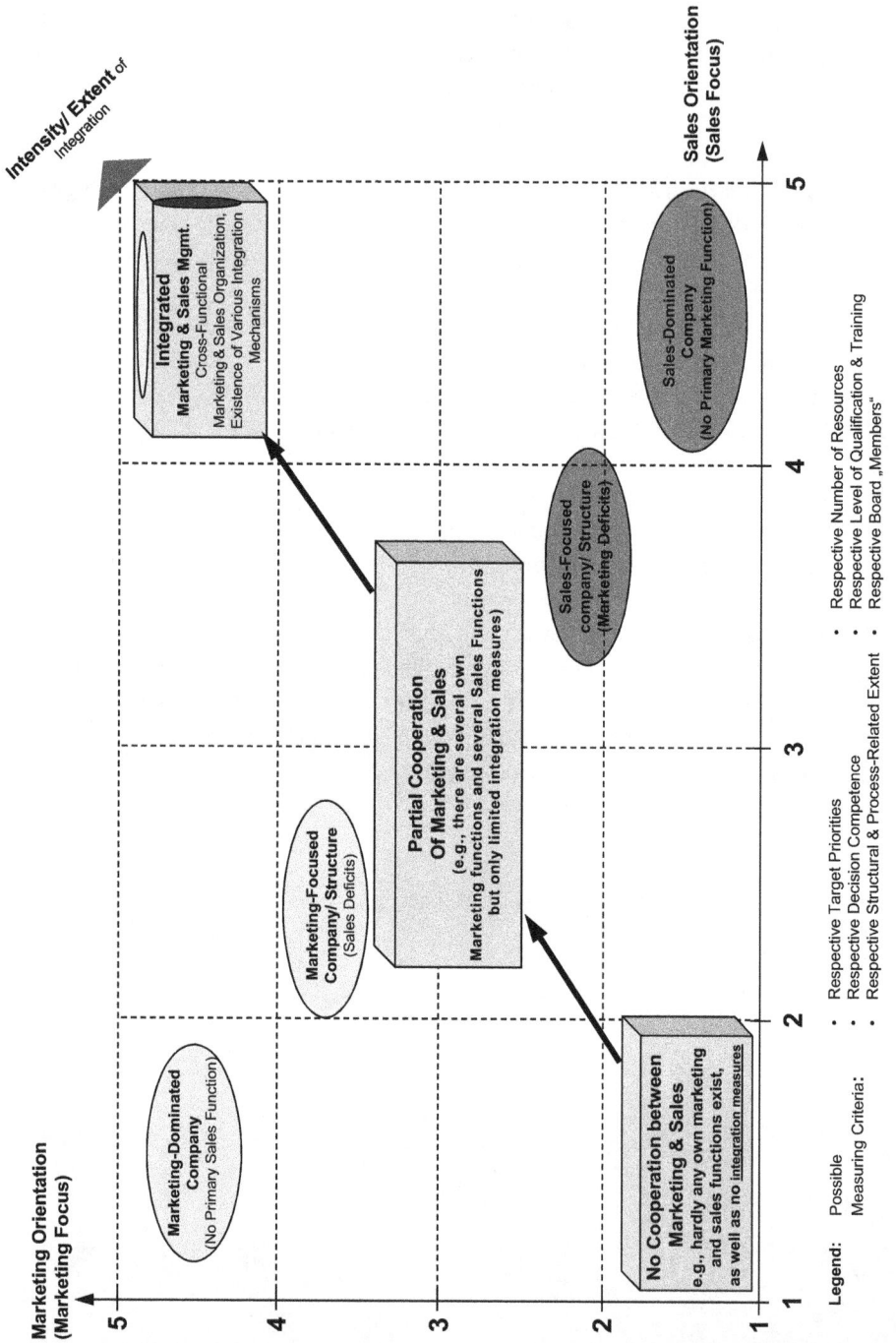

Fig. 10: Identification and integration matrix for B2B Marketing and Sales Management Companies (by Marketing and Sales Management) (© Prof. Dr. R. Hofmaier).

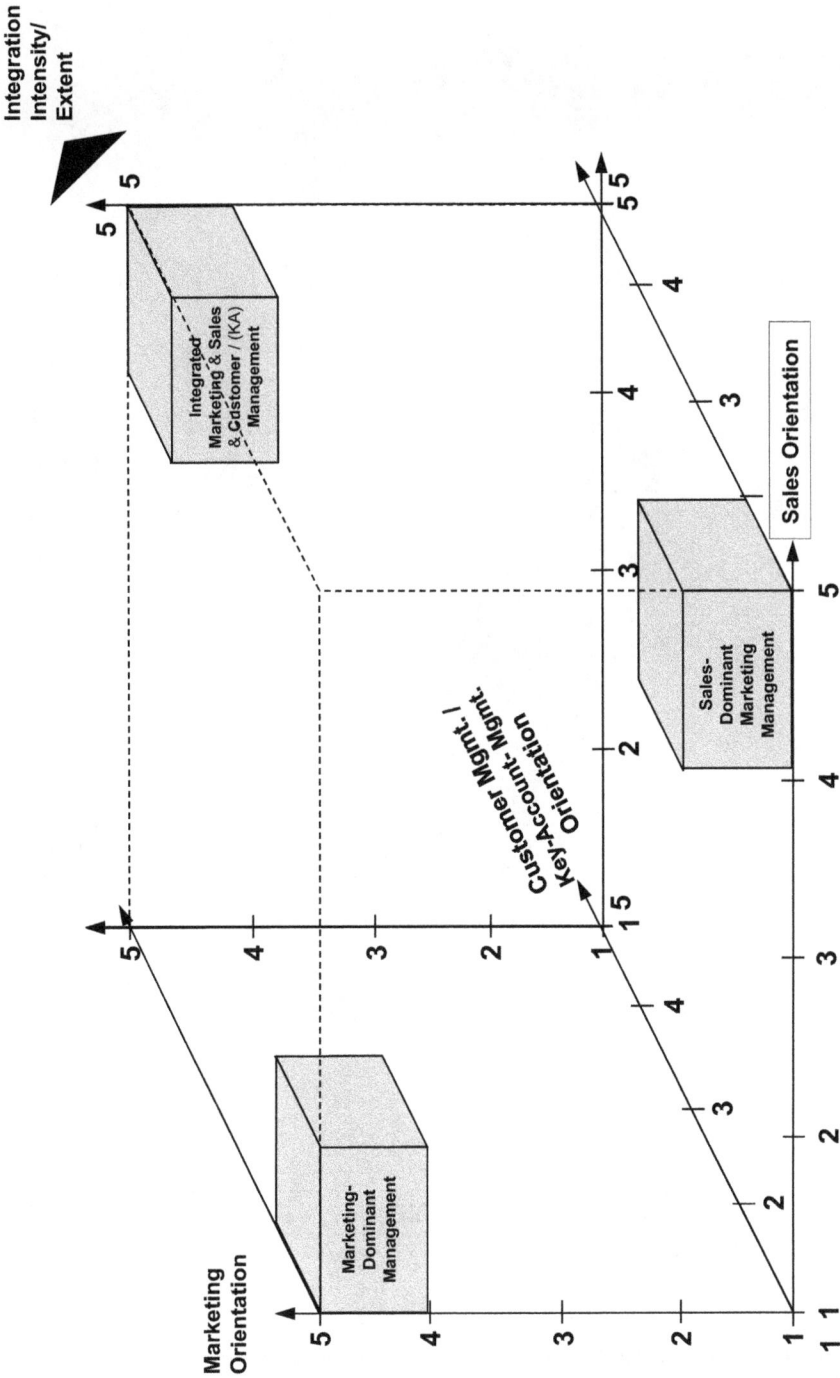

Fig. 11: Integration matrix for marketing, sales and customer (key account-oriented) management (B2B) (© Prof. Dr. R. Hofmaier).

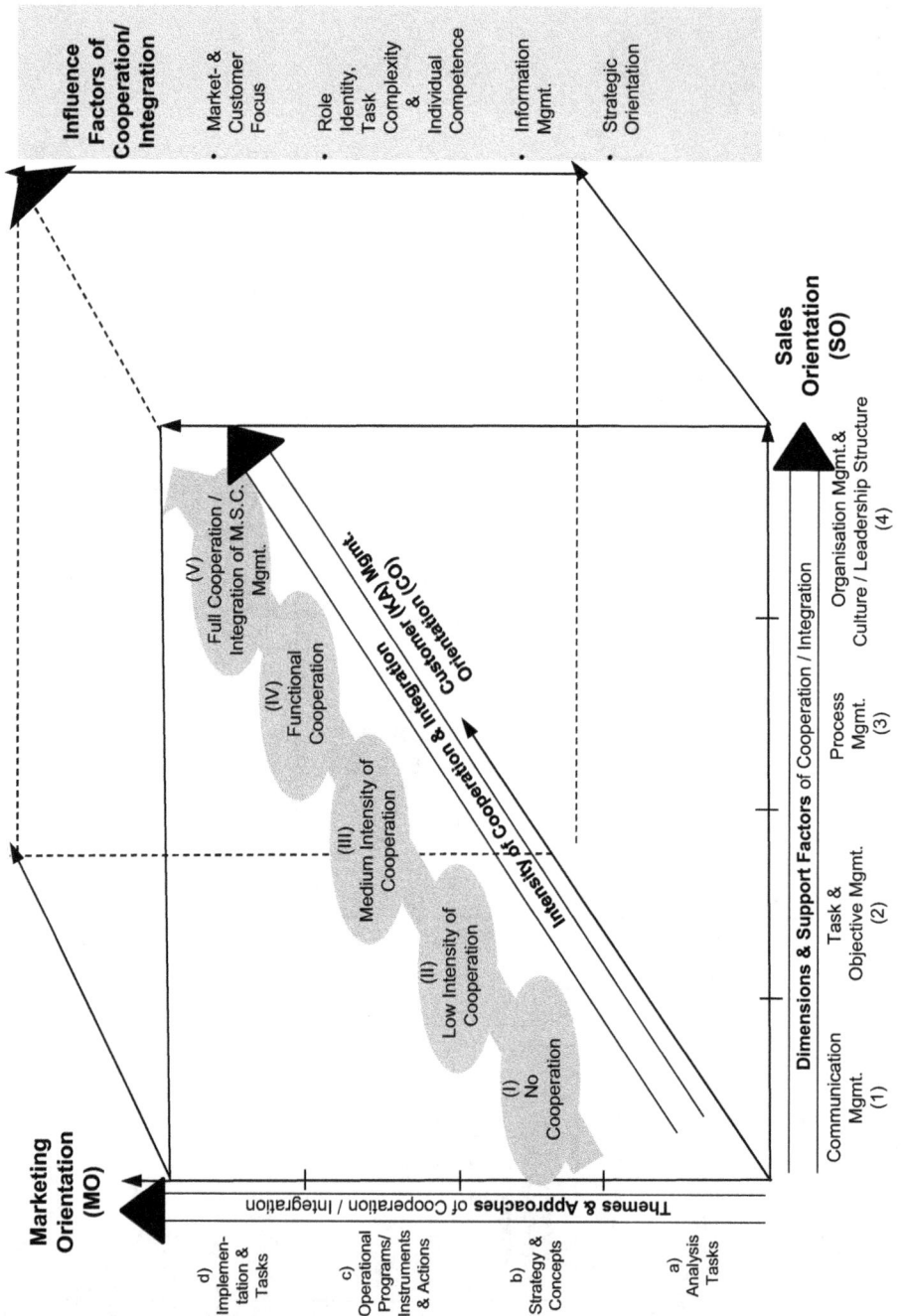

Fig. 12: Integration and implementation matrix for marketing, sales and customer management (MSC Mgmt.) (© Prof. Dr. R. Hofmaier).

References

Ansoff, J. (1966) Management-Strategien, München

Haase, K. (2006) Koordination von Marketing und Vertrieb, Wiesbaden

Hofmaier, R. (2014/2015): Empirical Studies of Marketing, Sales and Customer Management Integration in B2B Companies, Munich

Hofmaier, R. (2010/2013) Die Optimierung der Zusammenarbeit von Marketing und Vertrieb in Mittelstands- und Großunternehmen – Empirische Studien, München

Hofmaier, R. (2012) Möglichkeiten und Chancen einer konzeptionellen Fundierung und Weiterentwicklung des Key Account Management (B2B), in: FORUM Betriebswirtschaft München, Heft 01, S. 6–13

Hofmaier, R. (1999) Systematische Marktsegmentierung und Hit Rate-Optimierung (im Business-to-Business-Marketing), in Pepels, W. (Hrsg.) Business to Business Marketing, Neuwied, S. 130–139

Hofmaier, R. (Hrsg.) (1995) Erfolgsstrategien in der Investitionsgüterindustrie, 2. Aufl., Landsberg a. Lech

Hofmaier, R. (Hrsg.) (1993) Investitionsgüter- und High-Tech-Marketing (ITM), 2. Aufl., Landsberg a. Lech

Kotler, P. / Cox, K.K. (1988) Marketing Management and Strategy, 4. Aufl., London

Meffert, M. / Burmann, C. / Kirchgeorg, M. (2012) Marketing – Grundlagen marktorientierter Unternehmensführung, 11. Aufl., Wiesbaden

II Strategic marketing, sales and customer management (B2B)

To begin with, selected methods of strategic marketing, sales and customer management are important for the **integrative strategy approach.** Fig. 13 shows an overview of selected **methods** of fundamental **strategic goal setting,** (micro) **strategy definition** and derivation of appropriate **programmatic design recommendations** in the B2B sector.

Strategic Methods & Programs / Strategy Categories & Alignments	Methods for Strategy Determination, Targets and Program Options
(1) Basic or Norm Strategies	**Portfolio Strategy Method (MA-CP)** Launch-/ Acquisition-/ Growth-/ Harvesting-/ Disinvestment-/ Consolidation Strategies & Programs, etc.
(2) Market Expansion Strategies	**Eight-Cell Potential Matrix:** (for Market, Industry Segment, Application & Product/ Customer Segments) Market Segment Penetration/ Development or Expansion/ Product development/ diversification strategies & programs
(3) Competitive Positioning Strategies	**Competition Portfolio Method:** Differentiation strategies (e.g. Innovation/ Quality/ Service/ technology differentiation) versus Volume/ Cost Leadership & Customer Specialization Strategies & Programs
(4) Market Segment Strategies	**Market Segment Strategy Matrix:** Multisegment/ Selective Segment Expansion/ Segment Compression/ Segment Differentiation / Segment Specialization & Niche Strategies & Programs
(5) USP Strategies and Core Competency Strategies	**USP Development Method (Matrix):** Core Competence (CC-) Identification/ CC-Development/ Customer Value Development- & Value-Potentiality Differentiation Strategies & Programs
(6) Positioning Strategies	**Positioning** and **Profiling Comparison Method:** (based on Market, industry segment, Application & Customer/ Product Segments) Innovation, Quality-, Product range/ Program (Breadth/ Depth), Service, Design, Synergy, Application, Technology, Advancements & Profiling Measures, etc.
(7) Geographical Strategies	**Regional Strategy Matrix** Regional-, National-, International- and Global Strategies
(8) Marketing-, Sales- and Customer Program Strategies	**Strategic Derivation** (Strategic Marketing Mix) CPM - Integrative Customer Product Mgmt./ CSM - Customer Sales & Distribution Mgmt./ CDM/ KAM - Customer-Development-Mgmt. & Key Account Mgmt./ CRM - Integrated Customer Relationship Mgmt./ CCM - Customer Communication Mgmt./ CPrM: Customer Pricing Mgmt.

Fig. 13: Integrated Strategic Goal Setting, Strategy Definition and Derivation of Appropriate Programs (© Prof. Dr. R. Hofmaier).

1 "Traditional" marketing strategies

A first approach of basic strategy determination (classic marketing strategies) is initially based on so-called basic or **standard strategies**[7], which build on the information and findings of the SPOT and SPOS analyses.

1.1 Basic or standard strategies of marketing management

The first task is to create the **strategic actual portfolio positioning** in the individual assessed market segments compared to the overall competition and thus to derive a strategic actual portfolio (with different levels of aggregation: e.g., the overall company, individual business and product sectors, individual countries, etc.). Based on the actual position (based on the two dimensions MA = market attractiveness and CP = competitive position) (see Fig. 14), a fundamental basic or standard strategy can be derived. This strategy target is derived on the basis of the **actual position in the strategy portfolio.** For example, a basic growth strategy can thus be defined for the product area of measuring systems A (overseas) due to a relatively high market attractiveness, a consolidation strategy can be done for measuring systems B (DS), and a disinvestment strategy can be performed for measuring systems B (GY/AU/CH). For the main source of revenue, measuring systems A (GY/AU/CH), a selective strategic approach would be important, i.e. the short-term reduction of a "negative" contribution margin by lowering variable costs and maintaining the market position, and the medium-term product development and launch strategy (possibly an acquisition strategy) for a successor product in an attractive market. Whether and to what extent a harvesting strategy is to be considered for measuring systems C (EU), needs to be clarified in additional detailed analyses. Overall, it becomes clear that there has not been a previously successful base-strategic alignment for the business sector at hand, and that the current actual positioning status (see also Margins) should be seen as very critical. Product launches and growth products in attractive market are missing, as are viable opportunities of a sound absorption strategy, which is necessary for the implementation of necessary investments.

Fig. 15 a and b show which **main criteria** can be used both for the assessment of **market attractiveness** for the different segments as well as for the respective **(competitive) positioning** and how to calculate the overall positioning value for the actual portfolio.

---

[7] For classic portfolio methods and strategies, see also Kotler / Keller / Bliemel, 2007, pp. 96–100, and others; also, Homburg, 2012; Backhaus/Voeth, 2010.

Legend:

- Measuring Systems **A**
  (German-speaking: GY/A/CH):
  (X: 3.1 / Y: 1.9)

- Measuring Systems **A** (Europe):
  (X: 2.2 / Y: 1.8)

- Measuring Systems **A** (Overseas):
  (X: 2.9 / Y: 3.8)

- Measuring Systems **B**
  (German-speaking: GY/A/CH):
  (X: 3.0 / Y: 2.8)

- Measuring Systems **B** (Europe):
  (X: 1.7 / Y: 1.6)

- Measuring Systems **B** (Overseas):
  (X: 4.5 / Y: 1.6)

- Measuring Systems **C**
  (German-speaking: GY/A/CH):
  (X: 1.9 / Y: 2.4)

- Measuring Systems **C** (Europe):
  (X: 3.7 / Y: 2.8)

- Measuring Systems **C** (Overseas):
  (X: 1.6 / Y: 3.2)

Legend: Area of Circle: Equivalent to Revenue
Circle Segment "starting to the right": Positive Margin
Circle Segment "starting to the left": Negative Margin

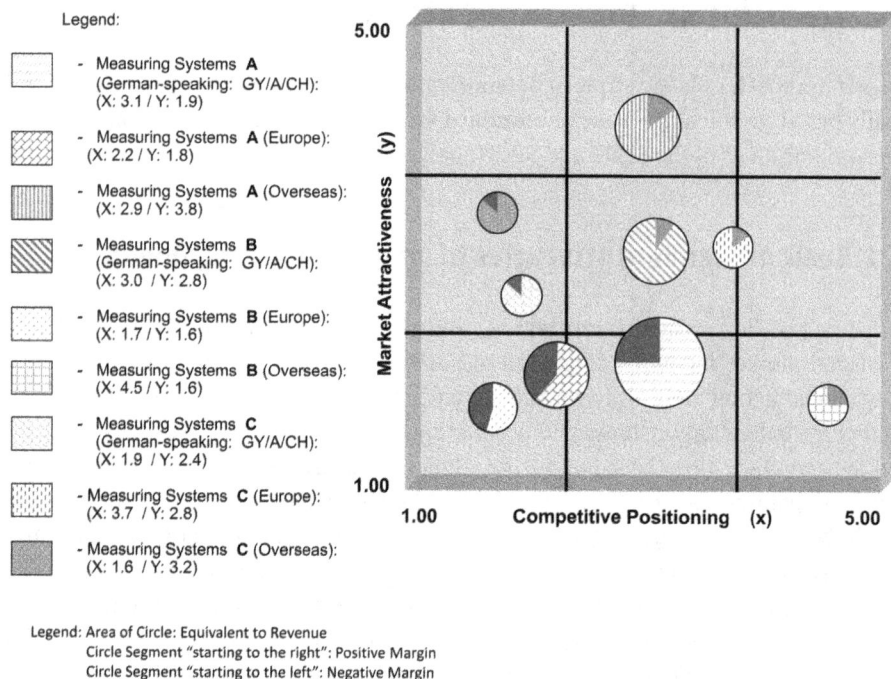

Fig. 14: Example of an MA-CP "Portfolio Strategy Analysis" (© Prof. Dr. R. Hofmaier).

1.2 Market expansion strategies

Besides the fundamental basic and standard strategies, market expansion strategies are to be determined in a further step. As is described in Fig. 5/Part I area strategies, eight different dimensions and strategies for the detection of growth potential (through market segment infiltration, expansion, product/service development, innovation and diversification, etc.) can be derived and developed through an integrated analysis of marketing, sales and customer perspective.

1.3 Competitive strategies

For additional overall strategic goal setting, the relevant competitive strategy[8] must be determined. In connection with previous strategy setting, what matters now is the alignment of the **specific** competitive marketing strategy (see Fig. 16). Here, **different forms of differentiation strategies** (especially for mid-sized and large enterprises in international competition) are selected in sophisticated and qualitatively demanding markets.

---

8 See the fundamental work of Porter, M. (1984) and Porter, M. (1985).

Criteria of **Market Segment Attractiveness (MA)**	Weighting	Short-term Characteristic			Evaluation (Negative ↔ Positive)					Overall Value: Evaluation x Weighting
		Best Case	Most Realistic Case	Worst Case	1	2	3	4	5	
1. Market Volume/ Market Potentials										
2. Market Development/ Growth										
3. Market Quality/ Profitability										
4. Market Occupancy: a) Pressure from Competition b) Barriers of Entry c) Supplier/ Buyer Structure										
5. Exogeneous Factors										
Sum: **Market Segment Attractiveness (MA)**										

Criteria of **Competitive Positioning (CP)**	Weighting	Short-term characteristic			Evaluation (Negative ↔ Positive)					Overall Value: Evaluation x Weighting
		Best Case	Most Realistic Case	Worst Case	1	2	3	4	5	
1. Business Position: a) Market Share b) Return on capital (profitability)										
2. Marketing Positioning: a) Product Quality b) Pricing (Price-Value) Level c) Sales and Service Positioning										
3. R & D Positioning: a) Technology and Development Expertise b) Innovation Potential										
4. Manufacturing Positioning: a) Production Process Flexibility b) Cost of Manufacturing										
5. Organization/ Staff / Process Positioning etc.										
Sum: **Competitive Positioning (CP)**										

Fig. 15a and b: Main indicators of an actual portfolio analysis and target portfolio alignment (strategy) (© Prof. Dr. R. Hofmaier).

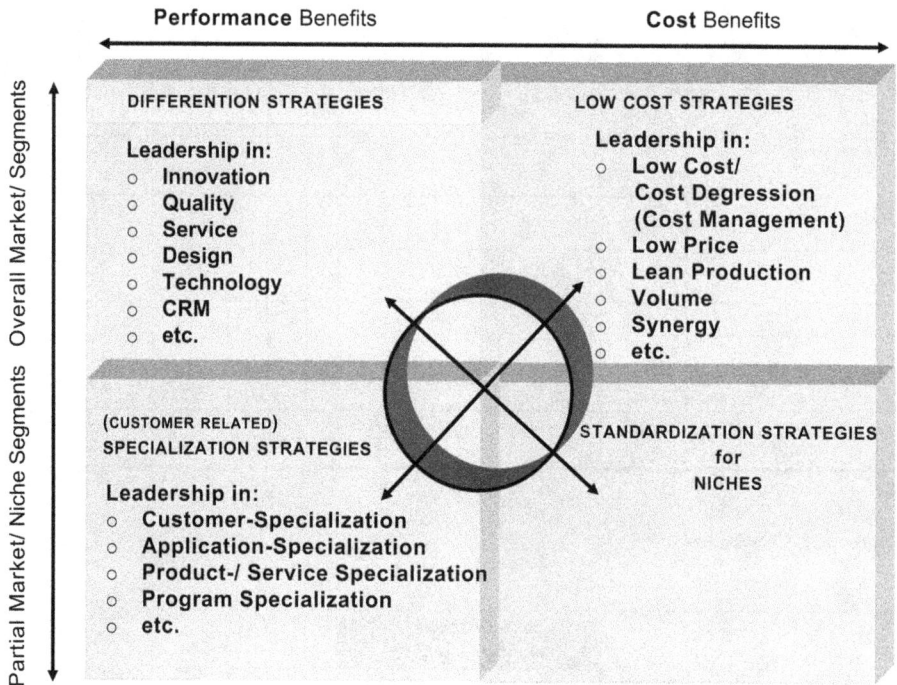

Fig. 16: Basic competitive strategies and their expressions (based on Porter)
(© Prof. Dr. R. Hofmaier).

These **differentiation strategies** often come in the form of innovative leadership (see for example the company 3M), but also as quality, service, design and technology leadership, etc., for implementation. In contrast, the so-called low-price strategies can also be relevant for broad market coverage, which can primarily manifest themselves as low-price, cost cutting, volume leadership, etc. Low-price strategies are especially relevant for those companies that specifically use cost-per-item decrease and experience-based curve effects and implement them in corresponding price leadership positions (e.g., low prices) due to their high production allocation and thus production volume.

Differentiation strategies for select sub-markets or specific market segments are especially important for **mid-sized companies** (see also **"hidden champions"**) in the context of expansion and the achievement of a "unique" preferred supplier position, because a me-too and thus price reduction strategy can often be avoided in the international competition and added values can be implemented through customer, application and product specialization.

In this context, it is often important to **combine,** for example, a "standardization" or cost-lowering/synergy strategy (internal) (see platform, module and packaging strategies) in addition to a differentiation strategy (external), in order to **take**

advantage of both strategic effects in international competition. A single-cause differentiation strategy is also increasingly replaced by a "multi-variable" differentiation strategy (e.g., a combination of quality and process leadership).

Niche standardization strategies are options for small market segments, which can carry out standardization and streamlining measures in such market niches, which make possible corresponding cost reduction effects at a relatively low production volume (see also so-called "virtual" companies).

However, it should also be noted that providers in so-called high-value or (high) quality market segments can certainly implement a top-down price-value differentiation strategy if the international competition systematically advances from below into higher value segments (bottom-up), in order to build a so-called **"defense corridor"**, while also offsetting the often declining market volumes in high-value segments with an infiltration of the underlying segments.

1.4 Market segment strategies

So-called **market segment (or segment focus) strategies**[9] can be typified by the following relevant focal points (see Fig. 17):
-   **Multi-segment expansion strategies:** Many, mostly horizontally established market segments with different products or services are being served. For example, a semiconductor manufacturer can offer his products and services both in many main segments (e.g., automotive/aerospace/IT/telecommunications industry), as well as in various sub-segments of a main segment (application and customer segments: e.g., ABS/assist-applications/OEM vs. system suppliers). Use of this expansion approach, combined with synergy effects (internal), can potentially be secured through strategic alliances and acquisition strategies, which allow the quick and competent implementation of the necessary completion of a comprehensive product segment offering.
-   **Selective expansion strategies:** Strategic segment focusing within a selective expansion strategy is the gradual segment expansion and infiltration on the basis of a previously limited segment range. Typical companies are those that established themselves over time with few products in few segments, and which now gradually address new segments with individual products. This often occurs in the context of a market expansion strategy in the form of a regional or industry, application and/or customer segment expansion (see successful foam, plastics, adhesives and LED manufacturers in select automotive, aerospace and construction industry segments).

---

9 See in detail Hofmaier, 1993, pp. 77–82.

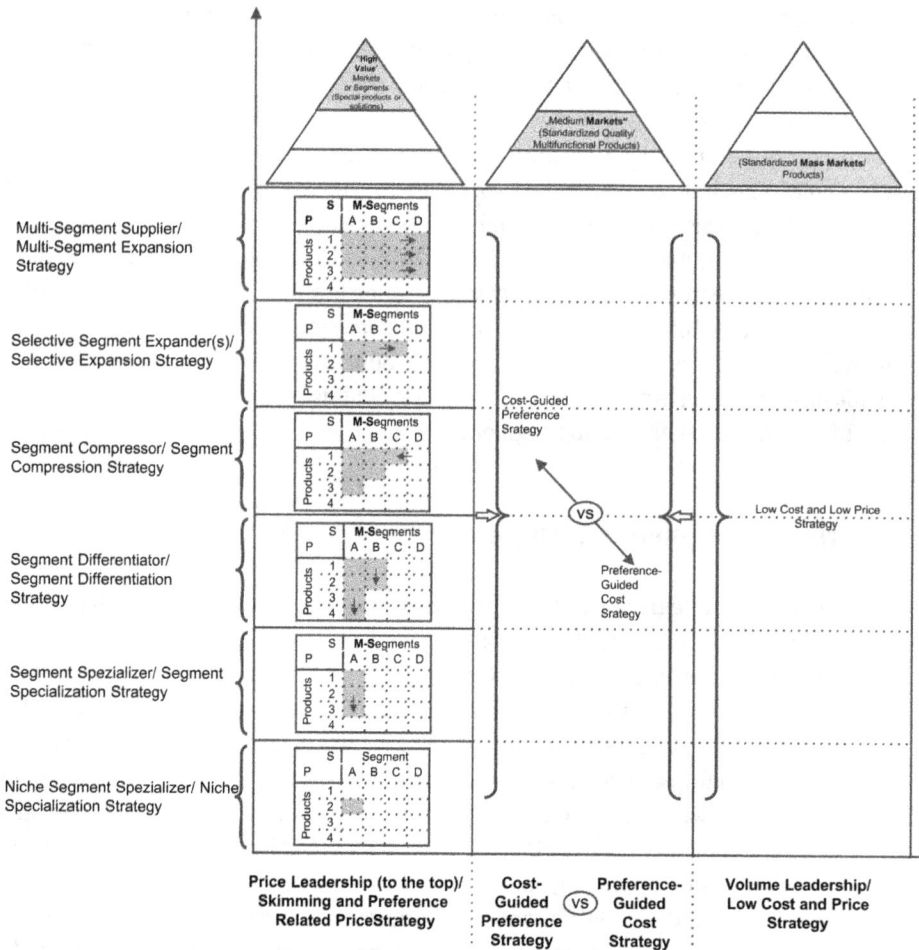

Fig. 17: Market Segment Strategies (Segment Focus Strategies) (© Prof. Dr. R. Hofmaier).

– **Segment compression strategies:** On the other hand, segment and customer-specific requirements and limited resource potentials can make it necessary to focus on select (growing in "depth") segments, in compliance with "economies of scale", while considering product- and technology-"connecting" competence effects (synergies). This can include a reduction in the range of marketing segments, possibly in conjunction with a segment differentiation in depth (see the successful strategic alignment of technical gas provider LINDE). Again, select outsourcing, insourcing and/or cooperation strategies can also lead to the timely desired growth of the company, as can be seen in the example of Japanese engineering companies with American partners or of select German-Chinese joint ventures.

- **Segment differentiation strategies:** These strategies might be required if a pooling of expertise and resources into a few segments must be carried out and additional order volumes can be generated by "extension" of a company's own product range in terms of program depth while using special skills. Because of technology, product and/or service skills, further areas of need can thus be developed in existing customer markets.
- **Segment Specialization Strategies:** Segment specialization can become the objective when the focus on (global/local) segment-specific customer demands allows for a greater ROI in the long term (capitalization of "unique" segment competencies/profitabilities) as a "fragmentation" in various market segments. (The successful segment specialization of some lathe, tunnel thrust, special drill and electronic component manufacturers may be mentioned here as an example.)
- **Niche specialization strategies:** They provide the possibility of a limited product line segment specialization because of very "close" and often (individual product-) bound competence and company resources. But exactly through that, entry barriers can be built for and defended against the competition, and a viable niche market return can be achieved. However, the danger here lies within a mid- to long-term-focused strategy that is too unilateral, when, for example, existing product technology, regional and customer benefits cannot be maintained or substituted anymore.

1.5 USP and core competence strategies

The **Unique Selling Proposition (USP)** and **Core Competence Strategies**[10] include the specific derivation of one, two or up to a maximum of three USPs, USP main attributes and core competence features in order to attain and claim a strategically important and **unique market leadership position** in the mid to long term. The development of **sustainable** USP marketing positioning contains the following steps, mostly in connection with (multivariate) differentiation strategies (see Fig. 18).

Starting with a market and customer main demand and the corresponding own core competence, which should be "unique" in the market, such as a so-called (A) leadership in innovation (see companies such as 3M, Apple, Intel, Putzmeister, Sennheiser, etc .), it must be examine whether this competence (core value) is also relevant in the short and mid-term future, and whether an obvious **added value** (qualitative and quantitative added value advantage) results for the customers. Accordingly, the own core competence must not only be maintained, but be specifically developed. In addition, important synergy benefits and a "continuous" usage benefit or added value must be attainable for the customer – even in the future (longer-term win-win advantage). It should be noted that this will also make clear competitive advantages achievable in the future.

---

10 For USP topics, see also Backhaus / Voeth, 2007, pp. 19–20, and others.

USP-Potential & Core Competence Features / USP Strategy Focus & Development	Core Competences, Individual Strengths, Performance Advantages & "Uniqueness"	Future Relevance & Possible Synergy Benefits	Ability & Possibility of Developing the Core Competence	Significant Improvement of Customer Values (Added Value) & Long-Term Win-Win Partnership	Additional & Clear Differentiation compared to Relevant Competitors	USP-Priority
A Innovation Competencies (Innovation Leadership)						
B Quality Competencies						
C Product Set & Program Competencies						
D Service Competencies						
E Design Competencies						
F Relationship & Customer Development Competencies						
G Process & Business Model Transfer Competencies						
H Integration, Application, Process & Technology Competencies						

Fig. 18: USP and core competence strategies (USP profiling) (© Prof. Dr. R. Hofmaier).

In addition, the so-called (G) **process and model transfer competencies** should also be noted here, which are increasingly combined with innovation and quality strategies and can both include process optimization opportunities (time, cost, resource savings, etc.) and focus on business transfer effects and thus business model improvements (including margin and resource models/improvements). (For business modeling, see also Johnson / Christensen / Kagermann, 2008, p. 51–53)

1.6 Positioning Strategies

Positioning strategies build on the SPOS analysis and the related profile comparison method (see Fig. 4). Through them, important profile indicators from customer evaluation and competition comparisons are being checked and necessary resulting defining programs and measures are derived. These can refer to corresponding improvement measures of innovation, quality, product program, service and design defining, etc.

1.7 Geographical Strategies

Also the **Geographical strategies** have to be considered within the overall strategy combination (Fig. 13 and Fig. 19).

Those strategies can be regional (within specific home markets and countries), national wide, international (step by step merging to similar neighbor countries and furthermore (countries)) and finally global (being global by going into the triade from f.e. Germany, West-Europe to Americas and Fast East Asia if this creates the most MSC challenge, attractiveness and (optimalizing) win win potential).

1.8 Marketing program strategies, sales and customer program strategies

The corresponding **program strategies** (Fig. 13) that are deduced from the previous strategies focus mainly on the strategic program mix of Customer Product Management (CPM), Customer Sales and Distribution Management (CSM), integrated Customer Relationship and Retention Management (CRMs), Customer Development and Key Account Management (CDM/KAM), Customer Communication Management (CCM) and Customer Pricing Management (CPrMs) (see also Part III–VII).

2 Strategy profile development and integrated marketing, sales and customer strategy map

In order to summarize and combine the strategy approaches that are to be tracked and integrated, the respective **combination possibilities** must be checked in terms of their objectives and implementation options, and must be converted into an **overall strategy**. This can be illustrated in a simplistic and compressed way based on the **strategy combination matrix** or **strategy profile matrix** (see Fig. 19). The gray parts show which (segment- and product-related) strategy combinations are possible as a prerequisite for subsequent specification and quantification.

This **strategy profiling** can be evaluated, coordinated and combined in multiple levels of aggregation within the company (segment-, product-, area-, region-related). Three additional **methodical approaches** can be used for defining and transparency, namely

- The **integrated marketing, sales and customer management strategy map (MSC Map)** and its **implementation matrix** (Fig. 20 and 21),
- the **strategy and process matrix** (Fig. 22), and
- the **integrated marketing, sales and customer management scorecard** (Fig. 23).

The **integrated marketing, sales and customer management strategy map** (Fig. 20) initially involves the strategic conditions and premises (impacts) that need to be defined in accordance with the general strategic corporate or divisional alignment. They can contain the necessary mid- and long-term financial, resource and innovation premises (see also the marketing, sales and customer scorecard in Fig. 23), as well as process implications and other change premises. The next step now is to derive, concretize and prioritize the respective **strategic marketing, sales and customer goals** in reciprocal consultation (for the following one to two years in respect to the most important market segments and product areas) and also **priorities and measurement criteria**. Such strategic marketing objectives would be, for example, certain market shares (quantitative), market positioning (quantitative/qualitative) and image goals (qualitative), while respective sales targets would be sales, turnover and acquisition targets, and respective customer goals would be, for example, customer group shares, key account market shares and KAM implementation, customer loyalty, preferred supplier positioning etc. (See for detailed figures the MSC-Scorecards in Part VII.)

In a further step (for more detail, see Part III), the **strategy-led marketing programs** and tools (Fig. 21), such as product programs (e.g., product line extensions, differentiations, specializations), single product programs (qualitative product design and product development, brand management), price and terms programs (e.g., price-value differentiation, condition spreading reduction), and the respective communication programs (e.g., the design of online communication programs, direct marketing, print and viral communication programs, event and sponsorship programs, etc.) are derived and

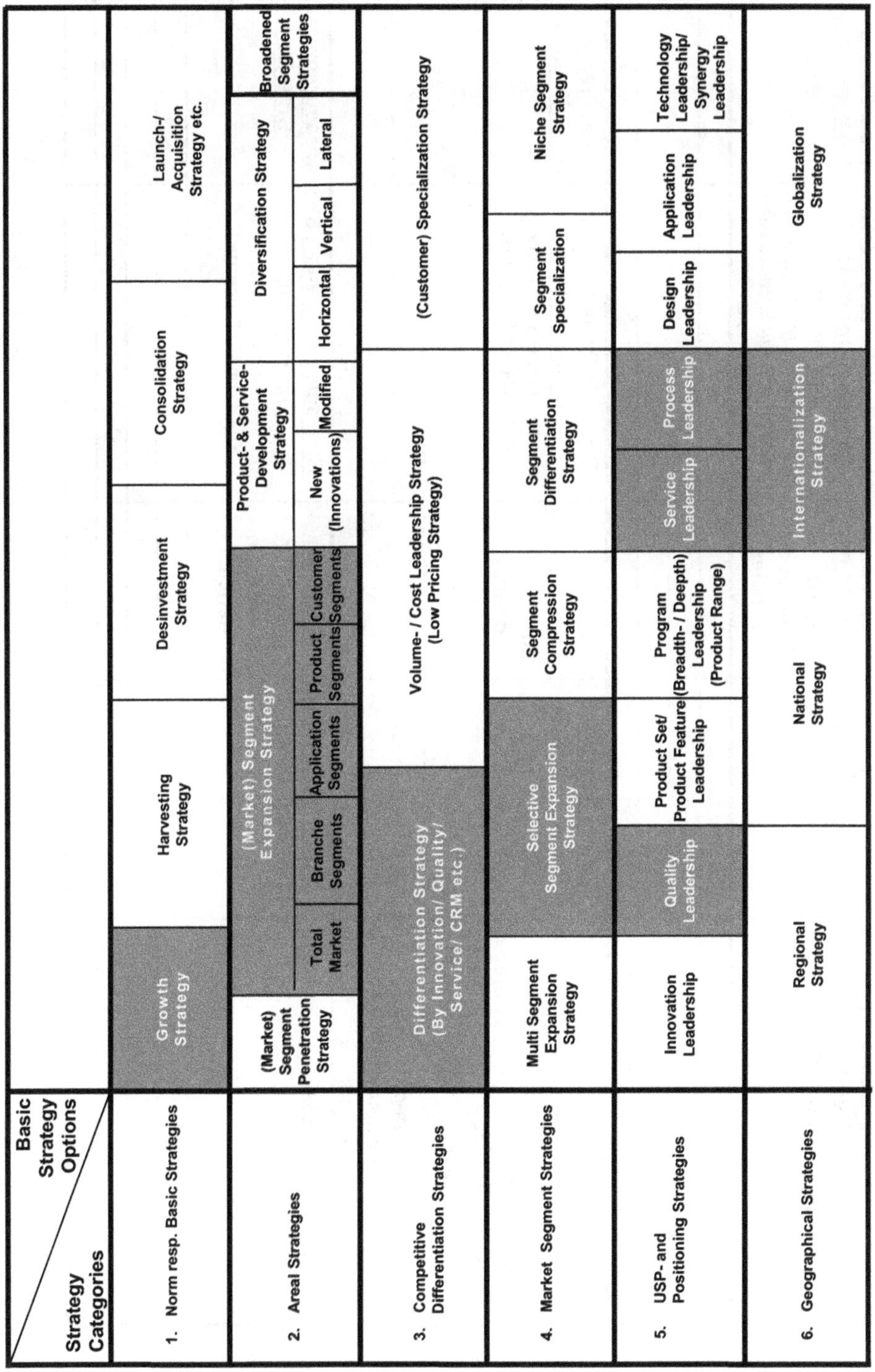

Basic Strategy Options / Strategy Categories										
1. Norm resp. Basic Strategies	Growth Strategy	Harvesting Strategy	Desinvestment Strategy	Consolidation Strategy	Launch-/Acquisition Strategy etc.					
2. Areal Strategies	(Market) Segment Penetration Strategy	(Market) Segment Expansion Strategy			Product- & Service-Development Strategy		Diversification Strategy			Broadened Segment Strategies
		Total Market	Branche Segments	Application Segments	Product Segments	Customer Segments	New (Innovations)	Modified	Horizontal	Vertical	Lateral
3. Competitive Differentiation Strategies	Differentiation Strategy (By Innovation/Quality/Service/CRM etc.)		Volume-/Cost Leadership Strategy (Low Pricing Strategy)		(Customer) Specialization Strategy					
4. Market Segment Strategies	Multi Segment Expansion Strategy	Selective Segment Expansion Strategy	Segment Compression Strategy	Segment Differentiation Strategy	Segment Specialization	Niche Segment Strategy			
5. USP- and Positioning Strategies	Innovation Leadership	Quality Leadership	Product Set/Product Feature Leadership	Program (Breadth-/Deepth) Leadership (Product Range)	Service Leadership	Process Leadership	Design Leadership	Application Leadership	Technology Leadership/Synergy Leadership
6. Geographical Strategies	Regional Strategy	National Strategy	Internationalization Strategy	Globalization Strategy					

Fig. 19: Strategy combination matrix (grid) (© Prof. Dr. R. Hofmaier).

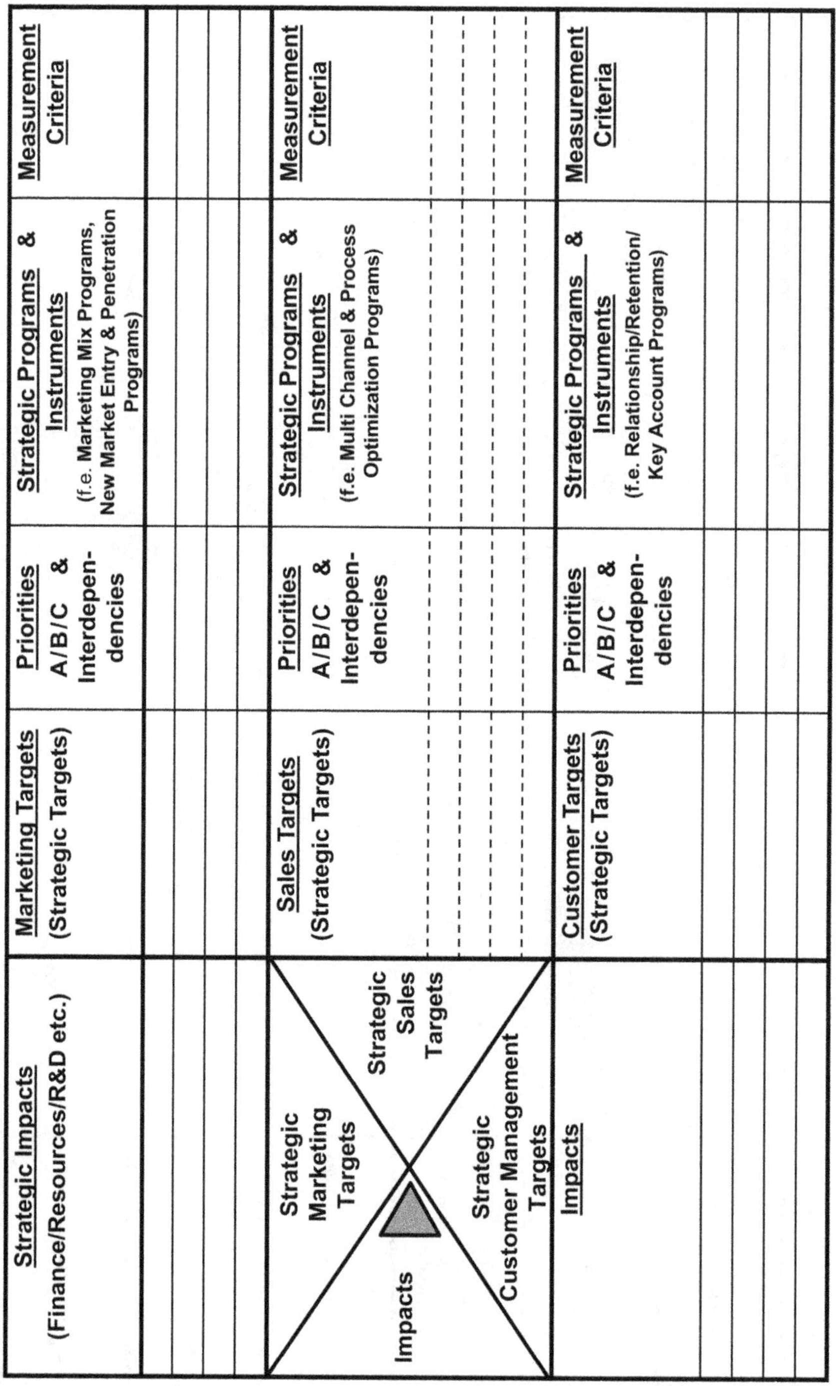

Strategic Impacts (Finance/Resources/R&D etc.)	Marketing Targets (Strategic Targets)	Priorities A/B/C & Interdependencies	Strategic Programs & Instruments (f.e. Marketing Mix Programs, New Market Entry & Penetration Programs)	Measurement Criteria

Strategic Marketing Targets — Strategic Sales Targets — Strategic Customer Management Targets — Impacts

	Sales Targets (Strategic Targets)	Priorities A/B/C & Interdependencies	Strategic Programs & Instruments (f.e. Multi Channel & Process Optimization Programs)	Measurement Criteria

	Customer Targets (Strategic Targets)	Priorities A/B/C & Interdependencies	Strategic Programs & Instruments (f.e. Relationship/Retention/ Key Account Programs)	Measurement Criteria

Fig. 20: Integrated marketing, sales and customer management "Strategy Map" (MSC Strategy Map) (© Prof. Dr. R. Hofmaier)..

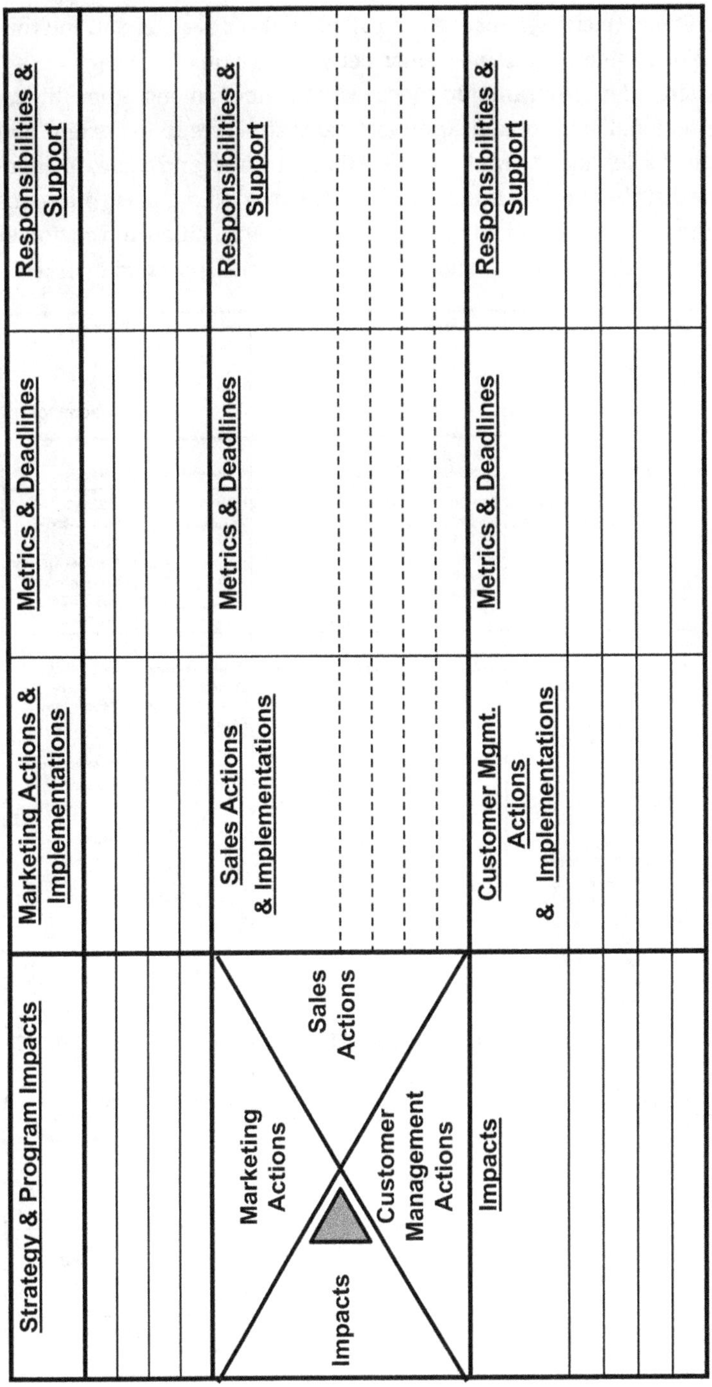

Fig. 21: Integrated marketing, sales and customer management program and implementation map (MSC Implementation Matrix) (© Prof. Dr. R. Hofmaier)..

are coded and monitored (metrics). But even so-called market development, internationalization and new business programs can be determined here.

The strategy-led sales programs and measures include, among other things, national and international sales organization and sales structure (type, extent and characteristics of field sales and internal sales distribution, direct and eSales, competence centers of the distribution cells and structure, etc.). In addition, these programs include changes and improvements for the respective sales, acquisition and customer processes and recovery processes, etc., and their individual measures and tools, etc.

PROCESS & ACTIVITIES / STRATEGY PROGRAMMES & FEEDBACK	Targets	Activities	Responsibilities	Support	Deadlines	Methods	PROCESS / SCORECARD
I. STRATEGY (1) Vision & Mission	V&M Statements	Statements Rev.	To be def.	To be def.	To be def.	To be def.	To be def.
(2) Define Strategy	• Markets & Sales & Customer Targets • Financial Targets • Process & HR Targets	• Strategy Workshops • SWOT-/ Feedback- WS etc.	Strategy Group/ Marketing & Sales/ Finance/ Process & HR	To be def.	To be def.	• Strategy Map • Strategic Priorities • Strategic Plan • Strategic Investment	• M&S&C Scorecard • Strategic M&S&C Targets • Strategic Measurement Criteria
II. PROGRAMS (1) Marketing Programs (2) Sales Programs (3) Customer Programs (4) Process Programs (5) HR (D) Programs (6) Innovation Programs	• MP Targets • SP Targets • CP Targets • Process Targets • HR Targets • Innovation Targets	• Product & Service Programs & Actions • Innovation Development Programs & Actions • Price Programs & Actions • Distribution Programs & Actions • Communication Programs & Actions • Lead Generation Programs & Actions • KAM-Programs & Actions • Customer Retention Programs & Actions • Penetration Programs & Actions	To be def.	To be def.	To be def.	Prod. Planning Methods & Implementation Plan	Operational Criteria & Measurement: • Product Range Criteria & Measurement • Product Development Criteria & Measurement
III. IMPLEMENTATION & INTEGRATION PROCESS	• Marketing Implementation Steps • Sales Implementation Steps • Customer Management Implementation Steps	• Marketing Actions • Sales Actions • Customer Management Actions	To be def.	To be def.	To be def.	• MMBO Activities • SMBO Activities • CMBO Activities	• Marketing, Sales & Customer Mgmt. MBO Measurements & Feedback
IV. MARKETING, SALES & CUSTOMER MGM. SCORECARD	Scorecard Targets & Criteria	Scorecard Management Actions	To be def.	To be def.	To be def.	Balanced Scorecard Methods & Coaching	Integrative Scorecard Management
V. FEEDBACK & PROGRESS Activities/Programs/ Strategy Impacts/ Adjustments	Marketing Feedback Impacts	Feedback Actions	To be def.	To be def.	To be def.	Feedback Mapping etc.	Feedback Scorecard

Fig. 22: Strategy and process matrix (© Prof. Dr. R. Hofmaier)..

Strategy-led customer management programs focus, for example, on specific key account and customer development programs (single-, cross- and up-selling programs, etc.), customer relationship, retention and customer loyalty programs (as part of an overall CRM strategy), as well as select trade fair and focus group programs and their individual tools.

The campaigns and tasks, measurement and time criteria necessary for these programs, and those responsible can be structured and matched through an **integrated marketing, sales and customer management implementation matrix** (see Fig. 21).

For further content support, the one **strategy and process matrix** be used as a back-up (see Fig. 22). It complements the previous approach, in which implementation priorities, methods and the linking with the scorecard that "finalizes" the strategy process (see Fig. 23) are produced.

The strategy and process map is being derived and specified in a triad with the marketing, sales and customer management scorecard (see Part VII) and the integrated strategy map for the respective market segments, product ranges, strategic objectives, program, action and task areas that are to be prioritized. At the same time, they once again make it possible to explicitly state who is responsible and supportive and to what extent. Only in this way, a targeted, integrated and specialized implementation of relevant strategic objectives, tasks and procedures are possible while considering respective directive and testing criteria as well as feedback measures. This allows any necessary corrections and changes to be directly controlled and subjected to a rolling revision, even for strategic objectives.

This way, even the necessary consideration of the particular implementation status and continuous tuning of the three integrative planning, management and control "dimensions" of marketing, sales and customer management are possible.

3 The integrated marketing, sales and customer management scorecard

For **finalizing** the integrated strategy process, the summarizing planning, management, implementation, testing and improvement of marketing, sales and customer management programs and activities is carried out both horizontally (based on the whole company) and vertically (temporal, regional, segmental, product- and customer group-led differentiation) through the **integrated marketing, sales and customer management scorecard**[11] (see also Fig. 23 and Fig. 88ff, and in detail Part VII).

With this MSC-focused scorecard, relevant initial conditions and variables, as well as the explicit **four main dimensions** (marketing/sales/customer management-related, financial, process- and employee-related strategy dimensions) are being

---

11 For fundamental methodology of the balanced scorecard, see also Kaplan / Norton, 1997.

agreed on and specified, and the different strategic marketing, sales and customer goals are being explicitly integrated and evaluated through relevant measurement criteria. Here, specific strategy objectives, strategy-led programs and activities are being legitimized, and the respective parameters are being detailed. Short-term adaptation and improvement actions can be performed in a timely manner by using appropriate feedback processes.

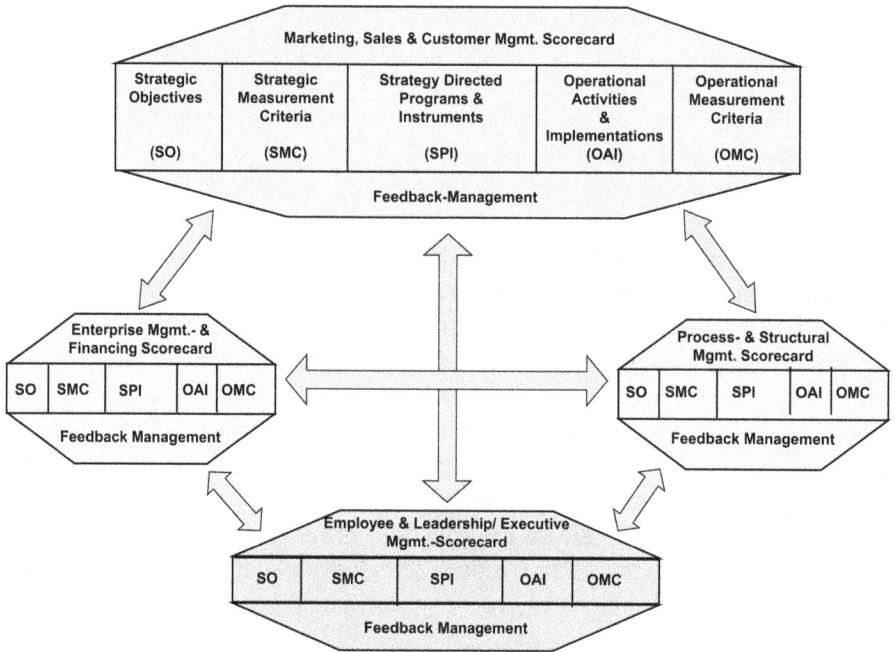

Fig. 23: The integrated marketing, sales and customer management scorecard (MSC Scorecard) (© Prof. Dr. R. Hofmaier).

By applying this integrated marketing scorecard, it is explicitly requested and implied that in addition to the marketing objectives and the corresponding sales and customer objectives and their tasks are already mutually developed, communicated, operationalized as well as sufficiently coordinated and evaluated while determining the strategy objectives. With an additional vote, these goals are explicitly aligned and integrated with the strategic objectives of the other dimensions.

References

Backhaus, K. / Voeth, M. (2010) Industriegütermarketing, 9. Aufl., München

Hofmaier, R. (Hrsg.) (1993) Investitionsgüter- und High-Tech-Marketing (ITM), 2. Aufl., Landsberg a. Lech

Homburg, C. (2012) Marketingmanagement: Strategie – Instrumente – Umsetzung – Unternehmensführung, 4. Aufl., Wiesbaden

Johnson, M.W. / Christensen, C.M. / Kagermann, H. (2008) Reinventing Your Business Model, in: Harvard Business Review, Vol. 6, pp. 51–59

Kaplan, R.S./Norton, D.P. (1997) Balanced Scorecard, Stuttgart

Kotler, P. / Keller, K.L. / Bliemel, F. (2007) Marketing Management – Strategien für wertschaffendes Handeln, 12. Aufl., München

Porter, M. (1985) Competitive Advantage, New York

Porter, M. (1984) Wettbewerbsstrategie, 2. Aufl., Frankfurt a. Main

III Integrated product, service and product development management

1 Implementation of integrated marketing, sales and customer management

For the following proceedings, please refer to the systematic classification of the so-called **"funnel presentation"** to illustrate integrated marketing, sales and customer management programs and measures, as it presents the respective tasks of marketing, sales and customer management priorities. As shown in Fig. 24a, b, and c, all strategy-led programs, activities and tasks can initially be assigned to those with appropriate **marketing priority** (Fig. 24a), i.e. marketing with its functionaries is the responsible spring-leader. Sales and customer management works as supplement and will be integrated accordingly (see the approach outlined in Part I/D). The situation is analogous to tasks with the respective **sales** (Fig. 24b) and **customer management priority** (Fig. 24c).

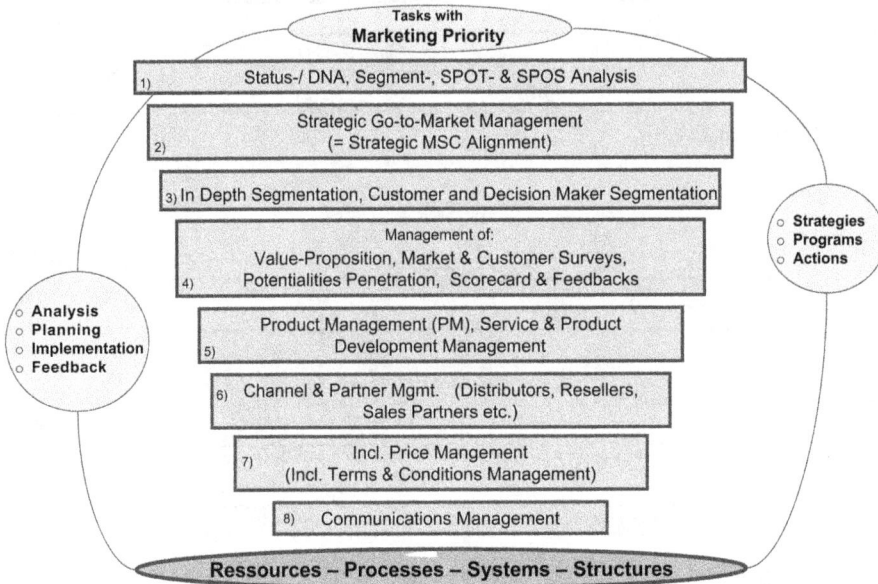

Fig. 24a: The marketing, sales and customer management (MSC) funnel with a focus on marketing (A) (© Prof. Dr. R. Hofmaier).

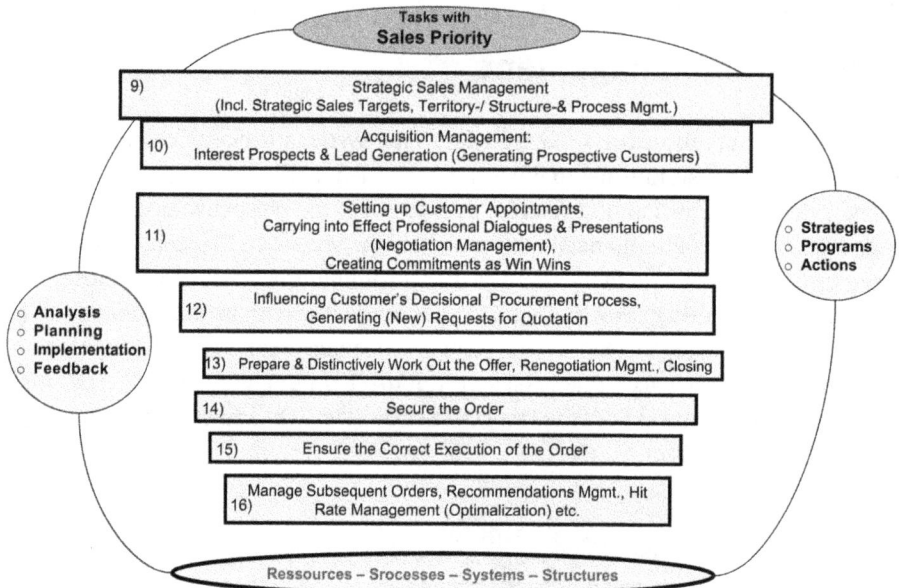

Fig. 24b: The marketing, sales and customer management (MSC) funnel with a focus on sales (B) (© Prof. Dr. R. Hofmaier).

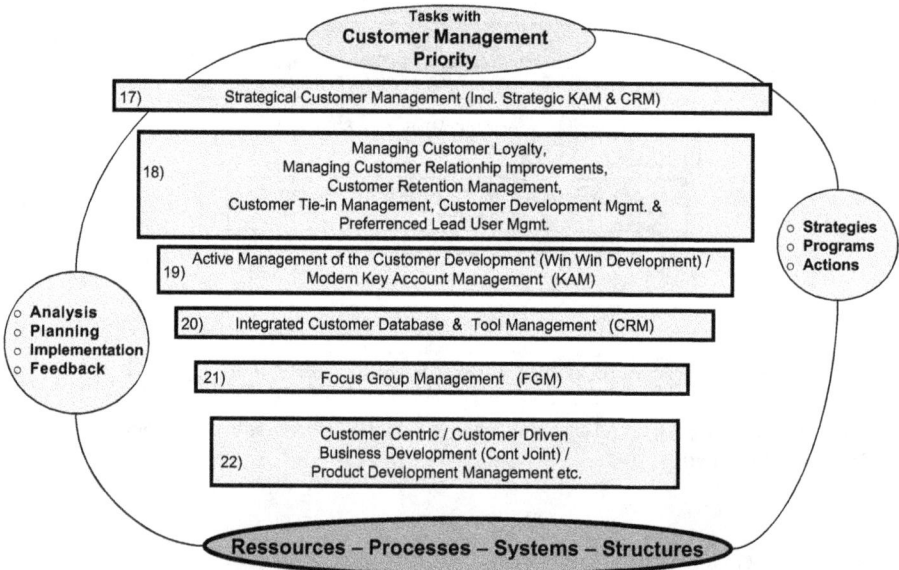

Fig. 24c: The marketing, sales and customer management (MSC) funnel with a focus on Customer Mgmt (C) (© Prof. Dr. R. Hofmaier).

The respective roles are divided into **analysis, planning, implementation** and **feedback tasks** according to the loop. Their implementation in companies usually first happens according to the defined **task** and **resource** classification, which is followed by a **process** to be defined and determined and with relevant **tools** and **systems**, before ultimately making potentially necessary **structural** adjustments. (This should also ensure the necessary flexibility and short-term response option.)

The "funnel presentation" clearly illustrates the individual topical relationships and classification. In regards to tasks with **marketing priority,** there is a focus on strategic marketing management and product management (PM) on top of market analysis. So-called control targets and main activities are to be performed mainly by the respective marketing managers, mainly product management. With these voting or "junctions" with sales and customer relation managers, it is important that the decision-making powers, areas of responsibility, time requirements and incentive opportunities are precisely defined. (The listed tasks initially have a strategic focus before they are increasingly concretized into individual programs, measures and individual tasks.)

To clarify step by step how high the need is for integration and when and how integration is possible, refer to the following summary matrix and checklist (Fig. 25 a and b).

The tasks of **sales management** mainly consist of the topics sales strategies customer acquisition, needs assessment, inquiry generation, offering, negotiation, order and follow-up contract management.

The present-day tasks of **customer management** refer primarily to (strategic) key account management (KAM), customer relation, retention and customer loyalty management (CRM) and focus group management (FGM). Special attention must be paid especially to the explicit tasks of business and interpersonal relation management, which are important for certain customer and decision-maker target groups (see Part VII: FGM). The management tasks of satisfaction- and loyalty-oriented customer management also gain importance here. In turn, the different measures of explicit customer loyalty gain importance. In this context, the relevance of overarching and potential-oriented key account management (KAM) (see Part VI) with its customer care support tools (CRM tools) is once again noticeable.

The integration or **implementation matrix** (Fig. 25a/b) shows how necessary the specification is of the respective objectives, sub-steps, activities, responsibility and support areas, measurement criteria, budgets and other integration measures. This implementation can be gradually introduced and be extended across all business units. The attainable success of such a process implementation ultimately also allows the parties "further development" in terms of one's area of responsibility, results in a better understanding of the overall connection of tasks, and is quite motivating with respect to assignments and the associated team or cooperation approach. It should be noted that such a procedurally-inclusive approach should also be supported and substantiated with necessary tools. Thus, the required cross-check is given, and the respective update tasks and access rights must be clearly defined.

Objectives, Activities & Process Steps / Marketing, Sales & Customer Mgmt. (MSC) Phases	Objectives			Tasks & Activities			Responsibility			Support			Measurement Criteria & Tools			Deadlines & Budgets			Specific Integration Measures & Actions		
	Marketing	Sales	Customer Mgmt.	Marketing	Sales	Customer Mgmt.	Marketing	Sales	Customer Mgmt.	Marketing	Sales	Customer Mgmt.	Marketing	Sales	Customer Mgmt.	Marketing	Sales	Customer Mgmt.	Marketing	Sales	Customer Mgmt.
1. Strategic MSC Analysis																					
2. MSC Overall Strategies & Marketing Strategy																					
3. Sales Strategy																					
4. Customer Mgmt. Strategy																					
5. Market Segmentation & Prioritization																					
6. Structuring of Sales, Customer Segmentation & Prioritization																					
7. Value-Proposition-, Market Survey-, Potenialities Penetration- as well as Scorecard- & Feedback-Management																					
8. Product-,Product Development-, Brand- & Service Positioning & Value-Proposition Mgmt.																					
9. Price & Condition Mgmt.																					
10. Channel & Partner Mgmt. (Incl. Sales Channels, Distribution Programs, E-Sales, Direct Marketing, Direct Sales, etc.)																					
11. Communications Mgmt. (Incl. Event & Fair Mgmt.)																					

Fig. 25a: Marketing, sales and customer management (MSC) integration matrix for step-by-step implementation (A) (© Prof. Dr. R. Hofmaier).

Objectives, Activities & Process Steps — Marketing, Sales & Customer Mgmt. (MSC) phases	Objectives (Marketing / Sales / Customer Mgmt.)			Tasks & Activities (Marketing / Sales / Customer Mgmt.)			Responsibility (Marketing / Sales / Customer Mgmt.)			Support (Marketing / Sales / Customer Mgmt.)			Measurement Criteria & Tools (Marketing / Sales / Customer Mgmt.)			Deadlines & Budgets (Marketing / Sales / Customer Mgmt.)			Specific Integration Measures & Metions (Marketing / Sales / Customer Mgmt.)		
12. Interrerests, Prospects- & Leads Acquisition Mgmt.																					
13. Customer Appointments, Dialogues and Negotiations Mgmt.																					
14. Customer Commitment Mgmt.																					
15. Proposal, Follow Up & Renegotiation Mgmt.																					
16. Closing & Order Mgmt.																					
17. Order Execution Mgmt.																					
18. Generate Follow-Up Orders & Mgmt., Recommendations & Hit-Rate-Optimization																					
19. Customer Loyalty, Customer Relations & Relationship(CRM), Retention & Retention Mgmt.																					
20. Customer Development- (Win Win Creation) & Key-Account-Mgmt. (KAM)																					
21. Customer Database & Tool Management (CRM)																					
22. Focus-Group-Mgmt. (FGM)																					
23. Customer Guided Business Development & Product Development / Conjoined Management																					

Fig. 25b: Marketing, sales and customer management (MSC) integration matrix for step-by-step implementation (B) (© Prof. Dr. R. Hofmaier).

2 Product Management (PM)

Product management (PM) for B-to-business companies refers to very different subject areas and includes the lead determination, coordination and control by the product manager (PM) for each of these areas in coordination with the necessary sales and relationship managers (see Fig. 26). The main topics include the establishing of an "optimal" **overall product and service program in range and depth** on one hand, and on the other hand, the detailed **individual product and service design and positioning** supplemented by market and customer-focused initiation and implementation of product development and innovation measures. Other priorities include brand management, customer satisfaction and loyalty management (to be controlled), distribution and partnership, pricing and term-based, communication and balanced scorecard management.

2.1 Product Program Management

Product program management initially involves analysis and design of the entire product program in terms of **range (diversification measures)** and **depth (differentiation measures)**. Mid- and longer-term program analyses include not only a program structure analysis with life-cycle-supported sales, revenue, profit contribution and positioning impositions for today and tomorrow (two to three years), but also overall portfolio and product-A/B/C/D-analyses and additional so-called complexity and synergy analyses. With a further step, this may result in the derivation and definition of **program strategies** with a focus on a product program expansion (horizontal, vertical and lateral diversification in range, multi-level differentiation in depth) and/or product program clearing in range (program specialization) and/or in depth (program reduction). A combination of different strategic orientations or combinations can also be selected (e.g., program diversification with differentiation or program specialization in conjunction with multi-level differentiation).

The following program-strategic approach concerns appropriate design measures in the broader sense. Thus, in addition to the previous program strategy, it must also be decided "outside in" which areas (from product development to production and sales) are to be carried out in-house with one's own offices or whether to make use of appropriate (development, production, sales) licenses or award such licenses. Usually, the strategic "favorability toward outside" and thus the respective marketing focus is in the foreground (see, for example, Apple's marketing, financial and design centers in the U.S. and their main procurement and production areas in Europe, Africa and Asia). Other areas include warranty service design, bundling management, and internationalization management. (This may, for example, justify different warranties and different prices at home and abroad and thus a corresponding price-value differentiation).

PM-Tasks and Proceedings / PM-Areas	Targets			Tasks			Responsibilities & Support			Deadlines			Measurement Criteria		
	Marketing (PM)	Sales	Cust. Mgmt	Marketing (PM)	Sales	Cust. Mgmt	Marketing (PM)	Sales	Cust. Mgmt	Marketing (PM)	Sales	Cust. Mgmt	Marketing (PM)	Sales	Cust. Mgmt
(1) Product- Program Management															
(a) Product Program Analysis — Program Structure Analysis (incl. A/B/C/D-Analysis), Product Lifetime Analysis, Program Portfolio-Analysis, Program Classification-Analysis, Sales, Revenue, Margen Analysis, Satisfaction, Loyality and Complaint Analysis, Complexity Analysis															
(b) Product Program-Strategies — Product Program Diversification, Product Program Differentiation, Product Program Specialization, Product Program Reduction															
(c) Extend Product Program Management (Broaden PPM) — Outsourcing/ Insourcing Strategies, Licensing Strategies, Service Strategies, Warranty Strategies, Bundlingmanagement, Internationalisation Strategies															
(2) Single Product Management and Product Development (PD incl. Positioning and USP-Mgmt.)															
(a) Single Product Management and Product Positioning															
(b) Product Development (PO) Management and Innovation Management															
(3) Brand Management															
(4) Customer Satisfaction, Loyalty and Feedback Management															
(5) Distribution and (Sales) Partner Management															
(6) Pricing and Term-Based Management															
(7) Communications Management															
(8) (Marketing-)Scorecard Management															

Fig. 26: Areas and approach of an integrated product management (PM) (© Prof. Dr. R. Hofmaier).

2.2 Individual product and product development management (PD) (lead-user-oriented product development)

Another focus of overall product management (PM) includes **individual product design** and **product development (PD)**. Here, product management is particularly responsible for the definition of the best possible product and service positioning in the relevant market segments as well as the timely production of the introduction of **modified or innovated** products and application solutions. The product developments that must be initiated and their firm development phases (deadlines, market launches and times, etc.) are among the main tasks of PM. Furthermore, the design of sustainable and expandable **innovation management** as well as corresponding brand management is important. Additional PM-decision areas concern customer satisfaction, loyalty and customer survey management, distribution and partner management (including numeric and weighted distribution), price and term management (see particularly target pricing and costing, price-value-differentiation, price levy strategies, etc.), as well as overall communication and (marketing) scorecard management.

For product development management (PD), the **procedure (process steps)** and the individual tasks of PD can be found in Fig. 27.

At the beginning of PD is the targeted locating of interesting product and service ideas through a broad exogenous and endogenous approach, with the support and mostly explicit control of PM in a team approach. (In addition to sales and customer management, research and development, quality management, production management are also particularly represented.) Exogenous mainly means the inclusion of important technological, market and innovation developments as well as the explicit inclusion and involvement of **lead users** ("lead customers") and opinion leaders – mostly starting with development, then the so-called prototype testing and through reference marketing. The integration of select, open-minded and innovative lead users and thus the respective connectivity with "development competent" lead staffers and team members to the **outside** (customer decision makers) and **inside** (development/idea/know-how providers from within the company) plays a crucial role here and is essential for successful innovations. An expert "knowledge management approach" and relevant knowledge and resource structuring, as well as the corresponding actions within the company (see the innovation scorecard in this chapter) are of prominent importance.

The range for the discovery of new or more leading product ideas and first PD concepts can be broadly defined (see also so-called "open innovation") in order to also have available the necessary product ideas and ultimately the product innovations for the right time to launch. With a market- and customer-focused approach, this is an essential function of integrated PM.

PD-Activities / PD-Phases	Targets	Steps & Tasks & Activities	Responsibilites & Support	Critical Milestones & Measurement Criteria	Deadlines	Communications & Knowledge Data Base
Phase I: **Marketing & Business Feasibility Analysis**		a) Idea Generation & Product Concept b) Market Opportunities c) Market Segmentation & Potential Analysis d) Position Analysis e) SWOT f) Marketing Penetration Plan	a) Resp.: PD-Team (incl. PM) b) Approval: Marketing & Business Mgmt. (incl. Strategic Mgmt.)/ Sales/ Finance R&D/Manufact. Mgmt. c) Support (s.a. Manufacturing)	a) Preliminary Marketing & Busin. Plan/ Finance Report b) Plan/Report Fundation & Plausibility c) Plan/Report/ Fundation & Plausibility d) Most realistic Business Opportunity	t.b.d	t.b.d.
Phase II: **Technical Feasibility Analysis**		a) R & Detailed Phase Plan b) Tests & Manufact. c) Product Evaluating & Design Review d) Detailed Cost & Fin. Plan	a) (s.a.) b) c)	a) R & D Fulfillment		
Phase III: **Development**		a) Updated Product & Manuf. Plan b) Business Case Validation	a) (s.a.) b)	a) (s.a.)		
Phase IV: **Scaling Up & Improvement**		a) Pilot Marketing & Sales Plan & Review b) Finance & Controlling Plan & Review c) Manufacturing d) Launch Plan & Total Verification		a) (s.a.) & Verification Criteria		
Phase V: **Pilot Marketing & Launching**		a) Customer Introduction & Multiplication Mgmt. b) Sales Launching Steps c) Deterred Marketing Mix Plan		a) (s.a.) & Audits		
Phase VI: **Market Introduction & Early Penetration**		a) Sales/Margin/Regional Plan: Verification & Application b) Updated Short Running Plans		a) (s.a.) & Business Plan Verification/Fits etc.		

Fig. 27: Market oriented and simultaneous product development (PD) (© Prof. Dr. R. Hofmaier).

A variety of select **creativity, brainstorming, association and simulation methods**[12] can be used for coming up with product ideas and designing the first product conception. The major methodological approaches for this primarily include a functional analysis, value chain analysis, and **"morphological box"**[13] (see Fig. 28). Especially the "morphological box" can be used at various aggregation levels in the first phase of PD.

In this procedure that incorporates several methods, it is important to do a systematic breakdown of product and application features, starting with the main, sub and partial features and their (modified, incremental but also "revolutionary") innovation alternatives (feature alternatives). Their respective added values for the product or the application solution and its "improved process integration" play an essential role that should be evaluated. Ultimately, the resulting new product or "solution" lines first lead to different product development approaches (from product modification, e.g., a product "facelift", to incremental or "revolutionary" product and application innovation).

The next step in product development (PD) phase I is the **marketing and business feasibility analysis**. Here, the methods listed in the marketing analysis (see Part I) are particularly applicable, which aid in deriving relevant marketing and business data in order to clarify as far as possible in advance and to "ensure" **successful overall marketing** throughout the product life cycle. **Simultaneously** or (where feasible) parallel in time, other main phases of PD are carried out step by step, such as technical feasibility analysis, pre- and prototype development and actual development, repeated detailed review and planning (scaling up), pre-marketing, and finally the actual launch. Especially during the prototype phase, but also in the context of pre-marketing, the **inclusion and assessment by lead users** (e.g., as pilot or reference customers)[14] can help. You can check out such a lead-user and customer evaluation in Fig. 29. Through such a lead user and sound customer survey (emerging and lead user-oriented PD), relevant requirements for product and service as well marketing "quality" and design can be recorded as well laid out in detail at the beginning of PD, but also in the prototype and scale-up phase, and target pricing, target costing and other potential data can be collected and verified.

In addition, such data and information can also be collected, substantiated and distinguished in the context of select customer surveys, such as **focus groups**.

Pre-marketing includes mainly the provision of a **launch package** via PM (again, in collaboration with sales and customer management), in order to make available necessary product literature, technical articles, application and reference examples, price-value arguments, tweaked positioning, specific added values and corresponding calculations, product flyers and data sheets, etc., and thus prepare a more effective market infiltration in time.

---

12 For select brainstorming and creativity techniques, see also Kleinaltenkamp / Plinke / Jacob/ Söllner, 2006.

13 For the "morphological box", see also Pepels, 2006, pp. 16–18.

14 For lead-user-oriented product development, see also v. Hippel / Thonke / Sonnack, 1999, pp. 3–5.

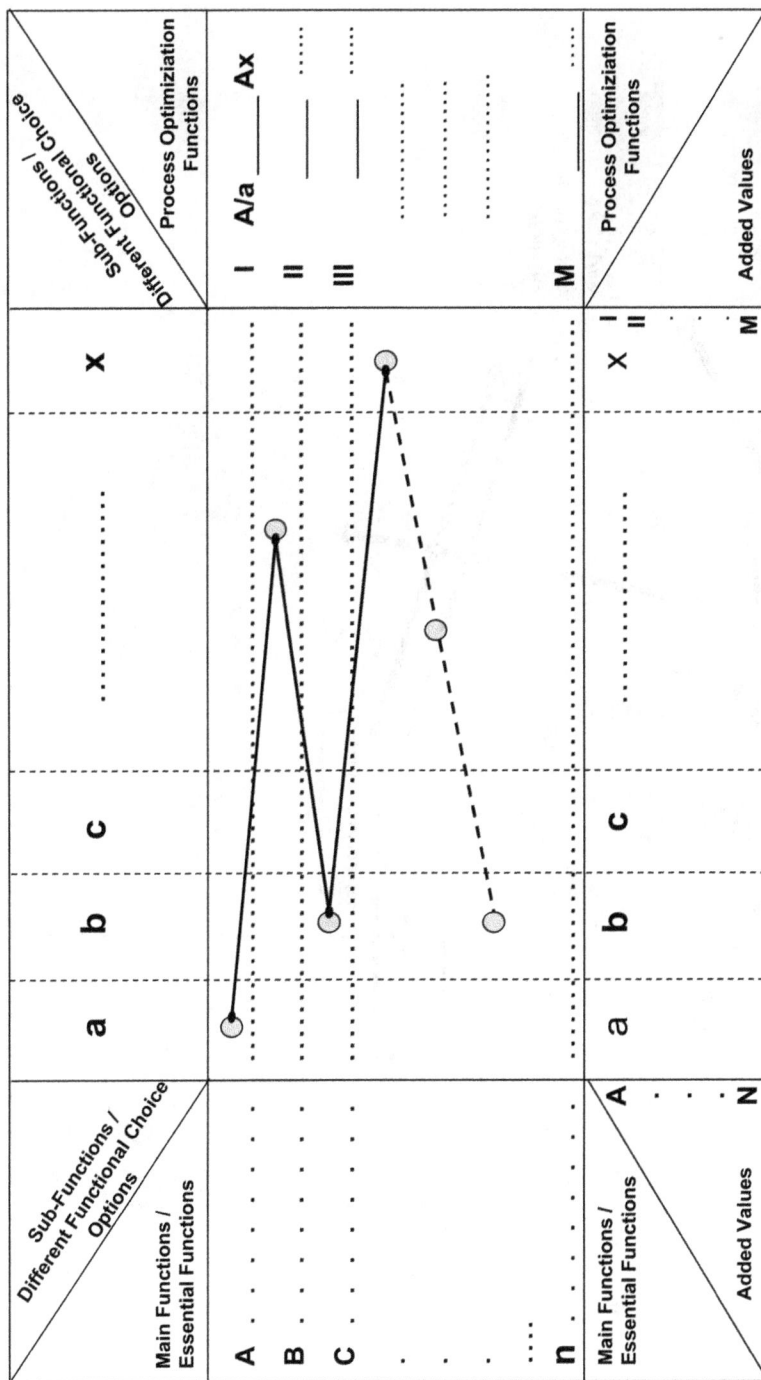

Fig. 28: Morphological box as a method of brainstorming, functional analysis and product concept development (© Prof. Dr. R. Hofmaier).

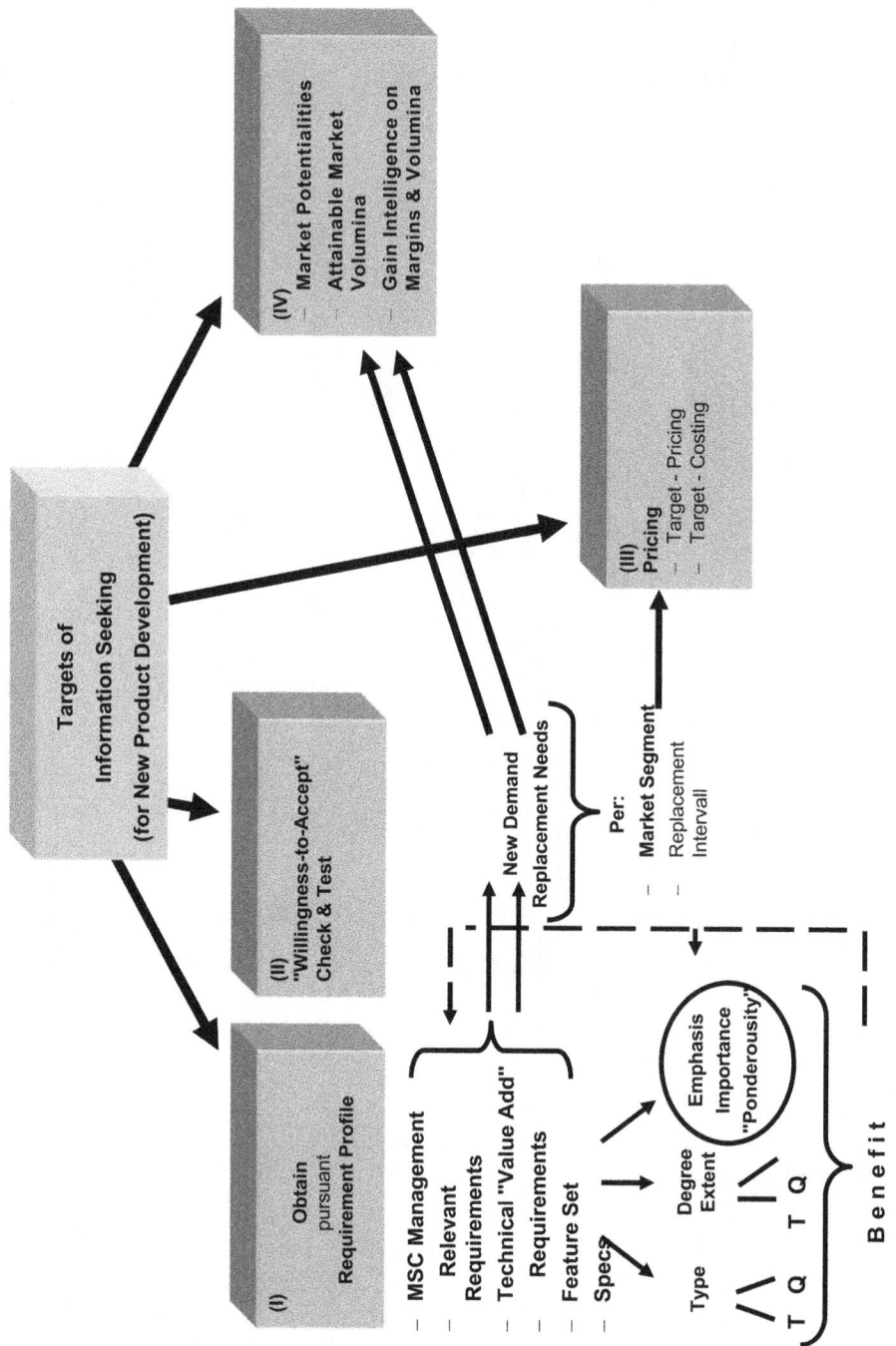

Fig. 29: Information retrieval in the context of market-oriented new product development (involving lead users) (© Prof. Dr. R. Hofmaier).

3 Service Management

Service management becomes more of a priority for B2B companies and their product management (PM). From a business perspective, it is increasingly important to develop and make available secondary and innovative **A-services** and **strategic services** for the expansion of relevant added values and preferred supplier positioning (see Part I/D and specifically Fig. 9: service development matrix and also Fig. 30a and b: **Service Process Matrix**). Since many companies often only provide C-services, but rarely A- and strategic services, relevant service developments **close a strategic "gap"**, can help improve sales and margins, and often allow effective cross- and up-selling strategy especially with bigger customers and key accounts. At the same time, they can provide important measures of (extended) customer loyalty and customer development.

Service Area / Service Categories	Business Services	Technical Services
(I) Strategic Services	❖ Strategic Project Management ❖ Prime Contractor Property Management ❖ International Project and Cooperation Management ❖ Total Cost of Ownership (TCO) Study ❖ Strategic Business and Marketing Feasibility Study	❖ Strategic Plant Management (Planning & Execution) ❖ Strategic (Conjoint) Application and Product Development ❖ Strategic R&D Studies ❖ Strategic Technical Feasibility Study
(II) Operational Services **A-Services** **(1) Pre Sales (Phase)**	❖ Customer Specific Business Service Development ❖ Customer Specific Offer and Implementation ❖ Customer Specific Consulting, Service ❖ Flexible Payment Opportunities (Vario-Fix-Payments etc.) ❖ Bundling Service ❖ Customer Specific Training and Coaching Service	❖ Customer Specific Engineering Services ❖ Customer Specific Programming Services ❖ Customer Specific Technical Service ❖ Development Offer and Implementation ❖ Prototyping Service ❖ Customer Specific Integration Service ❖ Configuration Service
(2) Sales (Phase)	❖ Best Practice Concepts ❖ Added Values Analysis and Management ❖ Customer Specific Service Integration ❖ 24 hours Business Consultancy Service ❖ Customer Specific Delivery Service	❖ Test Equipment Service ❖ Customer Specific Competence Studies

Fig. 30a: Service categories, opportunities and development matrix (practical examples) (A) (© Prof. Dr. R. Hofmaier).

(3) After Sales (Phase)	❖ General Replacement Service (No Argumentation / No Payment) ❖ Financial Service ❖ Recycling Service ❖ Warranty and Extra Ordinary Warranty Service ❖ User Meeting Service ❖ Bundling Service (Long Term) ❖ Logistic & Store Service for the Customer ❖ Marketing (Research) Service for the Customer ❖ Innovation Community Service ❖ Licensing Service ❖ Network Management Service ❖ Change Management Support "
(4) Customer Life Time (Phase)	

	❖ 24 hours Technical Services ❖ Virtual Testing ❖ General Technical Replacement Service ❖ Demo Units ❖ Technical Recycling and Re-Implementation Service ❖ Maintenance Servoce ❖ Interface Mgmt. Service ❖ Insurance Migration Service ❖ Up Grade / Up Date Service ❖ Technical Innovation Service ❖ Solution Management ❖ Lean Unit Pooling "

B-Services

(1) Pre Sales (Phase)	
(2) Sales (Phase)	❖ Common Warrenties ❖ Common Warrenty Support ❖ Common Financeial Service ❖ Common Terms and Conditions ❖ Common Dates of Payments ❖ Key Word Marketing for the Customer ❖ Common Insurance Service a.s.o.
(3) After Sales (Phase)	❖ Common Delivery Service ❖ Common Maintainance Service ❖ Common Installation Service ❖ Common Update Service ❖ Common Migration Service ❖ Common Technical Webinars ❖ Documentation Service a.s.o.
(4) Customer Life Time (Phase)	(Differentiation, Upgrading and Migration)

C-Services

(1) Pre Sales (Phase)	
(2) Sales (Phase)	(Differentiation, Upgrading and Migration)
(3) After Sales (Phase)	(Differentiation, Upgrading and Migration)
(4) Customer Life Time (Phase)	

Fig. 30b: Service categories, opportunities and development matrix (practical examples) (B)
(© Prof. Dr. R. Hofmaier).

4 Innovation Management and Innovation Scorecard

Successful PD management also requires the support of effective and efficient, if possible company-wide **innovation management**. In summary, such **holistic** innovation management (see Fig. 31) needs the listed **endogenous** and **exogenous determinants**, as well as corresponding task and knowledge management in all areas of expertise, but especially in the essential marketing (PM/market research/ direct marketing/online marketing/event marketing/distribution), sales (outside and inside sales/direct and online sales), customer (customer service/KAM/fair and event management), research and development, quality and production feature areas, etc. Finance, procedure, human resource, leadership and corporate culture management that promotes a climate of innovation should not dismiss this.

Besides these substantive **task priorities** and the required **"critical resources"** (mainly staff), company-wide settings, promotions and measures are important for this. This not only helps maintain overall innovation proficiency, but also purposefully develop and expand it. However, what is difficult here is adequate and timely assessment within the company. The application of the so-called **innovation scorecard**[15] can be helpful here, because it allows an anticipated **assessment of specific innovation status** from an internal and external perspective **(benchmarking)**. It allows to recognize innovation deficits in time, address first improvement measures "early", and thus implement necessary actions (see Fig. 32a–e). It is composed of **five different scorecard dimensions** and allows for weighting and evaluating historical, present and (expected) future innovation-related criteria and measures (internal and possibly external benchmarks can thereby be taken into account).

The **first scorecard (1)** contains the **necessary strategic and product/product-development management** issues, priorities and unanswered questions as well as actions of promising innovation or PD management. Significant competencies, programs and methods as well as relevant management options and results of innovation and development projects should be considered.

This scorecard (1) mainly provides information on the status of innovation-related resources, related interconnectedness, and the essential added-value approach. The **innovation process-focused scorecard (2)** is focused on corresponding steps and process-guided opportunities for support, especially appropriate programs and project methods, while the **innovation "structure"-focused scorecard (3)** takes into account the corresponding necessary structures, project organization and tools. The **fourth scorecard (4)** focuses on necessary **staff resource development** opportunities as well as the **necessary leadership** approach. The **fifth scorecard (5)** contains the corresponding definition of the **corporate culture** and the **supportive focus of top management**.

---

15 For the innovation scorecard principle and Fig. 30 in particular, see also Sommerlatte / Grimm, 2003, pp. 49–55.

Its company-specific selection and application allows the comparison of different corporate and business units with each other and based on time (compared to historical values and for the near future = "projective") **(internal benchmarking)**. However, **external benchmarking** can also be performed with one or more major competitors (at least partly) wherever possible. In any case, if it is properly applied and cross-functionally implemented with various functionaries within the company, interesting insights can be derived in time about innovation status and necessary "innovation and (additional) product development." (If used correctly, deficits in innovation alignment, in necessary product development and timely development and marketing of new products, in access of new and future-oriented market opportunities, can be largely reduced, and necessary measures for improvement can be taken.)

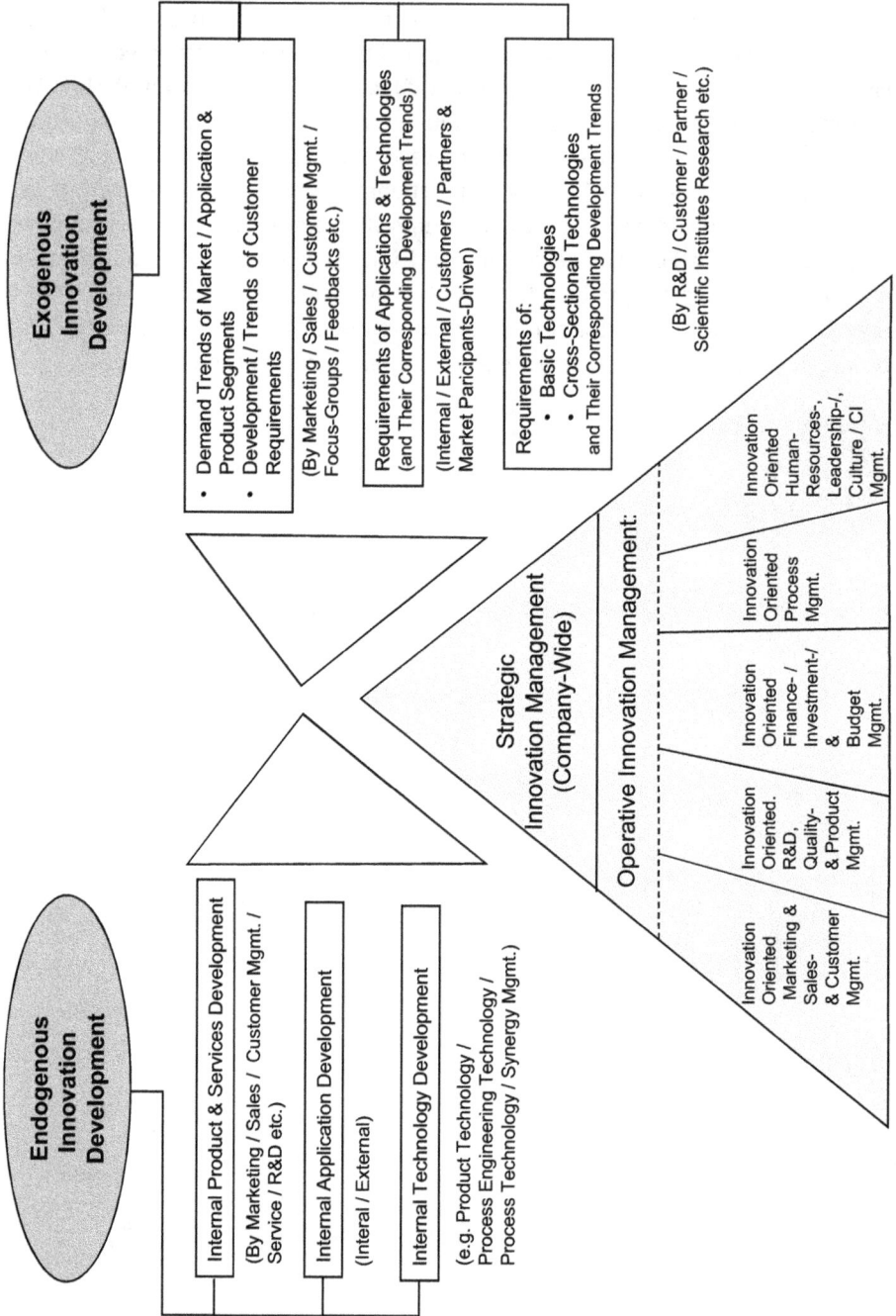

Fig. 31: Determinants of an Holistically Innovation Management (© Prof. Dr. R. Hofmaier).

»1« Innovative Strategy- and Product Development focused Scorecard (Strategy- & Product-Based Innovation Potentialities)	Score						Options for Action
	Past / History			Today And if Needed: Status Quo in 2–3 Years Time			Responsibility: Time Frame / Deadline: Support:
	Weight	Extent	Σ	Weight	Extent	Σ	Top Mgmt./ Commitment & Support
	1 2 3 4 5	1 2 3 4 5		1 2 3 4 5	1 2 3 4 5		Priority: 1 2 3 4 5
Core Competencies General R&D Development/ (Numbers/ Quality) Programs Specific Product Development Programs							
Status of Cruicial High Level / Top Qualifications (of Both Staff and Methods)							
Potential for Differentiation Innovative "Added-Value" Potential							
Cycle Times of: Innovation Projects & Product Developments							
Adherence of Planned Time-to-Market Introduction Deadlines							
MSC/ Management-Relevant Output of Successful Products and / or of Product Development / Product Design Projects							
Cost Cutting- and Synergy Effects being Enabled by Innovation							
Efficient Product Management of Product Development Processes							
Innovation Leadersip Innovation Guided "Preferred Supplier" Leadership							
Revenue Segment Share of New Products & Services in Relation to the Addressed Market Segments and Key Accounts							
Earnings Share of New Products & Services in Relation to the Addressed Market Segments and Key Accounts							
Total (Arithmetical Mean)							

Fig. 32a: Innovation Scorecard: Part 1 (© Prof. Dr. R. Hofmaier).

»2«

Innovation Process focused Scorecard

(Process-Based Innovation Potentialities)

	Score							Options for Action
	Past / History			Today — And if Needed: Status Quo in 2–3 Years Time				Responsibility: / Time Frame / Deadline: / Support:
	Weight	Extent	Σ	Weight	Extent	Σ		Top Mgmt./ Commitment & Support
	1 2 3 4 5	1 2 3 4 5		1 2 3 4 5	1 2 3 4 5			Priority: 1 2 3 4 5
Efficiency of: Searching / Scanning / Identifying Process for Innovations- and Product Development Ideas etc.								
Efficiency of: Creating Innovation- and Product Development Concepts								
Number of Approved Product Development Concepts (per Time Frame or Phase)								
Process-Guided Usage of: • External Innovation Ideas • Process-Guided Execution of Conjoint Development Cooperations								
Impact on R&D and Development Projects by: • Lead Users • Customers and Open Innovations								
Well-Targeted Follow-Up on Successfully Carried out Conjoint Developments								
Innovation-Oriented Know-how Transfer with: Lead Users, Selected Customers and/or Relevant External Partners (By Utilizing a Knowledge Data Base)								
Innovation-Oriented Customer Relationship Management								
Innovation-Oriented Customer Retention Programs & Management (Sharing Expertise, Pilot Projects, Product Clinics, Entrepreneurship Centers a.s.o.)								
Efficient Management of Over-All Product Development Process								
Total (Arithmetical Mean)								

Fig. 32b: Innovation Scorecard: Part 2 (© Prof. Dr. R. Hofmaier).

»3«
Innovation Structure focused Scorecard
(Organizational Structure Guided Innovation Potentialities)

	Score						Options for Action
	Past / History			Today And if Needed: Status Quo in 2–3 Years Time			Responsibility: Time Frame / Deadline: Support:
	Weight	Extent	Σ	Weight	Extent	Σ	Top Mgmt./ Commitment & Support
	1 2 3 4 5	1 2 3 4 5		1 2 3 4 5	1 2 3 4 5		Priority: 1 2 3 4 5
Number of Success of: Interdisciplinary Product Development and Innovation Teams							
Support of: Qualifications and Retention of Critical/ Predestinated Human Ressources							
Organizational and Structure-Supported Possibilities of Well-Targeted Search for Innovation and Product Development Options							
Role and Status of Product Development Organizations							
Efficiency and Transparancy of Innovative & Product Development Driven Competencies Networks and "Synergy Lobs"							
Organizational Structural Support in Respect of Cooperation with: Selected Lead Users and Selected Customers (In Regard to R&D Issues / Topics)							
Rapidness of Response and Success • To Build a First, Initial Concept and Its • (Lead User-Oriented) Realization							
Overcoming / Neutralizing of Innovation Hindrances/ Lacks							
Total (Arithmetical Mean)							

Fig. 32c: Innovation Scorecard: Part 3 (© Prof. Dr. R. Hofmaier).

»4« Innovation Staff Resource focused Scorecard
(HR- and Leadership-Based Innovation Potentialities)

	Score						Options for Action
	Past / History			Today And if Needed: Status Quo in 2–3 Years Time			Responsibility: Time Frame / Deadline: Support:
	Weight	Extent	Σ	Weight	Extent	Σ	Top Mgmt./ Commitment & Support
	1 2 3 4 5	1 2 3 4 5		1 2 3 4 5	1 2 3 4 5		Priority: 1 2 3 4 5
Innovation-Promoting and Leadership / Top Mgmt. Support							
Simultaneous and Cultivating Important ("Critical") Qualifications and Staff Retention							
Support of Facilitate Individual Options and "Predestinated Involvement" for Innovative Product (Ideas) Developments (Innovative Job Enrichments)							
Innovations Promoting Informations & Communications Management							
High Priorization of Important Product Development Topics, Concepts and Marketing Effectiveness							
Support Usage and Integration of External Know-how							
Support of Working with Partners, Cooperative Relationships, Open Source, Innovations a.s.o.							
Further Support of Facilitate Cooperation with Lead Users							
Support and Facilitate Company Involvement with External Experts and Bearers of Knowledge / External Knowledge Resources							
Ensure, Facilitate and Empowerment the Follow-Through of Innovative Concepts							
Total (Arithmetical Mean)							

Fig. 32d: Innovation Scorecard: Part 4 (© Prof. Dr. R. Hofmaier).

»5«

Innovation Culture focused Scorecard
(Culture and Transfer-Based Innovation Potentialities)

	Score						Options for Action
	Past / History			Today And if Needed: Status Quo in 2–3 Years Time			Responsibility: Time Frame / Deadline: Support:
	Weight	Extent	Σ	Weight	Extent	Σ	Top Mgmt./ Commitment & Support
	1 2 3 4 5	1 2 3 4 5		1 2 3 4 5	1 2 3 4 5		Priority: 1 2 3 4 5
Importance, Status and Encouragement of Innovation Accomplishments and Product Development Motivation and Performance							
Provising of Innovation-Relevant Know-how , Timeframe and Job Enrichment Possibilities							
Role, Relevance , Image of Internalization of Learning, Qualification and Creativity Mgmt.							
Furthering the Concept of Being Responsible for the Learning and Knowledge Development Process and Responsible Incentive Based Mgmt.							
Support, Utilize and Implement "extrinsic"and "intrinsic" Innovation-Supporting Motivation Management							
Ensure Systematic Support, Implementation and Usage of Know-how Guided Customer Feedback, Customer Relationship and Customer Mgmt.							
Total (Arithmetical Mean)							

Fig. 32e: Innovation Scorecard: Part 5 (© Prof. Dr. R. Hofmaier).

We now will only include a brief mention of the programs and measures of **price and condition management** and **communication management** in B2B markets as they refer to overall product management (PM).

Degression

PM-led pricing and term-based as well as communication management

Product management (PM) controls **price and term creation** in coordination with sales and customer management.[16] It is important to particularly note that the use and levy of achievable **upper price caps** during the launch of new products is being considered in the context of preferred supplier positioning, and that corresponding target pricing is being pursued particularly through sound focus group management (FGM) with corresponding price levy leeway. Likewise, opportunities from intra-segment- and inter-segment-related **price-value differentiation** should be used (see Part I), because they not only allow for better segment infiltration, but also for improved margin generation.

Communication management focuses on efficient development of specific individual communication concepts[17] (e.g., direct marketing, advertising, sponsorship, SEO and SEM concepts[18]), as well as the efficient combination of individual concepts into a unified business unit, business segment, or company-wide master plan (see in combination with sales activities also Fig. 35a). The respective **conceptual decision parameters** must be considered:

They include the definition of specific (individual and total)
- Communication goals (direct/indirect)
- Communication target group approach and outreach
- Communication budgets (and their dynamic assessment values)
- Communication content and visualizations
- Communication media choices, their combination and synergistic effects
- Communication periods
- Communication success control options (direct/indirect).

---

16 For detailed pricing and pricing development in B2B markets, see also Simon 2000
17 For general communication management, see also Meffert / Burmann / Kirchgeorg, 2012.
18 For SEO and SEM concepts, see also Bischopink / Ceyp, 2007

References

Hofbauer, G. / Sangl, A. (2011) Professionelles Produktmanagement – Der prozessorientierte Ansatz, Rahmenbedingungen, Strategien, 2. Aufl., Erlangen

Hofmaier, R. (2013) Product, Product Development and Innovation Management, Lecture Manuscript, München

Kleinaltenkamp, M. / Plinke, W. / Jacob, F. / Söllner, A. (2006) Markt- und Produktmanagement – Die Instrumente des Business-to-Business-Marketing, 2. Aufl., Wiesbaden

Meffert, H. / Burmann, Ch. / Kirchgeorg, M. (2012) Marketing – Grundlagen marktorientierter Unternehmensführung, Wiesbaden

Pepels, W. (2013) Produktmanagement: Produktinnovation, Markenpolitik, Programmplanung, Prozessorganisation, 6. Aufl., München

Simon, H. (2000) Power Pricing, Frankfurt a. Main

Sommerlatte, T. / Grimm, U. (2003) Kreativität besser managen, in: Harvard Business Manager, Heft 2, S. 49–55

v. Bischopink, Y / Ceyp, M (2009) Suchmaschinen-Marketing – Konzepte, Umsetzung und Controlling für SEO und SEM, 2. Aufl., Berlin

v. Hippel, E. / Thonke, St. / Sonnack, M. (1999) Creating Breakthrough at 3M, in: Harvard Business Review on Innovation, pp. 3–9

IV Integrated sales, customer acquisition and negotiation management

Integrated MSC management must now determine and incorporate the appropriate **sales approach**. This can be divided into **sales structure, sales process** (including multi-stage acquisition steps) and **negotiation approaches.** First, we will discuss the overall sales approach with its different distribution channels and organs according to respective customer types and kinds of customers (sales structure) (see Fig. 33), before we then focus on multimedia customer acquisition approach and sales fine-tuning based on select sales processes with respective "optimization" key figures. Finally, we discuss a "cross-cultural" negotiation management approach, which becomes more and more important these days.

1 Sales structure in the context of marketing and customers (MSC Management)

A national and international **sales structure** and its **distribution organs** can be generally designed with a focus on respective customer structure and therefore types of customers and **customer typology** (see Fig. 33).

At first, actual customers can be distinguished according to their **customer types** as **A, B, C and D customers.** This is mainly done based on criteria of actual sales, strategic potential (sales, margin development, know-how transfer, lead-user, disseminator potential, etc.), customer margin and customer growth/development potential (see Fig. 34a).

Due to today's increasingly limited resources within a company, the same effort and the same times of availability cannot be offered. Therefore, the respective division of resources and timing must be done according to **priorities**. Priorities develop based on criteria I to IV (Fig. 34a) and the resulting classification of customers and customer type status. An A-customer has a much higher potential for development, infiltration and thus sales, revenue and margins than a B-, C- or D-customer. In this respect, A-customers (usually key accounts) need a specific integrative marketing, sales and customer management and service approach, for example, through coordinated CRM, customer development and key account management (KAM). Such a KAM works in conjunction with the support of key account marketing (and possibly KA field sales – as well as technical KA service management). This can often lead to customer and business development potential that is far above average and manifold (see Part VI), which is usually not possible and implementable with other customer types (unfavorable cost-benefit ratio).

On one hand, it is therefore important to analyze, develop and tap **A-customers** based on their "diverse" potentials; on the other hand, all actual customers must undergo a corresponding screening in order to discover and possibly target even a **latent A-customer potential** (e.g., with a B- or just-acquired C-customer) (see target customer profile or "development arrow" in Fig. 34a). Only then we can speak of a "complete" or consistent A-customer profile.

If one were to analyse customers only based on their actual sales, as it unfortunately still happens quite often, but not according to their important criteria of potential, one might not recognize **"sleeping giants"** (key account potentials) and would leave a multitude of existing customer potential unused and disregarded.

Potential B2B Customers
(Value Bearing Potential Customers) **Existing Customers**

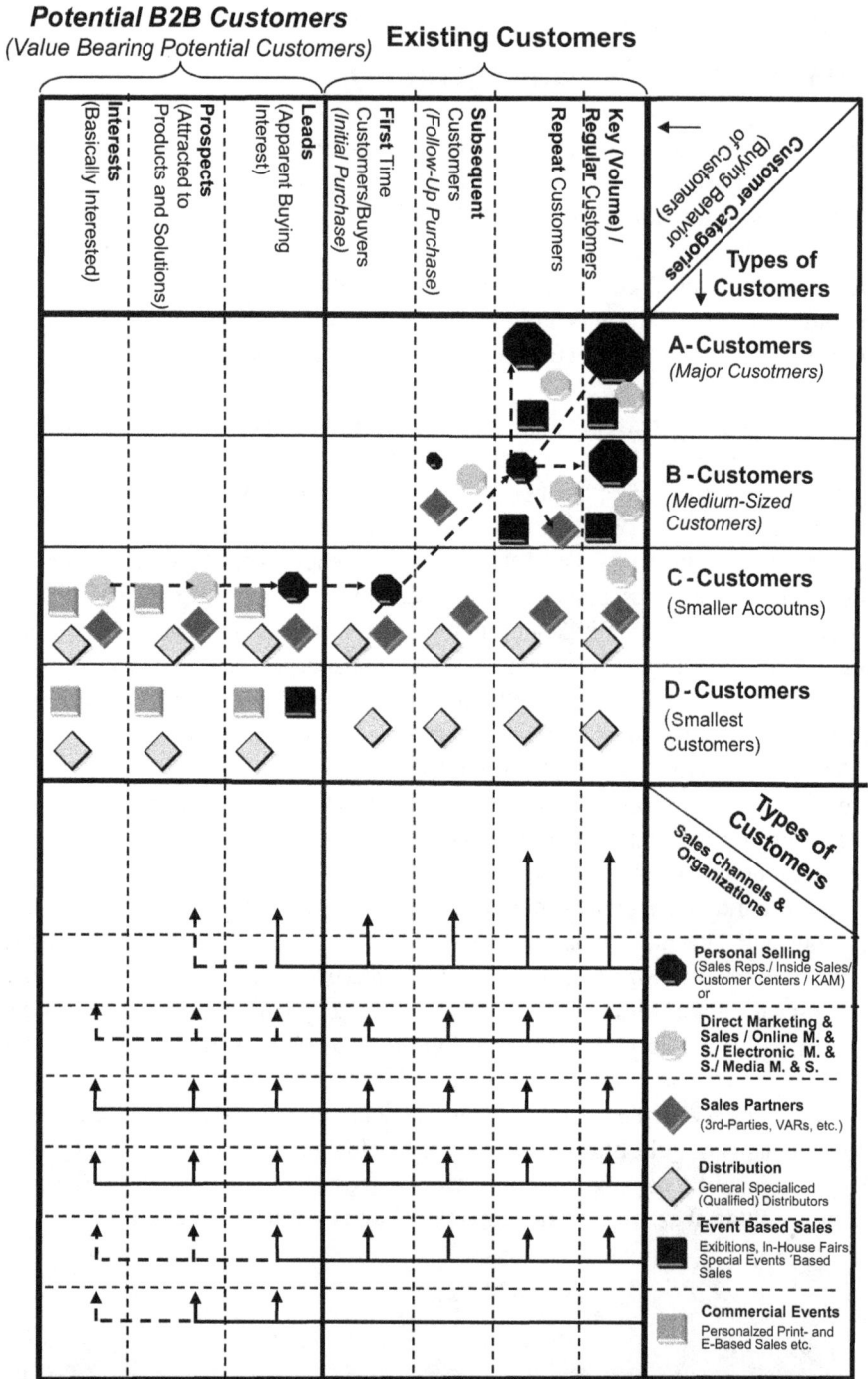

Fig. 33: Sales structure and distribution organs (within B2B customer context)

(© Prof. Dr. R. Hofmaier).

Criteria for Typing \ Types of Customer	A Customer	B Customer	C Customer	D Customer
(I) Actual Sales	X_1		X_0	
(II) Customer Strategic Potential	X_1			
(III) Customer Margin	X_1			
(IV) Customer Growth	X_1			

Legend: — · — Customer Profile "as Is"
---- Customer Target Profile
——➤ Customer "Development"

Fig. 34a: Customer Categorisation by Types and Criteria (© Prof. Dr. R. Hofmaier).

The overall sales structure presentation makes it clear that different types of custom-ers should experience different kinds of sales support through **different kinds of sales institutions** (Sales Representatives (OS)/Inside Sales/eSales etc.). However, A- and B-customers can be attended to not only with **personalized outside sales (OS)** and **inside sales (IS)** in its different forms[19], but also with **direct/e-marketing or eSales**, etc. (see also, for example, spare parts/repair services). But smaller C- and D-customers can also be attended to not only with inside sales (IS) or e-sales, but mainly also through **sales partners** (f.e. **VAR's**) and (technical) **distributors**, etc.. (For the acquisition, "special" channels and organs, such as event, PR and online-based distribution design, can also be used.)

Furthermore, it is important to note that actual and potential customers should be addressed and – where possible – built and "developed" differently according to their customer type (purchase status). First, **potential customers** are divided into so-called **interests**, that is, companies, which have a fundamental need for potential (depending on nature of the business, administration, production concept and mar-keting approach, etc.). They can thus be basically considered as customers and are mostly recorded, selected and contacted by the marketing division (especially at first by market research and direct marketing) and then by the sales department (inside sales, tele-sales, e-sales, customer competence center (internal/external, etc.) via fitting acquisition and address data management (see Part IV/B). In a second acquisi-tion step and once interest and need have basically been confirmed, such potential customers can be classified as **prospects** who then trigger the respective next acquisi-tion steps and sales process stages. When a product or solution requirement is specifi-

---

19 For the varying degrees and forms of internal sales office staff, see also frequently outsourced customer service centers, centers of excellence, customer competence centers, call centers, etc.

cally laid out and comprehensible, the actual sales process now starts, since this is already about specified **leads** that are now "attended to" as part of the sales process and its individual steps (request generation, quoting, and follow-up negotiations, etc.). If such a lead now buys for the **first time**, he/she turns into a launch customer, who can now be developed (depending on customer analysis and prioritization) into a follow-up **(subsequent)**, repeat, and, if necessary, up to a **regular customer**. (Conversely, so-called "lost" customers can be recovered as "sustainable" actual customers with specific "re-acquisition" ("lost status" I = short-term recoverable customer; "lost status" II = mid-term recoverable customer; "lost status" III = unrecoverable customer).)

Depending on customer status, different sales organs can be combined with customer support institutions as well as those responsible for marketing **(team selling)**. Basically, it depends on the **optimal selling mix**, i.e. a usefully integrated sales, customer care and marketing team (especially for larger customers) and thus a "team approach" through different levels of inclusion and support of internal service/inside sales, tele-sales, direct marketing, e-marketing and e-sales, online marketing and distribution partners.

Additional integratable distribution organs include, for example, **sales partners** (value-added resellers, system integrators, consultants, etc.) that can add their own value creation for customers (e.g., a system retailer who can take on software sales as well as hardware selections and implementation advice/care), or even **special distributors** (mostly specialized distributors), who present customers with product programs and assortment-building functions in order to facilitate his/her decisions among all the choices. **Additional** select, partly also (supplementary) special forms of distribution organs can be specific company or customer event measures, different trade shows (types of trade shows) and "special offers" in the context of PR, sponsorship and other communication activities (with direct follow-up or ordering options) (as well as various online/communication and other distribution media (see also Fig. 37a and b)). Overall, respective sales care and support can take place with varying intensity and varying scope of support (ideal situation illustrated by the arrow in Fig. 33).

Another possibility of Customer analysis and planning management can be described by the **present** account and **"target position" account portfolio** (see Fig. 34b). Using the necessary customer data base, the relevant accounts can be categorized based on their attractiveness and our provider position as "Question Mark Accounts", "Star Accounts", "Cash Cow Accounts" and "Migration Accounts". This provides the opportunity to position our present accounts based on these categories and to compare it with an "ideal typical" (benchmark oriented) account portfolio (based on branch and segment specific empirical studies). This will lead to a more guidelined and efficient positioning of our select accounts. According to the practical example (in Fig. 34b) basically more star accounts developed (out of the question mark accounts) and even more substantial cash cow accounts are needed. On the other side the second largest present account group of migration accounts should be reduced resp. transferred to less cost intensive sales channels (e.g. e-sales, resellers, distributors). In summary this account portfolio generally allows more distinctive and different planning and implementation of the multi channel sales and distribution organs and a more specific account and specifically key account management (see Part VI).

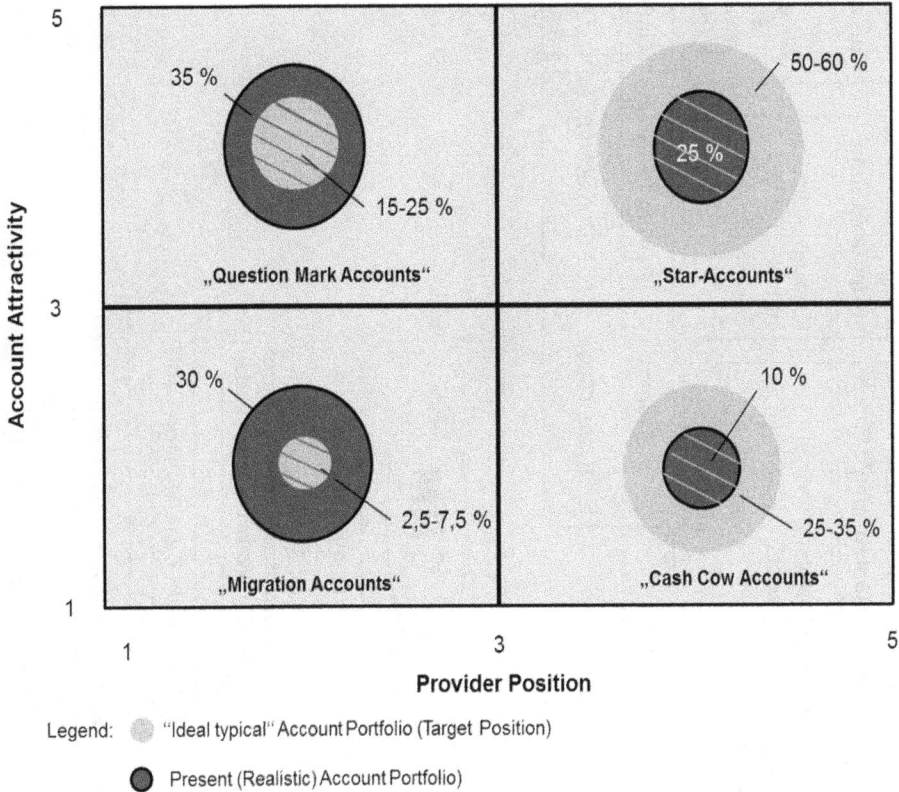

Legend: ⬤ "Ideal typical" Account Portfolio (Target Position)

⬤ Present (Realistic) Account Portfolio)

Fig. 34b: "Ideal Typical" (Target) and present account portfolio positioning by types of customers (practical example) (© Prof. Dr. R. Hofmaier).

2 Customer acquisition and its multi-functional approach

Possibilities of acquiring customers in B2B markets today are very diverse and result in a multiple **customer acquisition** approach with a corresponding mix of media and thus a diverse acquisition basis. Fig. 35 illustrates this with a **systematic overview:**

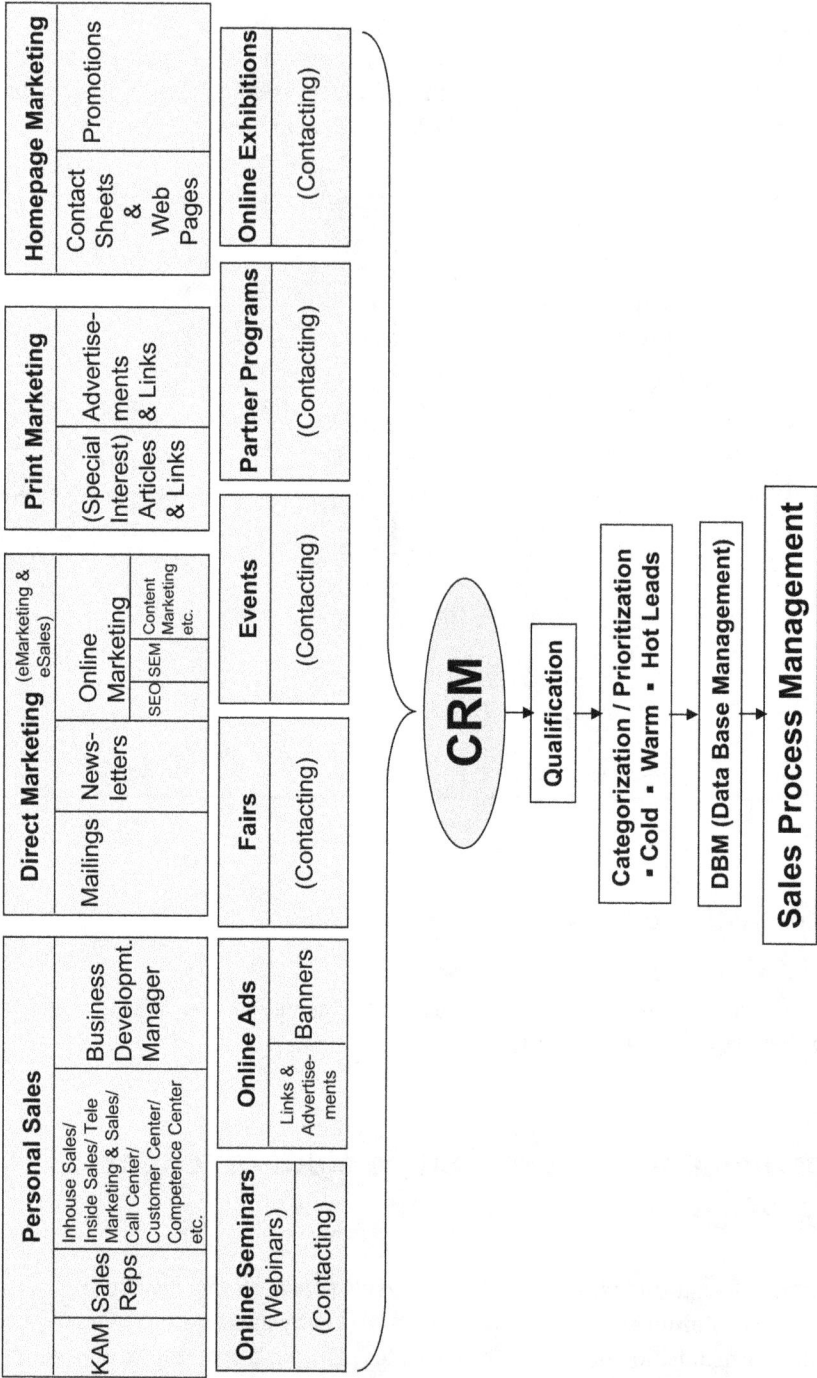

Fig. 35: Opportunities for winning customers (customer acquisition) and customer acquisition approach (© Prof. Dr. R. Hofmaier).

Personal sales and personal customer contact (measures of personnel sales, customer management and inside sales/tele-sales/marketing approach, etc.) represent a first approach to acquire select customers. Thus, the key account manager (KAMgr.) can – aside from actual KA-development and infiltration – facilitate a first sighting or contact of a potential new ("referred") national and inter-national (large) customer for the overall acquisition through his/her communication and information network. Along the same lines, external sales representatives as well as internal representatives (in-house/inside sales, etc.) in their various forms (call center/customer center/competence center, etc.) can be used specifically for this purpose. In addition, if present, business development managers can also be integrated and incorporated into customer acquisition.

A second approach involves so-called **direct marketing** (including e-marketing and direct sales/e-sales). Through select (electronic) mailing campaigns, newsletter distribution and the entire acquisition range of online marketing and content management (see Fig. 36, 37a and b), a variety of customer acquisition programs and measures can be applied and implemented. (We won't discuss individual instruments of online marketing[20] in depth.)

Another important B2B acquisition area is **print marketing**. Here, select technical papers and articles are especially important, particularly if they refer to relevant experiences of lead users and/or opinion leaders. These can be combined with appropriate advertising, PR and online measures. Another acquisition channel is website marketing. In addition to contact sheets and select sales promotions, it can address other (especially international) interested parties. Furthermore, so-called webinars, online advertisement, fairs/trade shows and events, as well as integrated partner programs and online exhibitions can be considered.

Fig. 37a and b summarize a detailed overview of select media-related support measures based on **content and levels of communication for customer acquisition** and care. Various print and electronic media marketing outlets can be selected and combined based on the required content after each phase for customer approach and acquisition.

---

[20] For detailed online marketing, see also v. Bischopinck / Leyp (2009).

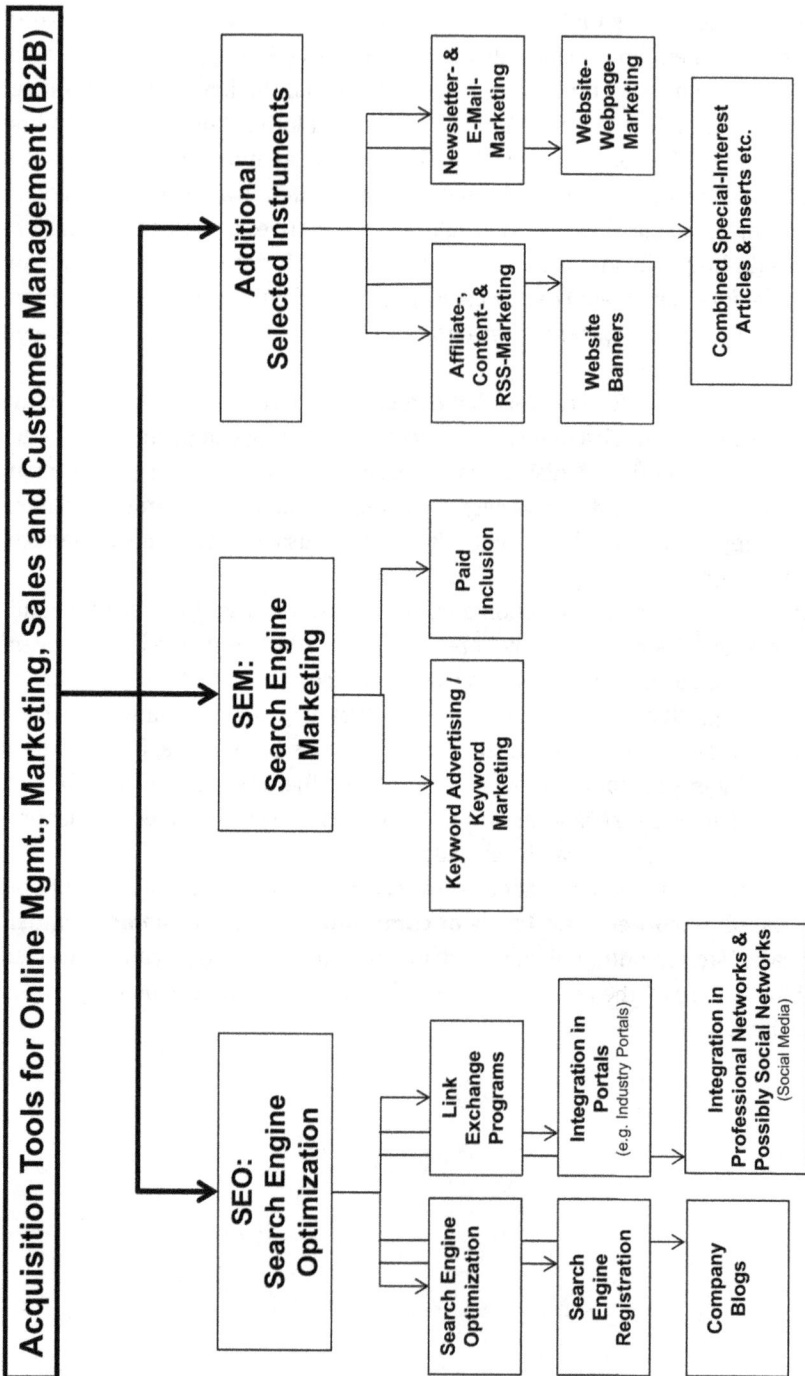

Fig. 36: Acquisition instruments of online marketing (B2B) (© Prof. Dr. R. Hofmaier).

Information & Communication Topics & Media / Acquisition & Communication Phases & Steps	Contents	Media
① Identification of Interested Customers	■ Identifying Interested Customers/ Decision-Makers and Initial Contact with Select Topics Relevant to Target Groups (Personal Competence Areas) according to Market, Application, Target Company Segments └ Decision-Maker Segments and Organizational Units └ Interest and Competence Potential	└ SEO/SEM └ Online Advertisements └ Websites └ SEA (Search Engine Advertisements) └ White Papers └ Webinars └ (Remarketing) └ Online-Videos └ (Online Marketplaces) └ Blogs └ (Online Shops) └ Specialized Online Events
② Demand/ Problem Identification	■ New (and Own) Product, Service, Integration Opportunities/ Feasibilities/ Trends └ Application, Technology and Industry Trends └ Product Inventions (and Application Options) └ Risk of Non-Consideration	└ Website Mgmt. └ E-Mails └ Newsletter/ └ Webinars └ E-Newsletter └ Virtual Events └ SEO/ SEM └ Tech-Days └ White Papers └ Application Events └ Print Newsletter └ Special Interest └ Print Magazines └ Conventions (Trade Magazine Articles)
③ Problemsolving (Finding Problem Solutions)/ Transparency	■ Exemplary (Own): └ Applications & Results (Technical, Economical, Sustainable) └ Application Differentiation and Opportunities/ Presentation of Possibilities └ "Reference" Applications/ Problem-Solving/ Comparison of Solutions	└ E-/ Printed Reference Reports: -- E-Media -- Print Media -- Websites -- Online Videos -- Webinars -- Tradeshows └ E-/ Print Case Studies └ Topical Communities └ Show Rooms └ Technical White Papers └ Select Customer Retention Events (See Chapt. VI) └ Tech-Days/ Focus Workshops └ IR/ Professional Articles in Select Media Specific to Target Groups └ Demos

Fig. 37a: Important communications concepts and their media (for integrated marketing, sales and customer management) (A) (© Prof. Dr. R. Hofmaier).

Information & Communication Topics & Media / Acquisition & Communications Phases & Steps	Contents	Media
④ **Optimized Problem Solutions/ Meeting Demand**	▪ Presentation of Own Specific Solution Advantages/ Added Values based on: └ Technical/ Professional Criteria └ Economic / Cost Benefit / Added Value Criteria / Calculation └ Situative/ Customer Specific Concretisation / Explicitation └ Different Competitive Advantages └ Further More Relevant Customer-Oriented Adjustments/ Explicitation / Necessities	└ Specific Customer Development and Retention Programs –– Outside Workshops –– Outside Focus Groups └ Specific E-/ Print- Documents like: –– Papers –– Brochures/ Flyers –– Application Studies (Cases) –– (Application) Reports └ Product / Application Videos etc. └ Special Websites └ Special ROI Studies With Customer Specific Application Methods/ Documents/ Reports/ Original Author Reports etc. └ Affiliate Marketing └ SEA (Search-Engine Advertisement)
⑤ **Customer Loyality (Customer Retention)**	└ User Guides/ Contents └ Installation Material └ ROI/ Added-Value-Measurements └ Selected and Specified Customer Retention Programs/ Actions/ Contents └ Product/ Feature Releases	└ Best (Implementation) Practices, esp. with: - Special User Forums/ Platforms - Special Communities - Special Events & Actions - Special Application Clinics - Focus Groups

Fig. 37b: Important communications concepts and their media (for integrated marketing, sales and customer management) (B) (© Prof. Dr. R. Hofmaier).

3 Sales processes and their optimization based on key performance indicators

In addition to designing a sales structure with various sales entities that need to be in tune with each other, the next decision concerns the alignment of **sales processes** and their **continuous optimization** based on **key performance indicators.**[21] Basically, there are **four distinct core sales processes** (see Fig. 38).

(1) The so-called customer acquisition process with the described acquisition institutions, practices and opportunities.

(2) The "classic" basic sales process, which is a continuous distribution approach, usually with actual products/services and actual customers, with the goal of achieving the corresponding revenue expansion.

(3) The so-called "cross-selling" distribution process with the goal of expanding product and service sales (usually adjacent, advanced, as well as new product, service and application areas), and finally,

(4) the so-called customer development and value management ("sales") process (mostly including "up-" and "strategic-selling"). This involves long-term and holistic customer infiltration on horizontal and vertical levels (especially cross-, up- and strategic selling) in the context of modern key account management (KAM).

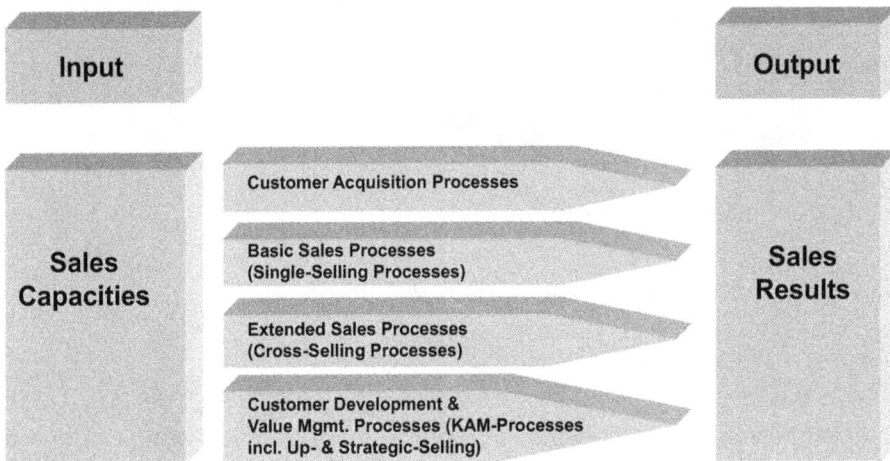

Fig. 38: The four core sales processes (including KAM) (© Prof. Dr. R. Hofmaier).

A compressed presentation with the **single phases** of the B2B sales process for the derivation of general **optimization options (hit rate optimization)**[22] is shown in Fig. 39 and 40.

---

21 For sales processes, see also Hofmaier, 1999, pp.130–139, and Hofbauer / Hellwig, 2012.
22 See also Hofmaier, 2011/2013.

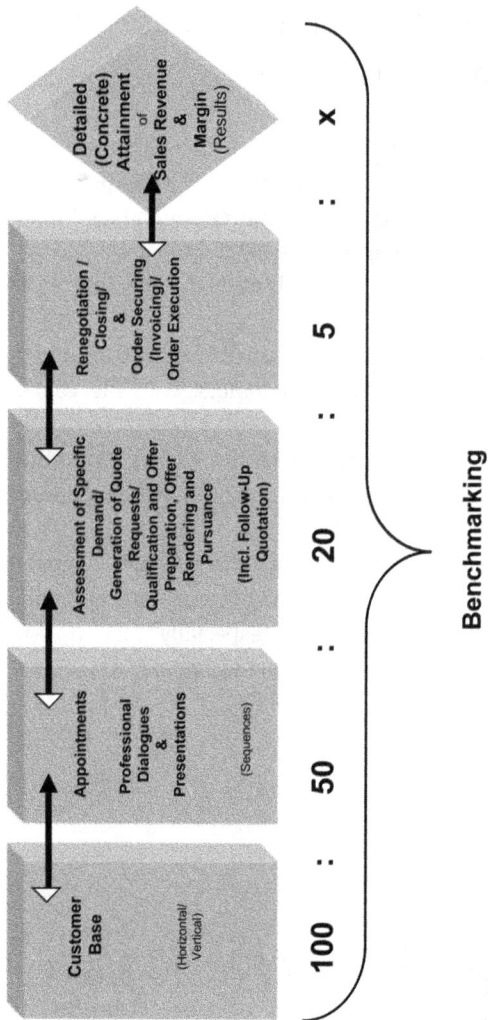

Fig. 39: The sales-hit-rate process within the overall context (© Prof. Dr. R. Hofmaier).

The **four basic steps and phases** in (personal) B2B sales begin with the assigned customer base, which is followed by the next process step with customer appointments, customer visits and talks/presentations that need to be done. After that follows (progressive) customer needs assessment, generation of requests for proposals, a corresponding request evaluation, preparation and submission of offers. When discussing the offer, there are usually renegotiations, which should eventually lead to closing and order placement with corresponding invoicing. The conclusion is the implementation of the contract with the relevant sales, revenue and margin targets.

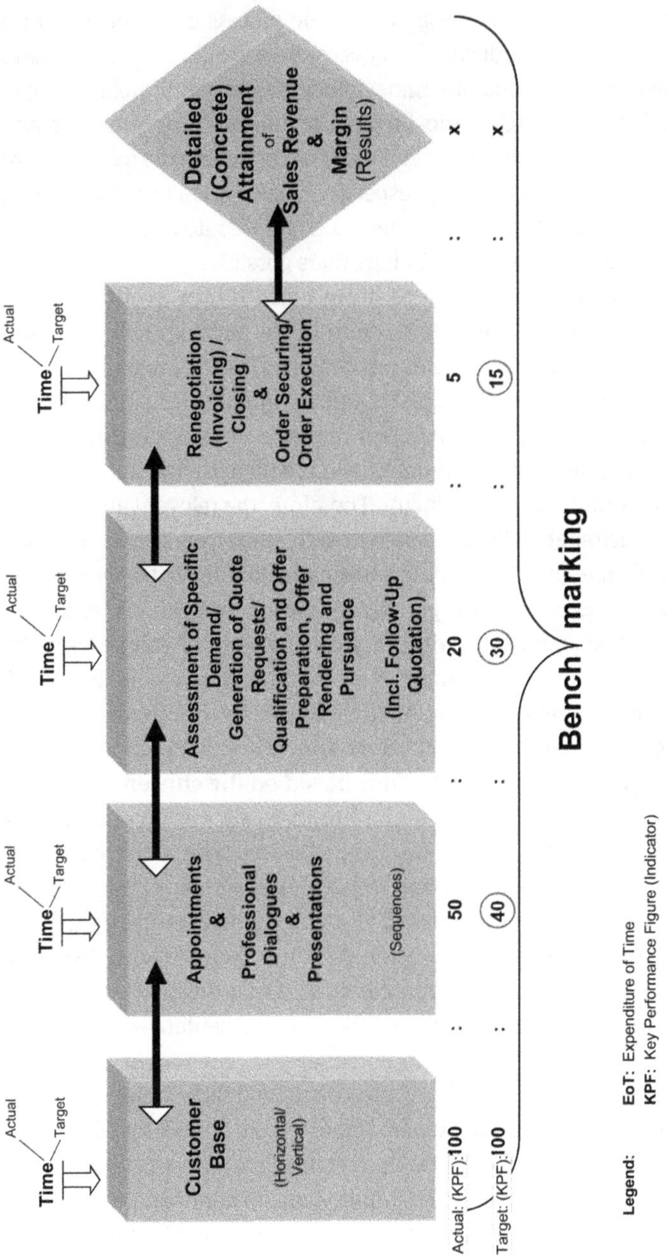

Fig. 40: The sales-hit-rate process and its optimalization approach
(© Prof. Dr. R. Hofmaier).

The respective **input-output relations** of the individual process steps can now be displayed in comparison to each other and can use **key account indicators** for sales process control, testing and improvement. Using these distribution process indicators (see also Fig. 42 and 44), the effectiveness of individual process steps as well as the entire sales process can now be designed in a transparent, understandable and optimizable way. Specifically, this means that **internal benchmarks** (in terms of sales territory, sales staff, and customers, as well as of past or present times) and **external benchmarks** (compared to the competition) can be set, supplemented by respective single and plausibility checks. Thus, if appropriate improvements are implemented, a target hit rate of 100: 40: 30: 15 (see Fig. 40) can make the desired success of tripling orders possible.

In addition to the individual process steps, **time distribution profiles** can be created, compared and optimized. This can be done by an (annual) task time and priority analysis. For example, individual sales rep activities (tasks) are recorded and paired with the respective time factor (time distribution). Often, sales rep tasks then end up with a high time factor (e.g., non-customer-related e-mail processing, phone calls, meetings, back-up and administrative tasks, etc.), which are not adding value in the proper sense, but require a high time factor. Therefore, the relevant and directly customer-related tasks (customer visits, preparation and follow-ups, etc.) usually get shortchanged in terms of time. (It turned out in some cases that the sales representative only had an average of about an hour per day for customer meetings, etc.) This "time recording" will now be juxtaposed with the **prioritization of sales rep tasks (A, B, C, D tasks)**. This often shows that there is far too little time for the few high-priority A-tasks (visits to customers/customer care), especially compared to the C- and D-tasks mentioned above. An appropriate **time allocation** (in conjunction with relevant organizational support) must now be done **based on the chosen priorities**, where, for example, customer preparations and follow-ups and customer conversations get a time factor of up to three hours a day instead of one hour, and where non-value-adding tasks get till only one and a half hours, for example, rather than six hours. The "right of way" rule to be observed calls for priority before urgency (!).

These time shifts and incongruities among priorities often follow "wrongly accented" cost reduction programs, for example, such as cutting back-office and office duty tasks (or resources) and assigning them to sales representatives. Sales force employees thus often work "on call" or based on urgency and therefore have less and less time for their main tasks (customer service and conceptual tasks). Even so-called "emailitis" (excessive and time-consuming e-mail inquiries, etc.) increases. This must now be reduced, redistributed and assigned the correct time budget according to priority. The few A-tasks get – as already mentioned – more time; in contrast, time budgets for B- and C-/D-tasks are reduced and, if possible, delegated (for example, to the support structure) or reorganized (see also the general reduction of emails (including e-mail processing in blocks) and of unnecessary forecasts and reports, as well as having the office staff take on proposal prep work and special tasks, such as handling complaints and interest research). Likewise, the implementation of travel times, customer visits and frequency of visits needs to be reorganized and thus simplified and cut. (Furthermore, D-tasks can usually be reduced and eventually "eliminated.")

It is important here that the entire sales process and its individual indicators be backed up and updated (database) in a **system (CRM tool),** and that the respective CRM tool (see Part V/D) be used consistently and actively by all participants in the process (marketing, customer management, etc.).

The following will now focus on an accordingly detailed sales process by presenting the so-called **sales funnel process** and its B2B-application[23] (see Fig. 41).

Based on the established marketing, sales and customer mgmt. strategy and goals, as well as the implications that need to be considered (e.g., application-specific conditions), **individual sales process steps and indicators** (depending on sales and customer area, responsibility, etc.) and their respective qualitative and quantitative sub-goals are to be defined and determined based on content, duration and other benchmark criteria. These sub-steps should be divided and assigned according to situational needs (customer size, number of customers, etc.). It is important to determine and know relevant decision-makers (see the decision-making matrix in Part VII) for customers, since these need to be involved and incorporated into the individual marketing and sales processes with a varying level of integration. These decision-makers can be divided into and assigned as **various division decision-makers** (according to special functions and hierarchy/ centralization levels), purchase decision-makers, co-decision-makers (decision-maker, gatekeeper, committees, etc.), as well as users (see Fig. 87 in Part VII). In addition, these decision-making target groups should be substantiated and integrated with appropriate information and measures (as well as a CRM tool created for this purpose).

The first step involves the **identification** and substantive "deposit" of relevant decision-makers. The second and third stages of the process involve defining necessary initial and intensifying **contacts** and supporting them with concrete objectives and an initial customer demand and problem-solving analysis. As part of follow-up contacts and other possible presentations, relevant **need-assessments** are specified and backed up with the best possible solution and **demand coverage approach/concept** (product/service concept) for the customer and one's own company (win-win-generation, clear added-value presentation). The ultimate aim is to use sufficiently necessary steps to generate a concrete and qualified request that can be covered and satisfied with a viable offer, after the final (demand) qualification. It is especially important here to showcase one's own strengths and positioning **advantages** as they apply to the customer and **differentiate** one's company from the competition (added-value creation), and, where possible, the related price-value ratio (modified based on preferred suppliers) as a **specific added value** for the customer (and the different decision-makers). The corresponding added value should be determined, calculated and decided both qualitatively and (where possible) quantitatively (e.g., by including calculation bases for customer contacts). A portion of the implementable added value for the customer should be **"exploited"** through a partial price that needs to be negotiated specifically for this purpose, in order to allow a preferred value for both sides.

---

23 See also in detail Hofmaier, 2011/2013.

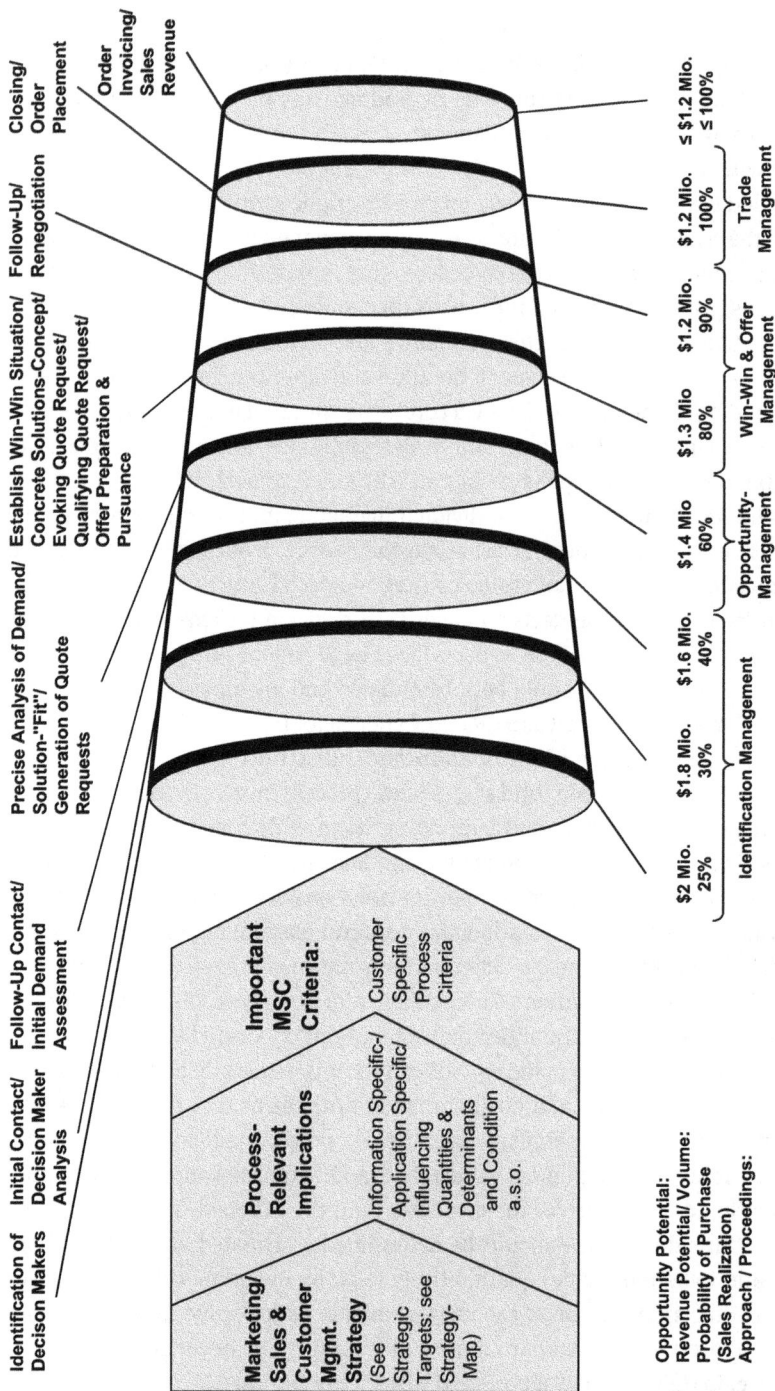

Fig. 41: Sales funnel process (© Prof. Dr. R. Hofmaier).

In a further step, **renegotiations** and, if necessary, adjustments can become necessary, until the closing and thus a specific order is eventually placed and issued. Finally, there is the **order billing** and order **execution**, before, if necessary, further process steps can be initiated regarding possible follow-up orders and additional **customer development** and penetration according to realistic cross-selling and up-selling measures (see KAM/Part VI).

The more precisely sales processes are defined, implemented and documented, and thus the more effectively an appropriate CRM system and meaningful customer database management can be put in place, the more these sales processes can be "redesigned" in a targeted and successful way and be improved with realistic benchmarks. Revenue potential, order volumes and closing probabilities can then be determined in a more **concrete way** according to the individual main phases and predictability can be improved in the medium term.

Sales hit rate optimization is explicitly devoted to this sales "steering and control" approach. Detailed analysis of the process steps and their individual input-output relations help improve sales and customer-oriented fine-tuning in time and proactively, so it thus not only supports gradual **win-win improvement**, but also especially **improved goal achievement** for sales, customer and marketing staff members and hence extrinsic and intrinsic motivation of employees. This must be backed by a sensible selected and implemented **integration-"able" CRM tool** that covers these processes accordingly, and that supports employees and their goal achievement (see also job enrichment).

Some **hit-rate key indicators** selected for sales process improvements can be found in Fig. 42. In addition to internal benchmarks, such indicators can also be used to specifically do plausibility and optimization analyses for external benchmarks, by questioning actual relationships and identifying opportunities for improvement or related cause-and-effect relationships and thus deriving mostly reasonable improvement suggestions. Thus, the hit rate can be improved in a more narrow sense, for example, when a poor (initial) quota of orders to inquiries can be optimized by distinguishing insufficient and, compared to the competition, inadequate offers through specific opportunities to improve the offers (e.g., implementation of long-term higher value-adding benefit to customers with targeted performance improvement and maintenance cost reduction). Likewise, the relation of supply requests to customer contacts can be improved through the more targeted approach of decision-makers, or the relation of acquired customers to existing customer potential can be made positive through better customer qualification and first-customer approach.

Additional hit-rate figures to draw on, such as efficiency of processing times and relevant qualitative success and earnings figures per customer and sales staff member, can also be selectively backed up and improved.

Level	Relation	2015	2016	2017
1. Hit-Rate (Narrower Sense)	Orders (x100) / Quote Requests	25%	35%	45%
2. Customer Potential Optimzisation = Penetration of High Potential Customers	Acquired Customers / Potential Number of Customers	5%	10,5%	18%
3. Efficiency of Customer Approach	Quote Requests (x100) / Customers	20%	30%	40%
4. Efficiency of Processing Time: • Customer • Offer • Order	Processing Time (Timebased Workload) / Order	40 Hours	35 Hours	30 Hours
5. ⊠ Revenue (Customer / Sales Person)	Revenue / Sales Person	0,5 Mill. $	0,6 Mill. $	0,7 Mill. $
	Revenue / Customer	0,25 Mill. $	0,3 Mill. $	0,35 Mill. $
6. Customer / Sales Person Profitability	Customer Profit (x100) / Customer Revenue	10%	11%	12%
	Sales Person Profit (x100) / Sales Person Revenue	20%	25%	29%

Fig. 42: Select key indicators for improvement of the sales process and hit-rate optimalization (ROS – Return on sales figures) (© Prof. Dr. R. Hofmaier).

In light of experience values gained from evaluating metrics, detailed sales process specifications, **such as for the introduction of a new product** or customer project and the acquisition of eligible customers, can now be planned and phased in (see also Fig. 43). As a result, appropriate distribution steps and results can be planned and implemented more accurately.

Overall, integrated marketing, sales and customer management, its management and control, can fall back on a **selected key indicator mix** (see Fig. 44).

These indicators can be divided into marketing, sales and customer metrics, as well as respective process and resource metrics. While the **marketing and customer metrics** contain corresponding segment shares, potential exhaustion levels, positioning, etc., and specific customer metrics focus on customer-relevant market shares and single-, cross-, up-sell ratios, customer satisfaction, loyalty and customer retention indices, etc., **sales figures** focus on sales, revenue, margin and profitability criteria. **Process indicators** primarily include the aforementioned hit-rate and ROS (return on sales) figures. **Resource-related** parameters mainly focus on motivation and qualification indicators related to employees, but also on appropriate development, position-filling and job enrichment, as well as leadership, culture and innovation indicators.

Not only can a few select indicators generally help lead the way, but upcoming steps, actions and tasks/measures, responsibilities and key performance indicators (measurement criteria), etc., can be determined for targeted planning for introducing a new product or a new solution or project approach, and thus the respective short-term goal achievement all the way to the final orders can be directly lead, controlled and improved. Figure 45 shows the necessary implementation. This **implementation matrix** shows how the corresponding phases, tasks and procedures (CRM-based) can be determined and implemented for the respective sales process stages. This improves the required transparency, makes short-term feedback, polls, and additions possible, and supports the integration of consistent and effective marketing.

Main Focus of Proceedings / Customer Acquisition & Order Process		Goals & Tasks	Responsibility & Support (Who?)	Time Frame & Man-Days (Until When? Ressources?)	Measurement Criteria	Budgets/ Risk Factors, etc.
Starting Point / Goal Setting/ Situation:	15	Customer Oders for a New Product/ Project to be Billed in 2015: $ 50 Mio Target Revenue				
(0) Scheduling of Customer Calls & First Explorative Discussions	50 → 40	Pre-Selected Customers Approach Potential Customers				
(I) Identify & Verify Demand	30	Conduct Customer & Demand Verification Talks				
(II) Generate Quote Requsts	20	Generate Quote Requests				
(III) Compile Offers / Follow Up on Offers (Closing)	20	Submit Offers				
(IV) Order Placement / Win Purchase Order	15	Secure Orders				
(V) Order Billing	15	Execute Orders & Prepare Repeat Orders				

Fig. 43: Hit-rate – target planning for new product introduction (© Prof. Dr. R. Hofmaier).

Select Marketing, Sales & Customer Management Planing, Drive & Control Key Performance Indicators

Marketing & Customer Mgmt. Key Figures

- Market Pentration / Market Share
- Customer Specific Market (KA) Penetration / Customer (KA) Market Share / Share of Wallet
- Share of New Customers
- Share of new Product/Service Share
- Customer Satisfaction Level
- Customer Loyalty Level
- Customer Relationship & Customer Retention Level
- USP & Image Criteria
- Various Positioning Key Figures
- Single-, Cross-, Up-, Strategic-Selling Key Figures (KAM)

Sales Key Figures

- Market
    - Revenue
    - Sales
    - Margin
- Customer Revenue / Sales / Margin
- New Customer Revenue / Sales / Margin
- New Product Revenue / Sales / Margin
- Quality of Sales
- Various Sales Positioning Key Figures

MSC-Process Key Figures

- Sales Process / Sales Related Hit-Rate Key Figures (ROS Figures)
- Acquisition-Process Key Figures (Incl. Acquisitions Mix Key Figures)
- New Product Development Key Figures
- Marketing & Customer Mgmt. Process Key Figures
- Various MSC Process Key Figures

MSC-Staff Key Figures

- MSC-Motivation Index
- MSC-Qualification Index
- MSC-Development Index Indicators (Incl. Job Enrichment Key Figures)
- MSC-Leadership Index
- MSC-Culture Index
- MSC-Innovation Index

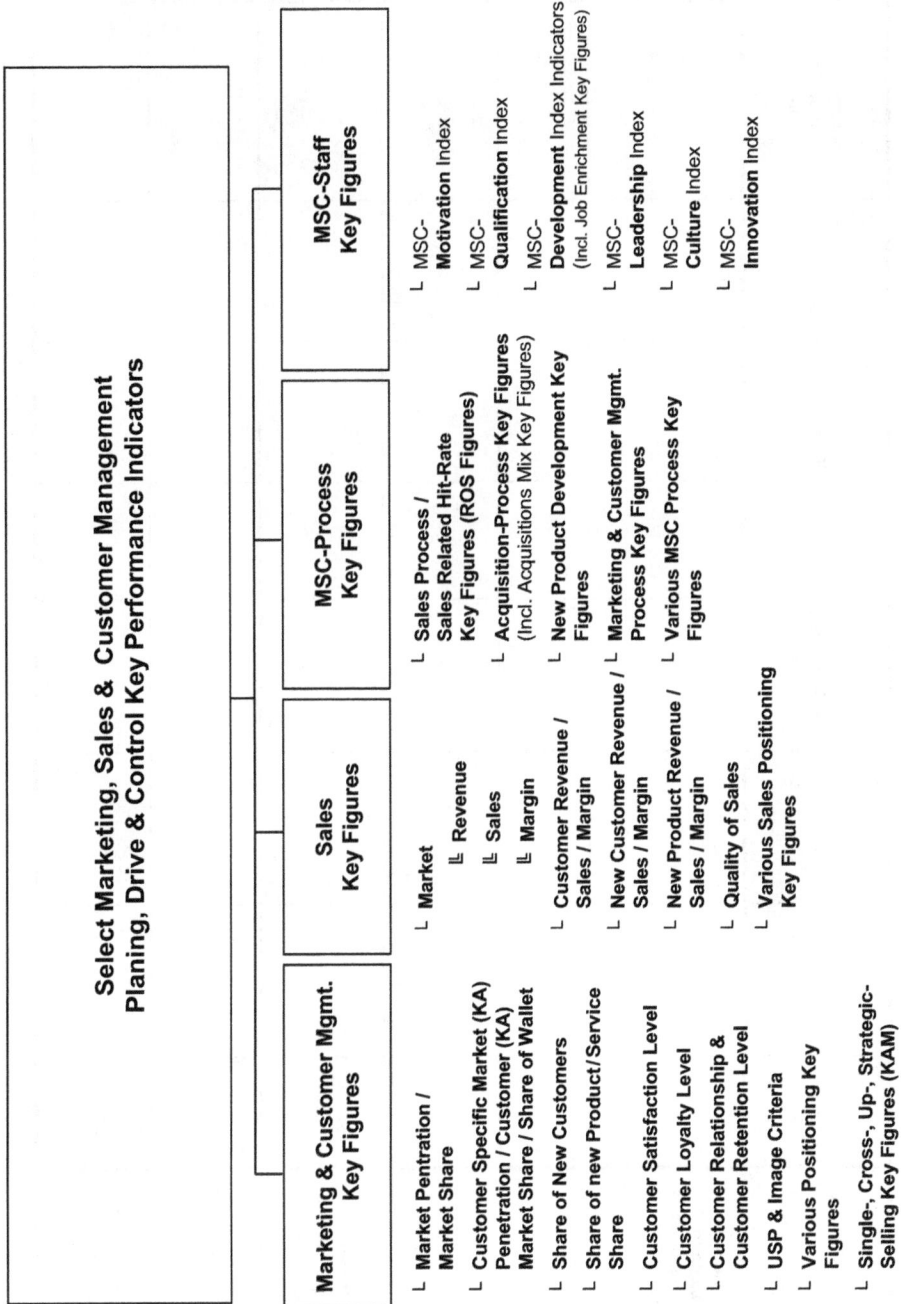

Fig. 44: Select marketing, sales and customer management (MSC) planning, control and monitoring indicators (© Prof. Dr. R. Hofmaier).

Steps & Measures / Phases	Objectives	Tasks & Contents	Actions & Measures	Responsibility & Support	Time/ Dead-Line	Budgets	Key Figures/ Measurement Criteria	Consequences/ Follow-Up Measures etc.
Basic Data Collection / More Detailing of Customer and Decision Maker Key Figures								
Customer Demand & Quote Request Generation								
Quote Request Qualification & Offer Compiling								
Offer Pursuance / Renegotiation & Closing								
Order Placement & Execution								
After-Sales- & Subsequential Measures								

Fig. 45: Implementation approach for sales-hit-rate optimalization (© Prof. Dr. R. Hofmaier).

4 Cross-Cultural Negotiation

Dennis Zocco[24]

Negotiating is the process of communication in which two or more parties jointly attempt to reach a single- or multi-issue agreement that has value to all parties. Negotiations take place constantly, both intra-company and inter-company. As example, a product manager negotiates with a division president for more resources; a human resource specialist negotiates with an employee for a salary increase; a media buyer negotiates with an advertising agency account executive for online advertising placements; a customer service representative negotiates the resolution of a delivery problem with a key account customer.

Negotiating across **cultures** presents an added dimension of complexity to the communications and protocols involved in the negotiating process. Consider a German media buyer negotiating ad rates with a Japanese media broker; an Indian software sales representative negotiating the terms of an engagement with a Swedish utility company IT specialist; an Italian human resource manager negotiating a compensation package with a prospective Mexican plant manager. Negotiating across these cultural divides, with their differences in approaches to agreement focus, interactive style, time sensitivity, decision-making hierarchy, and relationship value, presents complex challenges to a negotiator.

Culture has been defined in many ways. According to Max Weber, the late 19th and early 20th century German sociologist, philosopher, and political economist, "The concept of culture is a value-concept. Empirical reality becomes 'culture' to us because and insofar as we relate it to value ideas. It includes those segments and only those segments of reality which have become significant to us because of this value relevance."[25] Talcott Parsons, a 20th century American sociologist defined culture as consisting of "…those patterns relative to behavior and the products of human action which may be inherited, that is, passed on from generation to generation independently of the biological genes."[26] One of the simplest definitions of culture, the author of which is unknown, is that culture is what remains after all else is forgotten.

Every organization has multiple interactions with its customers, with **marketing**, **sales**, and **customer service** having the **greatest impact on customer decision-making**. Each contact point represents a segment of a long-term negotiation, often occurring across diverse cultures, that spans the entire customer engagement includ-

---

24 Prof. Dr. Dennis Zocco is professor of Finance Management and Director of the "Master of Science in Executive Leadership Program" (and is also specialized in "Cross-Cultural Negotiation") of the School of Business at the University of San Diego (USA).

25 Weber, M.,1949, p. 76.

26 Parson, T.,1949, p. 8.

ing many of the organization's functional areas. Consider the following as an illustration.

Christian, a salesperson from an equipment company in Hanover, Germany, is preparing to travel to Sao Paulo, Brazil, to negotiate the sale of his company's industrial equipment with Daniella, a potential buyer from a Brazilian agribusiness company. The interest of the Brazilian company in the products of the German company was generated by a marketing campaign made effective through rigorous marketing research. As a result of that interest, Christian was able to schedule a meeting with Daniella to begin the negotiation for the sale.

Christian had never been to Brazil and had no experience negotiating with a Brazilian. So he met with the marketing team that produced the campaign targeted to the Brazilian agribusiness company. He asked them what factors they considered in designing and implementing their campaign. The marketing team gave Christian valuable information that resulted from their extensive quantitative and qualitative marketing research. Christian learned that Brazil's economy is the sixth largest in the world (behind only the U.S., China, Japan, Germany, and France) and is considered by many economic experts to have the potential to move up in the rankings in the next few years. Recently, however, Brazil's GDP growth has slowed and inflation has become a problem. Christian also learned that the agribusiness sector has continued to thrive as it is focused mainly on exports and that Daniella's company is one of the leaders in the sector.

Christian considered the information he gathered from the marketing team valuable in his preparation for his negotiation with Daniella. In his experience in the sales division of his company, he knew that the marketing team has worked closely not only with the company's sales teams in their preparations for upcoming sales negotiations but also with customer relations in providing updated market information on the Brazilian economy, the manufacturing sector, and specific companies. He decided to contact other members of his company's sales and customer service teams assigned to Brazilian accounts.

The sales personnel experienced in negotiating with Brazilians gave Christian useful information based on their experience. He learned that in the Brazilian culture time is viewed much differently than in the German culture, and that he should expect the negotiation to proceed slowly, that interruptions would take place during the negotiation, and that some meetings will not start or end on time. He also learned that Brazilians are more relationship-oriented than detail-oriented, as are Germans, in their approach to negotiations. They told him that they learned from interacting with the company's Brazilian sales teams that Brazilians are much more emotional in their negotiations than are Germans, but it is a way of making a point rather than being angry. He learned that the native language of Brazil is Portuguese, not Spanish as is the case in other South and Latin American countries and that Daniella will expect Christian's business cards to be printed in Portuguese as well as German.

Christian's company had other Brazilian customers, so he assumed he could learn even more about how Brazilian's negotiate from the customer service specialists assigned to those Brazilian accounts. When he spoke with them, they told him that they are involved very early in customer engagements, providing the marketing and sales specialists with valuable feedback on strengthening as well as deepening the company's relationship with the customer.

Christian believed he was much better prepared for his upcoming negotiation with Daniella after his conversations with his company's marketing, sales, and customer relations teams, but the most important takeaway was that the **integration of those three areas of the company** provided coordination, consistency, and clarity (Koordination, Übereinstimmung, und Klarheit) in his company's approach to the cross-cultural sales negotiations that were taking place on a daily basis.

Of course, Christian would perform his own research focusing on the Brazilian cultural norms and business protocols, the Brazilian negotiating and communicating styles, and the state of the Brazilian economy and agricultural industry. He would also research Daniella's company by reading its annual report, press releases, and public information. His own research would be extensive and based on a strong base of information he received from his own company's marketing, sales, and customer services areas.

Daniella likely will be preparing for the upcoming negotiation in the same way as Christian, increasing the probability that the negotiation will be successful for both companies. Christian and Daniella will form a strong, trusting, and professional relationship as each will have the foundation for adapting to each other's cultural influences on their negotiation. The teams that will support Christian and Daniella in the negotiation will include representatives from marketing, sales, and customer service, and this **integrated approach** will increase the likelihood that they will develop a forward-looking agreement that has value for all parties.

This fictional account of Christian's preparation illustrates the **power** of an **integrated marketing-sales-customer service approach** in implementing a **successful cross-cultural negotiation** within an organization and providing **coordinated, consistent, and clear interactions** with the customer. Organizational success in cross-cultural negotiation requires a commitment to excellence in continued development of cross-cultural negotiating skills throughout the organization and a recognition and reward structure that aligns performance with the organization's mission and core values.

Exhibit 1 below represents a **bottom-up approach** to **building a successful cross-cultural negotiating** organizational capability with the **integration of marketing, sales, and customer services** as its foundation. Let's look at each building block of organizational cross-cultural negotiating success.

Cross-Cultural Negotiating Pyramid

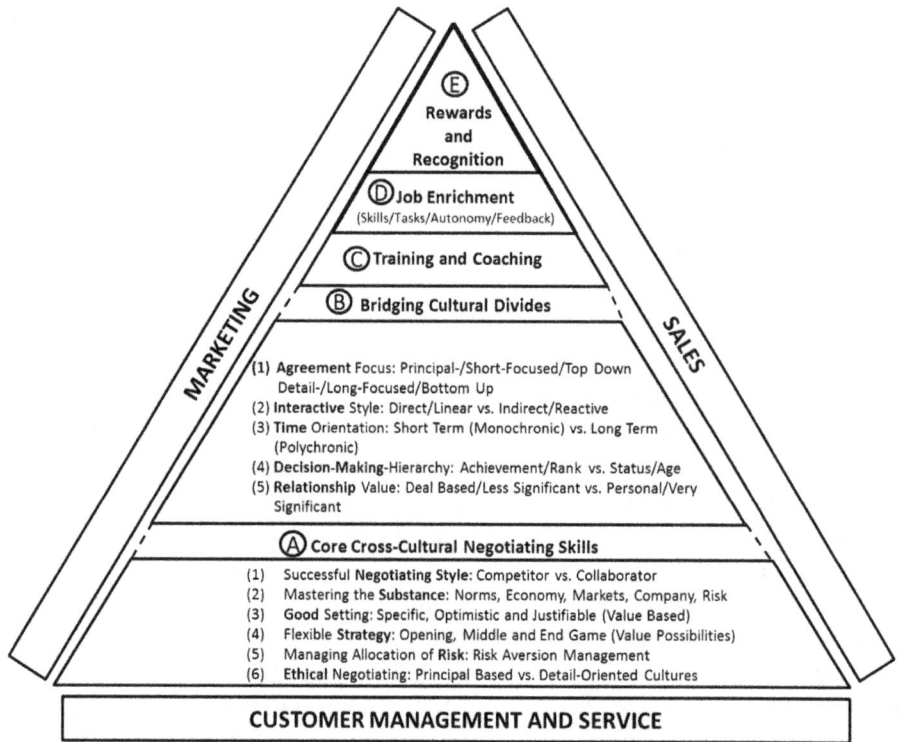

Fig. 46: Building Blocks of Organizational Cross-Cultural Negotiating Success.

4.1 Core Cross-Cultural Negotiations Skills

There are seven core skills essential to successful negotiating, either within one's own culture or across cultures. They are

1. developing a successful negotiating style,
2. mastering the substance,
3. establishing specific, optimistic, and justifiable goals,
4. understanding the other party's interests,
5. developing a flexible strategy,
6. assessing and managing the allocation of risk, and
7. negotiating ethically.

Core Skill #1: Developing a Successful Negotiating Style

Negotiators' styles can be summarized into two distinct categories: competitive and collaborative. These styles are found in varying degrees in all cultures.

The **Competitor**. This type of negotiator sees the negotiation as a win/lose battle where concessions by the other party are additions to the "score" while their own concessions are subtractions. They play the game for a "shutout", that is, they negotiate for an agreement in which they have all the value and their counterparts have none. The characteristics of a competitive style are easily recognized. Competitors are very reluctant to provide information, but expect answers to all their questions. They use tactics such as stalling for time, presenting ultimatums, and asking for concessions to save the relationship. The best way to deal with a competitor is to stress that their behavior has short-term costs (reciprocal competitive behavior or the negotiation resulting in no agreement) and adverse long-term consequences (limited or no continued business).

Competitive negotiating styles, in varying degrees, can be found in cultures existing in the United States, Italy, China, Spain, South Korea and Russia. Most negotiators from these cultures ultimately strive for a positive long-term relationship and an agreement that provides value to all parties. However the approach at achieving those objectives is somewhat competitive.

The **Collaborator**. Negotiators adopting this style take more of a problem-solving approach to the negotiation with more of a win-win rather than win-lose focus. Collaborating negotiators are much more willing to strategically exchange information that will lead to a better understanding of each other's interests. Collaborators rely on the trust that results from a strong relationship and search for ways to create value throughout the negotiation. Collaborators are skilled at recognizing value-creating opportunities through the strategic exchange of concessions. Within this style, successful negotiators are competitive in two ways: achieving their goals and utilizing leverage when available. Collaborative styles are found in Germany, Japan, Austria, the United Kingdom, and Thailand.

Although the cultures throughout the world have a predominant negotiating style, each negotiator brings his/her own personal style to the negotiating table. Variations of country- and cultural-based negotiating styles may result from regional, ethnic, or industry influences. For example, in the situation described above where Christian (a German sales rep) was preparing for a negotiation with Daniella (a Brazilian prospective customer), Christian learned that although the national language of Brazil is Portuguese, the second most spoken language in the country is German due to a large population of German descent. Therefore, even though Christian is prepared to find Daniella's style of negotiating more in line with the competitive nature of the Brazilians, Daniella may be of German descent and therefore may have the more collaborative cultural influence of her German heritage.

Another illustration of cultural differences in negotiating style within a country would be in the United States, where negotiators in the northern and eastern regions will likely have a competitive style while those in the southern states have a collabora-tive style. The western coastal region of the U.S. has a more casual, cooperative nature although two of the most competitive industries – entertainment and high-tech – are located in this region. Farther south in the Americas, Argentina has a collaborative style of negotiating, yet over half of the population has some Italian descent, which culturally has a competitive style.

Core Skill #2: Mastering the Substance

The term **mastering the substance** is widely-used among experienced, profes-sional negotiators. It relates directly to the knowledge a negotiator acquires before, during, and after the negotiation. To **master the substance**, a negotiator must have or acquire extensive knowledge of the market or environment within which the nego-tiation takes place as well as the motivations and interests of all involved parties. Mastering the substance in cross-cultural negotiations goes farther in that it refers to researching and understanding international markets as well as the cultural influ-ences the parties bring to the negotiation.

The knowledge mastery necessary to succeed in cross-cultural negotiation is in **six areas**: cultural norms and business protocols, negotiating and communicating styles, state of the economy, market condition, company condition, and political risk.

Cultural Norms and Business Protocols. Marketing programs, sales negotia-tions, and customer relationships can be sabotaged through inadvertent violations of a country's cultural norms and business protocols. In many cultures they often are as important as the positions taken in a negotiation.

As examples, although Arabic is the native language of Morocco, the language of business in that country is French. Exchanging business cards in Japan, China, and South Korea is done with both hands, giving and receiving. Not reading the business card would likely be considered an insult. However, in Thailand, India, Turkey, and Indonesia, a business card is always offered and accepted with the right hand only.

Gift-giving is a tricky affair. In the United States, Northern Italy, Spain, Australia, and Germany, giving a gift in a business situation may call into question the motive for the gift. It is best to avoid gift-giving in those countries. However, in China, Japan, South-ern Italy and South Korea, giving gifts in a business setting, even gifts of significant value, is culturally acceptable.

In Japan, never refer to a person by their first name unless asked to do so. In China, never openly show frustration or anger, especially to one of advanced age or high professional or political status as it will cause that person to **lose face**. In Spain, never use aggressive tactics such as ultimatums or walk-outs as they will be taken as a personal affront.

State of the Economy. Economic conditions and expectations have an important influence on the risk/return trade-offs in international negotiating decisions. Econ-omies around the world do not move in synchronization. Asian economies may be booming while Europe is in a recession. Although the increase in multinational trade has dampened these differences, they still exist, and economic activity can change quickly.

For example, a German salesperson preparing for a negotiation in Switzerland would master the substance of the Swiss economy by learning that Switzerland has the nineteenth largest GDP in the world, but the fourth highest per capita GDP behind only Luxembourg, Qatar, and Norway. It has the highest employment rate among the OECD countries and was ranked first in economic competitiveness by the World Economic Forum and first in innovation by the World Intellectual Property Organization. A German negotiator knowing this information would surely impress his Swiss counterparts and potentially be able to utilize the information to support a negotiating position.

Economic information about world economies can be found at the International Monetary Fund and the World Bank. Most countries have their own economic statistics government offices, for example, the *Swiss Federal Statistics Office* in Switzerland, *Destatis* in Germany, *Istituto Nazionale di Statistica* in Italy, the *Statistics Bureau of the Ministry of Internal Affairs and Communications* in Japan, the *National Bureau of Statistics* in China, the *Federal Reserve Board* in the United States, and the *Bureau of Statistics* in Australia.

Market Condition. Supply and demand conditions in world markets are dynamic and can shift quickly and dramatically. Price volatility in some markets is high, especially those involving natural resources. Negotiators, in mastering the substance for markets and industries, need to research the current supply and demand conditions as well as the pricing structure and the existence of shortages or surpluses in the markets in which they are negotiating. This information could serve as leverage points in the negotiation and can be found at the same sources that provide economic data. Often industry professional organizations have their own publications and websites that provide valuable information for a negotiator.

Company Condition. The Internet provides a wealth of information about specific companies, although care should be taken to verify the sources. All publicly-traded companies as well as most private companies have their own websites that displays product and management information. Publicly-traded companies provide electronic access to their **annual reports** (corporate philosophy, mission statement, financial performance, product descriptions, research and development results), **press releases** (new product announcements, management changes, annual and quarterly earnings reports, factory openings/closings), and **quarterly earning conferences**. Google, Bing, and Baidu have search alerts that provide notification when any news is posted on the Internet involving a particular company. Also, a company's **Corporate Social Responsibility Report** can provide valuable information in the mastering the substance phase of the negotiation.

Political Risk. Risk of a political nature differs from the normal business risk negotiators see in any potential agreement. It refers to the uncertainty of business outcomes based on political, non-market actions in a country. These actions might be shifts in fiscal or monetary policy or a change in ruling political parties and positions regarding the encouragement of trade with outside nations. Local politics presents another, often more complicated, form of political risk. In countries where consensus decision-making is a strong cultural influence, local political or union leaders may be important stakeholders who are absent from the negotiating table. Countries considered to have high political risk are Russia, Venezuela, Vietnam, Egypt, and Greece, while countries with low political risk are the Scandinavian countries, Northern ans Western European, and Northern American countries.

Core Skill #3: Setting Specific, Optimistic, and Justifiable Goals

Negotiating goals give direction and trigger powerful psychological "striving" mechanisms that are in play both consciously and subconsciously during a negotiation. Successful negotiators take great care in setting negotiating goals that are specific, optimistic, and justifiable, resulting in what are called Maximum Plausible Positions (MPP).

Goals should be **specific** enough to provide a clear value-based target. Quantitative negotiating issues should have quantitative targets that can be translated into a measurable benefit to the company. Examples of quantitative negotiating goals might be to have a customer agree to buy one hundred product units at one thousand euro per unit, or to have a client agree to a three-year, five-million euro marketing program that includes both print and online advertising.

Qualitative goals should be identified so that some scalable measure of success can be applied to the degree to which the goal is achieved. For example, qualitative negotiating goals might be to finalize the relationship-building phase of the negotiation so that the details of the negotiation can be discussed during the next meeting, or for a company's customer service specialist to get approval for his company's sales representative to meet with a division head to allow deeper sales penetration into the company. A test as to whether a goal is specific enough to be useful is to be able to write the goal on a notepad. Successful negotiators often take that notepad into the negotiation so that they can refer to the goals they are trying to achieve.

The rationale for **optimistic** goals is that they trigger powerful psychological and behavioral commitments to the best possible outcome of the negotiation on each issue. By setting less than optimistic goals, you mentally concede anything beyond that goal, so you seldom have a better outcome.

Justification for goals is extremely important in that it separates an **optimistic** goal from what might be considered an **outrageous** goal. Although optimistic goals may not be accepted by the other negotiating party, they have logical justifications based on economic and market conditions. Outrageous goals have no justification in either economic or market conditions and may antagonize the other side or cause the party having an outrageous position to lose credibility.

A cultural component of negotiation goal-setting exists. Expect negotiators from Saudi Arabia, Russia, India, China and Japan tend to have very optimistic goals. These negotiators will likely make large concessions toward a final agreement. Goals closer to market conditions can be expected from negotiators from Germany, the United States, Canada, the United Kingdom, South Africa, Austria, and the Scandinavian countries. Opening offers from negotiators from these countries will likely be closer to their reservation (final) level so that concessions will be smaller to arrive at a final agreement.

Core Skill #4: Understanding the Other Party's Interests

The American author, F. Scott Fitzgerald, once said: "The test of a first-rate intelligence is the ability to hold two opposing ideas in the mind at the same time, and still be able to function." This concept holds true for negotiators. The task of having your own interests and those of your counterpart in mind while you negotiate an agreement is not an easy one, but a necessary and beneficial one. Ignoring the other party's interests in a negotiation hinders the ability of both parties to create value in the negotiation and jeopardizes the opportunity to forge a long-term, trusting relationship.

A better approach is to convince the other parties involved in the negotiation that to arrive at an agreement that has value to all parties, all negotiating parties should be willing to make concessions of varying degrees to reach an agreement that addresses everyone's interests. The relative size of the concessions made will depend upon the amount of leverage each party holds in the negotiation.

Concession-making can reveal the value parties place on the issues. For example, negotiators typically make larger initial and overall concessions on issues of less importance to them and smaller concessions on issues of greater importance. By mentally tracking the concessions, a negotiator can either validate your preliminary judgment on the extent to which the other parties value the issues or revise those judgments.

Interests can be uncovered by asking open-ended questions and having the patience and confidence to listen carefully to the answers. Information received from your counterpart is the foundation for creating value in the negotiation. You get that information by listening, not talking. Negotiators from Asian cultures use this approach very effectively.

Core Skill #5: Developing a Flexible Strategy

Negotiating **strategy** establishes a roadmap for the journey to agreement and provides stability, continuity, and direction for tactical behaviors. **Tactics** are short-term, adaptive moves designed to enact and pursue a higher-level strategy. They are used when necessary to keep the strategic journey on course to agreement.

No negotiation strategy, regardless of how well it is researched and designed, will progress exactly as planned when implemented. Each negotiator must react to the actions of the other parties as they implement their strategy. No matter how much preparation takes place, negotiations involve people, possibly from a different cultural background, and it is very difficult to anticipate with complete accuracy how people think, act, and react. Furthermore, information acquired through the process of negotiation will influence and alter strategic direction. For this reason, a **flexible** strategy is important.

Developing and implementing strategy as a chess master would provide significant benefits, as many of the elements of success in chess can be adapted to success in negotiation. In chess, there are three phases to a game: an opening game, a middle game, and an end game.

The **opening game** in a negotiation involves gaining rapport and building a relationship with the other party, managing the issues to be negotiated, establishing opening positions, and anticipating reactions to those positions. The length and focus of this opening game will vary based on culture. Those cultures that are relationship-based rather than contract-based will want longer opening games to determine whether a strong relationship can be forged between the parties. That relationship will serve as the basis for moving on to the middle game. Negotiators from contract-based cultures will want to spend the time in the opening game on agenda-setting and presenting opening positions, then move quickly into the middle game. Relationship-building for contract-based cultures takes place through performance on the contract after the contract is signed.

The **middle game** has the negotiators engage in strategic information exchanges. This stage of the negotiation involves the expression of each party's interests through statements and concession patterns. In this important stage, negotiators explore areas of **value creation**, implement strategic concession-making, if necessary, and build momentum for a final agreement.

Cultural differences in the approach to the middle game abound. Inability to adapt to contrasts in **negotiating style** (competitive vs. collaborative) and **communication style** (direct vs. indirect) can cause frustrations and lost opportunities for value creation. Different cultures have different attitudes toward exchanging information. Negotiators willing to **share information to explore value creation** in a negotiation are normally from Germany, France, Austria, India, and the North American and Scandinavian countries. Negotiators who view information as a leverage point and are reluctant to share information are from the Asian, Middle Eastern, and Latin American countries as well as Spain, Portugal, Turkey, and Russia.

The **end game** involves periodically testing for a final agreement and, if it does not exist, uncovering areas of resistance. When the reasons for resistance to agreement are found, all parties try to develop low-cost solutions to the agreement obstacles and then re-explore possible agreement packages to determine the one that has the optimal amount of **total value possible for all parties**. Often in cross-cultural negotiations, barriers to agreement exist because negotiators are unable to bridge the cultural divides described below.

The **integration of marketing, sales, and customer service** can provide **significant benefits** not only in developing a **consistent strategy** for important negotiations in a customer engagement, but also in overcoming obstacles to an **agreement**. When obstacles are difficult to detect, shared insights among the three functional areas can provide **valuable information for breaking down barriers**.

To illustrate the cultural differences in implementing a strategy, the planned opening game of a **German sales negotiator** with a potential customer would be a review of the issues and the order in which they will be negotiated. The middle game would be a sequential negotiation on each issue with all parties presenting opening positions and supporting them with facts. Agreements on those issues would be achieved along the way. The German negotiator would be reluctant to return to issues already agreed upon. He would make some concessions during the negotiations on each issue, but they would be small ones as opening positions would be close to reservation levels. The objective of the end game for the German negotiator would be to review of the interim agreements and combine them into an overall agreement package that describes in detail the obligations of all parties. The German negotiator would expect all parties to honor those obligations.

If the potential customer was another German or possibly an American, the negotiation would progress as planned. But assume that the customer was a Roman. The strategy would not unfold as planned. The opening game of the Roman negotiator would be to take considerable time to establish a **comfortable and trusting relationship** before the issues are addressed. The time would be spent at lunches and dinners discussing the background and families of the negotiators and possible the history and current political situation in Italy. The negotiation issues might be addressed only in passing. The Roman's middle game might be unstructured. The issues likely would be discussed in no particular order, possibly with no agreement achieved before moving from one issue to the next, and then possibly returning to previously discussed issues. Emotions would enter the discussions to demonstrate the commitment by the Roman to positions taken by either side. The Roman might make a concession on a particular issue, then take it back in order to make an even larger concession on another issue. The Roman's end game would be a summarization of the discussions that took place in the middle game with the final agreement both lengthy and detailed, but the commitment to the agreement would depend more on the personal relationship that had developed between the parties than the agreement itself. Both parties would need to adjust their strategic plan to make the negotiation successful.

Core Skill #6: Assessing and Managing the Allocation of Risk

Most business agreements involve future performance, and since the future is not known with certainty, risk exists in most negotiated agreements. Consider a simple cash transaction at a swap meet where a music CD is purchased at a negotiated price. The buyer has some expectation that the CD in the case (1) has music on it, (2) has the music represented by the label, and (3) has music of an acceptable quality. Without actually sampling the CD by playing it in its entirety, the risk to the buyer is that the CD will not perform as advertised and expected. For the seller, cash in the national currency is received as a result of the negotiated and agreed-upon price, so there is no risk in receiving the cash. However, the risk taken by the seller agreeing to the transaction is that the seller might have been able to sell the CD to the next potential buyer at a higher negotiated price.

By multiplying the number of issues in this simple CD transaction by a factor of ten and multiplying the monetary scale of the transaction by a factor of a hundred thousand, the risk in a typical high-level multi-national transaction can be appreciated. A critical element in negotiating that is often overlooked is the assessment and management of the allocation of risk among the negotiating parties.

Risk aversion is a psychological concept adopted by the fields of economics, finance, marketing, and management. It refers to the degree to which a person is willing to engage in an activity in which more than one outcome can occur. The wider the range of possible outcomes (or possibly the existence of a negative outcome), the greater the perceived risk. A negotiator with a high degree of risk aversion would be willing to accept an agreement with low perceived risk and sacrifice expected return while a negotiator with a lower degree of risk aversion would be willing to accept an agreement with higher perceived risk as long as the expected return would compensate for that higher risk.

Cultures can be characterized by their **degree of risk aversion**. Cultures with higher risk aversion are Asian, Latin American, Middle Eastern, German, Spanish, and Italian. Negotiating with these cultures will require greater proactive effort in anticipating perceived risks and proactively finding ways to mitigate them. Culture that exist in North America, Scandinavia, and Australia have a lower degree of risk aversion, that is, they are willing to accept greater levels of risk in an agreement. Therefore, the burden on negotiators facing counterparts from high risk-averse cultures is to present a higher return potential as compensation for taking on the greater risk.

Ways in which different cultures pursue risk mitigation varies. In Asian and Latin American cultures, negotiators mitigate risk through relationship building. If problems arise in the performance on the contract, they expect to rely on the relationship between the parties to resolve the problems. In contrast, in North American and German cultures, contracts are laden with details that represent legal obligations for the parties' performance on the contract. Although relationships are relied upon to resolve problems, these cultures are more likely to ultimately rely on applicable laws and legal remedies.

Core Skill #7: Negotiating Ethically

Potter Stewart, a former Associate Justice of the United States Supreme Court, once said that ethics is knowing the difference between what you have a right to do and what is right to do. What a negotiator **has the right to do** is dictated by the laws of his country and the country of his counterpart, both of which should be obeyed without question. What **is right for a negotiator to do** depends on the business and social norms and protocols of the cultures involved in the negotiation.

Most cultures operate under established contract law for international transactions. For example, the Principles of European Contract Law governs international transactions for the twenty-seven member states in the European Union. Also, seventy-nine countries have ratified the United Nations Convention on Contracts for the International Sale of Goods (CISG). These conventions have enforcement provisions that protect the parties involved from damages due to non-performance.

Yet in some cultures, especially those that favor **principle-based contracts** (for example, Italy, Spain, Portugal, Brazil, Japan, China, and Saudi Arabia), signed contracts resulting from a negotiation are viewed as merely a formality to the stronger ties represented by the **relationship** between the parties. **Detail-oriented cultures** (for example, Germany, Austria, Spain, Argentina, the United States, and South Africa) will consider signed contracts as an ironclad document that will **guide future actions**. In these cultures, violation of a contract term would be considered a significant breach not only of contract law but of the ethics involved in the business relationship between the parties.

Consider a contract signed by a German seller and a Portuguese buyer. Non-performance by the Portuguese buyer on any of the terms of the contract would be seen by the German seller as unethical and a legal violation, but the Portuguese buyer would see it as merely a business-condition adjustment to the verbal agreement overriding the contract. This situation would likely be encountered by a customer service specialist after the marketing and sales specialists negotiated a signed contract. The consistent and clear communications between the German and Portuguese companies **across the marketing-sales-customer service continuum** would allow a contract performance problem to be resolved without damaging the business relationship. These adjustments may have implications on potential redesigns in marketing and sales strategies.

An especially perilous area of cross cultural negotiation is gift giving. In some cultures, gift giving is a valued element of the social and business interaction. In others, gift giving could be considered bribery and be subject to criminal sanctions.

In the past several decades, anti-bribery (and anti-corruption) conventions and legislation have emerged around the world. The first international convention directed at preventing corruption was the *Inter-American Convention Against Corruption*, enacted in 1997 by the Organization of American States which includes Northern, Latin, and South American countries. Other international efforts to prevent corruption includes the *Anti-Bribery Convention* of the Organization for Economic Cooperation and Development which has all thirty-four members as signatories as well as non-members Argentina, Brazil, Bulgaria, Columbia, Russia, and South Africa; the United Nations' *Convention against Corruption*; the Economic Unions' *Conventions against Corruption*; the Council of Europe's *Criminal and Civil Law Conventions on Corruption*; and the African Union's *Convention on Preventing and Combating Corruption*.

Individual countries have also taken measures to prevent bribery. In 1997, Germany enacted the *German Anti-Corruption Act*[27] *(Gesetz zur Bekämpfung der Korruption)* which applies to both public and private sector transactions but imposes penalties only on individuals, not companies. The UK has its very stringent Bribery Act of 2010 and the United States has it *Foreign Corrupt Practices Act*[28].

Within the context of these laws and conventions, what is culturally **right to do** may present a dilemma to the cross-cultural negotiator. In some cultures, such as those in Germany, the United States, Italy, Portugal, and France, gift-giving in a business setting is rare. However, in many other cultures, such as those that exist in China, Japan, South Korea, Thailand, and Saudi Arabia, gift-giving and the mutual exchange of gifts is often a courtesy expected as part of the relationship-building process. Some laws make an exception for "token" gifts when there is no country law prohibiting the giving of gifts to facilitate a business transaction. For example, the U.S. allows gifts for "promotion, demonstration, or explanation of products or services" or "the execution or performance of a contract with a foreign government or agency thereof."[29]

Organizations and their legal counsel should provide guidance to negotiators in the area of bribery and corruption practices and laws, as well as the culture-specific customs related to these areas. Company policy on gift-giving should be clear regarding purpose, timing, value, appropriateness, transparency, and record-keeping. If these policies or the laws of the negotiator's country would result in violation of the customs of the culture in which the negotiation is taking place, the negotiator should express awareness of the cultural norm and explain the laws that restrict actions that would allow him to follow those norms. An excellent resource for the cross-cultural negotiator is the Business Anti-Corruption Portal at *http://www.business-anti-corruption.com*.

4.2 Bridging Cultural Divides

The space across the negotiating table represents more than just the physical difference between two negotiators. It could also represent a cultural divide that encompasses a complex set of differences in the ways in which the negotiators think, perceive, communicate, and behave toward each other. The coordination, consistency, and clarity in negotiating that an integration of marketing, sales, and customer ser-

---

27 U.S. Foreign Corrupt Practices Act.
28 15 U.S.C., 2006.
29 See S. REP, 1977.

vices makes possible requires a high level of skill in **recognizing and adapting to cultural divides in five areas:** agreement focus, interactive style, time sensitivity, decision-making hierarchy, and relationship value (see Fig. 2).

Agreement Focus. The objective of any negotiation is to arrive at an agreement among the parties that addresses the interests of the parties. Culture influences the process and final form of the agreement. For example, Chinese, Japanese, Indians and Spanish negotiators use a top-down approach. They strive for agreement on the overriding principles of the transaction in the initial stages of the negotiation, then address the specific details support those principles. In contrast, negotiators from Germany, the United States, Austria, Italy and Argentina take a bottom-up approach and build an agreement by addressing the details first, then build from them to the general principles of the transaction.

The principles-focused, top-down approach results in shorter contracts than those produced in a details-focused, bottom-up approach to negotiating. Cultures preferring principles-focused contracts feel comfortable without the details because they place great importance on the business and personal relationship between parties in guiding performance on the contract. They rarely resort to legal means to resolve problems. They take a threat of legal action as disrespectful. They value flexibility in business arrangements, with terms adjusting as business conditions change.

In contrast, cultures preferring the details-focused, bottom-up approach have longer contracts with significant detail to guide future performance. These cultures tend to have an extensive legal system and rely on it to resolve contract problems.

The agreement focus cultural divide in a transaction involving a Swiss seller and a Thai buyer would be very wide, whereas the divide between a German and a Venezuelan or a Spaniard and a Malaysian would be narrow. For example, the marketing approach of the Swiss seller to the Thai buyer would be to stress the overall benefits of the product rather than the detailed specifications. The sales negotiation would likely be skewed more toward the top-down approach, drilling down to the detail from higher-level principles. The resulting contract would be shorter than the normal Swiss contract and have less detail. That places a burden on the Swiss customer service specialist to work with the Thai customer to interpret the parties' obligations from a principle-focused contract. The **integration** of customer service with marketing and sales provides the customer service specialist with a high-level, principles-based understanding of the agreements made throughout the marketing and sales negotiations.

For companies contracting for business across *agreement focus* divides, management, negotiators, and legal counsel may want to review their standard contracts for reasonable modifications to address the differing cultural views of an agreement.

Interactive Style. A successful negotiation requires clear, unambiguous interaction between all parties. Cross-cultural negotiations often present significant **interactive style** divides, with challenging differences in communication – verbally and non-verbally – and temperament. Richard D. Lewis, in his book, *When Cultures*

Collide, categorizes cultures around the world as a continuum between three major types: linear-active, multi-active, and reactive.

In **linear-active cultures**, people tend to be introverted, patient, private, task-oriented, and comfortable in established procedures, agendas, facts, and statistics. Lewis places Germans, Swiss, North Americans, Scandinavians, Austrians, and British in the linear-active category.

Multi-active individuals are extroverted, inquisitive, unpunctual, and emotional. They combine their social and professional lives and are people- rather than fact-oriented. According to Lewis, multi-active cultures are Latin American, Arabian, African, Spanish, Southern Italian, and Portuguese. Those cultures representing a combination of linear-active and multi-active communication traits are the Dutch, French, Czechs, Northern Italians, and Russians.

The third of Lewis' cultural categories is **reactive**. Communicators in this style are patient, calm, and respectful. They avoid confrontation and are good listeners. They are reactive rather than proactive, need to see the whole picture before making a decision, search for the *truth* among the facts, and must feel comfortable both socially and professionally with a business partner before continuing on with a negotiation. The reactive group is comprised of Asian countries (Japan, China, Korea, and Vietnam) as well as Finland, Turkey, and Malaysia.

Consider interactive divide between representatives from a North American and South Korean companies. **Interaction adjustments** would need to be made across marketing, sales, and customer service, and the integration of those functions would allow a consistent and effective adjustment. The North American **marketer** would have a more subtle marketing approach, focusing on the similarities in the missions and core values of the two companies and the benefits of a long-term relationship. The **sales representative** would tone down his normal approach and reinforce the marketing message by taking more time at the beginning of the negotiation in building a relationship with the customer representative. The sales representative would be prepared for a longer and more trying negotiation process than he might expect with another North American customer, with periods of silence and contemplation by the South Korean. The **customer service specialist** would be prepared to have indirect communication with the South Korean customer, with the added challenge of reading between the lines of statement. The cultural concept of **saving face** – maintaining dignity, avoiding embarrassment, and protecting reputation – would be an imperative in interacting with the South Korean customer.

Time Orientation and Sensitivity. There is no wider time orientation and sensitivity divide than the one that exists when a negotiation takes place between representatives from the United States and China. The U.S. negotiator wants to complete the negotiations in a short period of time under the concept of *time is money*. The Chinese negotiator has no time limit preconceptions, places no time constraints on a negotiation, and takes a long-term view of the implications of the negotiation. The history of both nations provides insight into this cultural divide. The United States is slightly less than two hundred and fifty years old. China's history dates back nearly four millennia to the Shang Dynasty in 1700 BC.

In his 1984 book entitled, *The Dance of Life: The Other Dimension of Time*[30], Edward T. Hall introduced the term *polychronic* to describe the way individuals address multiple topics *simultaneously*, and *monochronic* to describe how individuals address multiple topics *sequentially*. This divide between the way people from different cultures process tasks presents a time-dimension challenge to cross-cultural negotiators. North American and Northern European cultures tend to have a monochronic orientation while Latin, Asian, and Middle Eastern cultures are predominantly polychronic.

Consider a negotiation between a monochronic German customer service representative and a polychronic Mexican customer to resolve several issues of concern to the Mexican. The German enters a negotiation with a detailed list of concerns and a strategy for addressing the most important ones first, getting agreement on the resolution, and then sequentially working down the list until all issues are resolved. The Mexican counterpart enters the negotiation without an agenda, is more comfortable discussing issues in no particular order, refuses to come to an agreement on any issue before all issues are discussed and re-discussed out of order, and is constantly interrupted by phone calls and visits from relatives. The sense of monochronic order and progress of the German negotiator is disrupted by the polychronic approach to the negotiation (and life) of the Mexican customer. **Customer service specialists** experienced in cross-cultural negotiating would understand that a polychronic/monochronic divide exists and would **bridge the gap** by not viewing his counterpart's contrasting time and task orientation as a tactic or impediment and would make adjustments to facilitate communication and progress.

Decision-Making Hierarchy. Individualism and collectivism are strong forces within cultures. Collective cultures, such as those that exist in Asian and Latin American countries as well as Germany, Austria, Sweden, Portugal, Egypt, Indonesia, and Russia, tend to be hierarchical in their approach to decision-making. The process of making a decision is relatively slow and deliberate. Status within the hierarchy is based on age, position, and education. Negotiators expect their counterpart's team to be aligned in status and number. Lesser status or fewer members may be considered disrespectful. **Decisions** are normally made by individuals with the highest status, normally a person senior – by age and longevity – in an organization. Stakeholders in the negotiation may be silent or absent. For example, trade union or local bureaucrats may have considerable influence in the decision-making process but not directly participate in the negotiation. In family-owned businesses, the head of the family may never attend a negotiation meeting, but will make the final decision on any potential agreement.

Individualistic cultures such as those that exist in the United States, Canada, the United Kingdom, Switzerland, Denmark, France and Italy value personal initiative, entrepreneurship, and risk taking. Hierarchies play a much less prominent role in

---

30 Hall, 1984.

decision-making. Achievement is the primary status determination. In these cultures, a negotiator is far more likely to find the ultimate decision-maker sitting across the table either alone or with a support team of specialists. However, there will be no doubt as to the leader and ultimate decision-maker.

Decisions are made throughout a customer engagement across the marketing-sales, customer service functional coalition. Often these decisions are interrelated and coordinated. Recognition and adaptation to decision-making hierarchy divides across cultures provides for a more favorable outcomes, stronger relationships, and deeper penetration along sales-generating paths within the customer's organization.

Relationship Value. All cultures value a strong, trusting, **long-term relationship** between business partners. In that respect, the divide between cultures is narrow. However, the time allocated to developing the relationship and the position of relationship building in the negotiation process differs among cultures. On a continuum of importance placed on relationship-building in cross-cultural negotiations, Asian, Latin, and Middle Eastern cultures are at the high end and North American and Northern European cultures are at the lower end.

Cultures placing **more** value on **relationship-building** will engage in that activity at the **beginning** of the negotiation process, as failure to develop a strong, initial relationship could preclude further deliberations to arrive at an agreement. Those cultures placing **less** emphasis on **relationship-building** will do some **rapport-building** in the opening phase of the negotiation, but want to begin discussions on issues quickly.

Realization of this cultural divide in relationship building places different responsibilities on marketing, sales, and customer service. When dealing with higher relationship value cultures, the role of establishing the relationship falls mainly on marketing and sales, while customer service is responsible for maintaining and strengthening the relationship. For lower relationship value cultures, the responsibility for establishing, maintaining, and strengthening the relationship falls mainly on customer service.

The primary reason for relationship-building by all parties in a negotiation is risk mitigation, especially for new accounts in a cross-cultural setting. The reason why higher relationship value cultures place great emphasis on relationship building is that within those cultures, the relationship is the primary means by which problems are resolved. These cultures tend to have a less developed legal infrastructure, so the natural recourse when contract problems arise is to call on the relationship between the parties to work out a solution. Using litigation to resolve contractual problems would be considered an affront to the relationship and would likely have dire consequences.

In lower relationship value cultures, the legal system is much deeper and comprehensive in its guidance on contractual transactions. Contracts in these cultures tend to be long and laden with product and performance details as well as legal remedies for any party damaged by non-performance. The structure of the contract serves as risk mitigation for all parties involved. Problem resolution depends much less on the business relationship than recourse to legal remedies.

An important issue in bridging the **relationship value** divide is the continuity in representing the relationship and whether the relationship is represented by the individual or the company. In those cultures that are more hierarchical in their decision-making process, the relationship tends to be more centered on the company rather than the individual. Therefore, a change in personnel in marketing, sales, or customer service will have little effect on the relationship and business will continue as normal. However, in more individualistic cultures with less hierarchy, the relationship is considered more on an individual rather than company basis. A change in the person representing the marketing, sales, and customer service contacts with the customer will seriously influence the relationship. Therefore, continuity in the representation of those three areas is critical, and if a change is made in personnel, it should be gradual with the incumbent facilitating a new relationship-building effort for the new person.

4.3 Training and Coaching

Acquiring and enhancing cross-cultural negotiating skills is essential in multinational organizations. *Training* is directive in that it is designed to provide individuals with the opportunity to acquire knowledge, skills, and expertise. *Coaching* differs from training in that it is non-directive and focused on enhancing skills already learned. Let's look at approaches for using both in providing a means by which cross-cultural negotiators can succeed in an organization.

Training. As presented above, succeeding in cross-cultural negotiations requires two tiers of expertise—a core level of cross-cultural negotiating skills and the ability to recognize and bridge cultural divides. Expert, experienced trainers can be brought into an organization from the outside or developed in-house to provide classroom instruction. Experiential learning in the form of mock negotiation exercises also can be used. In this latter approach, situations can be created for the trainees that will be similar to those that will exist for them in their future negotiations. Experienced negotiators can be brought from the field into the training sessions to assume the role of a negotiator from another culture, thereby creating realistic cultural divides for the trainees to bridge using their newly-acquired skills. The mock negotiations can be videotaped and viewed after the experiential learning exercise to identify areas where skills were applied correctly and incorrectly. Progress can be tracked for each skill throughout a series of exercises.

When the training is complete, the trainee should be assigned to a cross-cultural negotiating team led by an experienced negotiator. These **apprentice or associate negotiators** will be able to observe the direction of the negotiation and participate in various aspects until they are ready to lead a team of their own.

An **important element** of the training is for the trainee to understand the **synergistic power of cooperation between the marketing, sales, and customer service functions**. Trainers should emphasize the importance of teamwork, with the exchange of information a critical component of everyone's success.

Coaching. Experts in any field are susceptible to falling into bad habits or allowing certain skills to be underutilized. A coach can recognize areas in which cross-cultural negotiating skills can be enhanced. A good way for coaching to take place is for negotiators to develop a debriefing report for every negotiation. An experienced coach can identify areas in which performance can be improved. When appropriate, coaches can accompany cross-cultural negotiators into the field to observe performance. Coaching should be positive and encouraging. Those coached must be made to understand that coaches will offer constructive criticism aimed at making them better negotiators. Annual performance reviews are opportunities to identify areas in which cross-cultural negotiating skills need to be enhanced. A coaching schedule as well as follow-up debriefings can be developed.

Coaching is a skill and should not be assumed to be possessed by everyone with expertise in cross-cultural negotiating. Coaches must have observation and motivation skills and a desire to assist others in realizing their potential.

4.4 Job Enrichment

Cross-cultural negotiating is an intellectually and physically challenging activity. It allows the employee the opportunity to experience the wide variety of cultures of the world and interact with individuals within those cultures in a meaningful and rewarding way. Proactive organizations search for **job enrichment opportunities** for their cross-cultural negotiators.

The formalization of job enrichment thinking and theory began in the 1950s with the American psychologist, Frederick Irving Herzberg.[31] Subsequent research by J. Richard Hackman and Greg Oldham[32] [33] produced a job enrichment model in which five core job characteristics lead to three critical psychological states that produce three personal and work outcomes. Figure 2 below illustrates the model. Let's look at how the model illustrates opportunities for job enrichment in the area of cross-cultural negotiations.

The need for **skill variety** is apparent in the seven cross-cultural negotiating core skills described above as well as the experience in bridging the five cultural divides that negotiators face when negotiating across cultures. **Task identity** refers to being an integral part of the job from start to finish. Of course, the negotiation starts with

---

31 Herzberg, 1987.
32 Hackmann / Oldham, 1976.
33 Hackmann / Oldham, 1980.

mastering the substance, setting goals, and developing a flexible strategy and progresses through implementation of that strategy, bridging any cultural divides that may exist, and crafting an agreement that has value for all parties. The **integration of marketing, sales, and customer service provides additional opportunities for job enrichment** in that the negotiator, as part of that integrated team, is involved in the task at an earlier stage (marketing) and remains with the task (the customer engagement) into the more mature customer engagement stage (customer service). **Task significance** refers to the ability of the negotiator to understand the role of the cross-cultural negotiation within the context of the overall mission and goals of the organization. Again, the inclusion of the negotiator into the **integrated** marketing-sales-customer service team, regardless of where within those three functions the negotiator operates, **provides a context for the significance of the task**. Within the job enrichment model, these three core job characteristics — skill variety, task identity, and task significance — allow the negotiator to experience a greater sense of meaningfulness with the job.

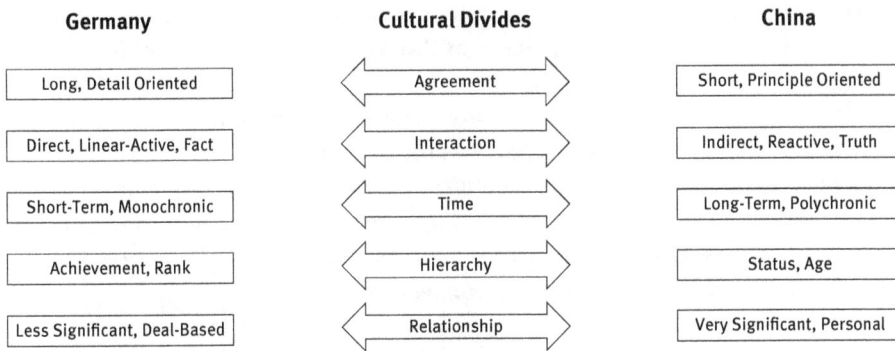

Germany	Cultural Divides	China
Long, Detail Oriented	Agreement	Short, Principle Oriented
Direct, Linear-Active, Fact	Interaction	Indirect, Reactive, Truth
Short-Term, Monochronic	Time	Long-Term, Polychronic
Achievement, Rank	Hierarchy	Status, Age
Less Significant, Deal-Based	Relationship	Very Significant, Personal

Fig. 47: Cultural Divides Between Germany and China.

Cross-cultural negotiating requires a significant degree of **autonomy** in that, within the clearly-defined organizational mission and ethical behavior guidelines, the negotiator should be allowed the freedom and discretion to apply the core cross-cultural negotiating skills described above and effectively bridge cultural divides. Inflexibility by imposing excessive organization restrictions can cause suboptimal negotiator performance and value creation during the negotiating process and loss of job satisfaction. Flexibility, autonomy, and control during the negotiating engagement promotes as sense of responsibility for and ownership of the outcomes of the negotiation.

Job feedback refers to the degree to which the cross-cultural negotiator is provided information about performance effectiveness. Post-negotiation debriefing reports and meetings can assist in the feedback process. The marketing-sales-customer service team approach, with its **multiple touch points** throughout the customer engagement, can also provide valuable peer-to-peer feedback.

Core Job Characteristics   Critical Psychological States   Personal and Work Outcomes

Skill Variety

Task Identity   →   Experience
                              meaningfulness of the
                              work

Task Significance   High internal work
                                                                         motivation

                                                                         High quality work
                                                                         performance
Autonomy   →   Experience
                              responsibility for the   High satisfaction with the
                              outcomes of the work   work

                                                                         High work effectiveness

Job Feedback   →   Knowledge of the actual
                              results of the work

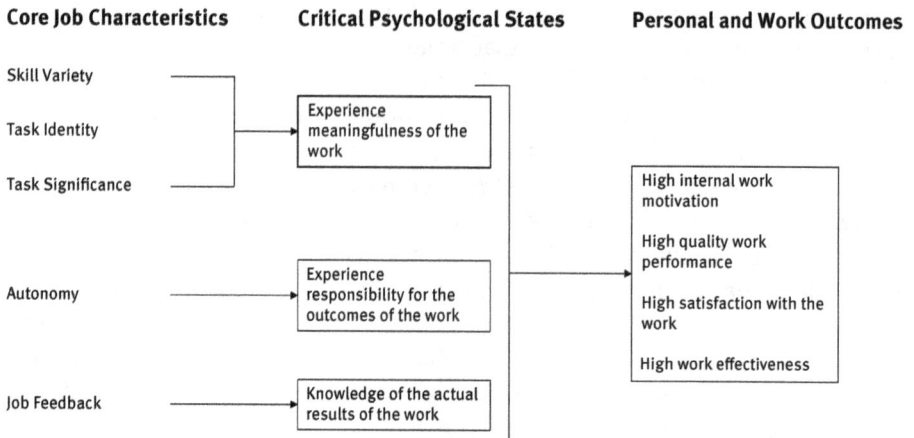

Fig. 48: Hackman and Oldham Job Characteristics Model (Hackman / Oldham 1976/1980).

Two additional organizational job enrichment initiatives that are being used effectively are the formation of **natural work teams** and **vertical loading**, both of which fit perfectly within the **team approach of the marketing-sales-customer service integration**.

The formation of **natural work teams**, comprised of marketing, sales, customer service and other functional areas provides the negotiator with an enriched sense of responsibility, involvement, and accomplishment in building a successful customer engagement. The team approach allows implementation of the second job enrichment initiative – **vertical loading**. In this method, structure is put in place so that the employee is involved throughout the customer engagement.

4.5 Rewards and Recognition

The use of employee rewards and recognitions is a means by which management motivates high-level performance in line with the strategic direction, mission, and core values of the organization. Measuring performance in the complex function of cross-cultural negotiation is challenging yet required if a well-defined rewards and recognitions program is to be an incentive for high performance and is consistently and fairly applied.

Questions that need to be addressed in implementing an **incentive program** are:
1. What type of performance is being motivated?
2. Can the performance be measured?
3. What level of performance would merit an accolade?
4. Should the accolade conferred be in the form of a reward, award, or recognition?
5. Should the accolade be on an individual or team basis?

Let's apply each of these questions to the cross-cultural negotiator.

1. **Type of Performance Motivated.** The three value-based performance criteria are customer satisfaction, customer sales penetration, and customer sales. Customer satisfaction relates to building a strong, trusting relationship with the customer and addressing the customer needs in a superior manner. The chain of satisfaction extends along the marketing-sales-customer service continuum and then beyond into an organization's functional areas. Although some cultures place higher value on relationships than others, all cultures eventually value a strong relationship with their business partners. Customer sales penetration refers to opening additional sales avenues within the company, potentially taking share away from competitors. Again, the marketing-sales, customer service team approach can **facilitate** this performance. Customer sales are the most quantifiable performance measure and represent the organization's contribution to the growth of the customer's business.

    In addition, high proficiency in applying the core cross-cultural negotiating skills and bridging challenging cultural divides should also be motivated through the organization's reward and recognition program.

    A critical element of any reward and recognition program is to align the performances motivated with the organization's strategic and operational objectives as well as its mission and core values.

2. **Performance Measurement.** Some areas of performance can be measured quantitatively, such as performance against sales quotas or initiating sales with new customers or in new areas/divisions of existing customer organizations. Others, such as the application of core skills, bridging cultural divides, and strengthening the customer relationship need to be evaluated qualitatively even though success in these applications can be related to the more quantifiable performance measures.

3. **Performance Level.** Performance that would merit an award or recognition needs to be set at levels that differentiate the top five to ten percent of performers from everyone else. Ambitious, yet attainable, performance goals trigger a psychological striving mechanism in individuals and motivate all employees to emulate the top performers. Quantitative performance levels worthy of recognition are based on past top performance and derived from optimistic projections of overall organization performance. Qualitative accolade-worth performance is somewhat more difficult to set. An example of negotiator or negotiating team high performance would be signing a contract with a customer situated across wide cultural divide or a customer service specialist rescuing a customer on the verge of severing the business relationship.

4. **Reward, Award, or Recognition.** A reward is normally monetary, such as a spot cash payment, a salary increase, or a bonus. An award is a token, such as a trophy or plaque. A recognition is a broadcast over one or more media of a special performance. The best policy is to have a mix of all three. For negotiating performance

that results in higher profits for the company, possibly a combination of cash payment (allowing the negotiator to directly share in the profit generated) and recognition would be proper. For exceeding a sales quota, a quasi-cash payment, such as a vacation or time off, would be appropriate. For service *beyond the call,* usually given at regular intervals, an award would be best.

5. **Individual or Team.** This decision is not always an easy one, as an individual showing outstanding performance usually has support within the organization. The integrated marketing-sales-customer service **team approach** to cross-cultural negotiating will itself promote **superior performance**. So recognition of that team effort in producing superior performance is critical. Many organizations have a peer-to-peer recognition program that allows for individual recognition within a group.

Although cash awards are the most tangible means of motivating superior performance, don't underestimate the power of non-cash rewards and recognitions. The results of a recent survey of 291 companies by the Aberdeen Group, an American research firm, in support of their research study *"Sales Performance Management 2012: How Best In Class Optimize the Front Line and Grow the Bottom Line"*, show that organizations that give non-cash rewards and recognitions had (1) an average annual increase in revenues of 9.6% versus 3.0% for all others, (2) a 1.6% annual increase in team quota attainment versus 2.2% for others, and (3) a 2.1% annual increase in revenue per sales full-time employee versus a 0.7 decrease for others.

That completes the explanation of the building blocks of organizational cross-cultural negotiating success as illustrated in Fig. 46. Now let's take a quick look at how those building blocks can be utilized in conjunction with key account management (KAM).

4.6 Cross-Cultural Negotiations and Key Account Management

The organizational commitment to excellence in cross-cultural negotiating cuts across the company's functional areas and is especially illustrated by key account management (KAM). Assume a German company producing advanced technology batteries for hybrid vehicles has identified one of its customers – an American automobile manufacturer – as a key account. The German company has organized its **KAM team** as comprising an account manager, a marketing specialist, a dedicated sales account executive, and support by customer service representative. On a less dedicated level will be specialists in procurement, research and development, quality control, product management, and production management.

The German company realizes that at any one time, every person on the key account team could be negotiating across different cultural divides. Therefore, each person would have had to have taken the organization's in-house core negotiating skills and cross-cultural negotiating skills training to qualify to be a KAM team member. With this training requirement, the German company knows that team members will be representing the company by successfully applying high-level core cross-cultural negotiating skills and bridging cultural divides throughout the American customer's global organizational network.

On a particular day, based on information provided by the *account and customer service representative* on the account, the *account sales executive* and the *account product manager* are in the American automaker's New York headquarters negotiating with the president of the commercial vehicle division to be the automaker's battery supplier for a new line of hybrid short- to mid-range commercial vehicles. The morning meeting was scheduled for two hours, had an agreed-upon agenda, and started and finished on time. The negotiation on pricing was detail-oriented. The discussion was direct and took each issue – performance, pricing, quality, durability, delivery – sequentially. No decision was made but a follow-up meeting was scheduled for a future date. The division president had more of a competitive negotiating style than the Germans but, overall, the cultural divides were narrow between the German and American negotiators.

While the account salesperson stayed in New York to continue negotiations with the automaker's division president, the account manager flew south to one of the American automaker's hybrid vehicle test facilities in Mississippi where the German *key account product manager* was meeting with the automaker's Vice President of Research and Development and a few of his research engineers to negotiate the cost of an enhancement of the design of the battery to add more power generating efficiency. The account manager met his product manager and the American vice president at a local plantation restaurant where the negotiation was taking place.

The German account manager found the culture in Mississippi, a state in the Deep South of the United States, completely different than the one he left in New York City. The discussion was much more casual and relationship-oriented, with a diminished sense of urgency in coming to an agreement. The American vice president, a native of Mississippi, had a negotiating style that was more collaborative and team-oriented and less formal and structured than the president of the commercial vehicle division in New York City.

At the same time, a *Research &Development specialist* on the key account team was in Italy negotiating a technology transfer agreement with the president of a small company that had developed a new polymer that would substantially increase the power-to-weight ratio of the German company's hybrid vehicle batteries and result in a value-added for both the company and its key accounts. The German R&D specialist and Italian company president had never met before. Prior to the trip to Italy, the German R&D specialist mastered the substance of the upcoming negotiation by reading about the Italian company and its polymer research. He was also prepared for wide cultural divides in interactive style, time sensitivity, decision-making hierarchy, relationship value, and temperament, and a narrow divide in agreement focus.

Meanwhile, the German *account procurement manager* was in Australia negotiating a price increase with the sales manager of the company's supplier of mineral nickel used in the manufacture of the hybrid vehicle batteries. Australia is a leading producer and exporter of mineral nickel and prices have been increasing with the increased production of stainless steel, of which mineral nickel is a component. Before that meeting, the German procurement manager met with the marketing, sales, and customer service teams who have knowledge of the culture, communication style, and negotiating protocol of Australia. As a result of the valuable information provided by those teams, the procurement manager was prepared to face an Australian negotiator with a collaborative, win-win approach. The procurement manager prepared brief statements supported by verifiable facts concerning the state of the mineral nickel market, as Australians value brevity and supportable facts. The German manager was pleased that he was of equal status in management with the Australian negotiator as Australians are more trusting of equals.

That very same day, the German *quality control specialist* was in Mexico at one of the American automakers hybrid vehicle assembly plants. There was an issue with variations in battery dimensions and negotiations were underway at resolving the issue to the satisfaction of all parties. The German production specialist found his negotiating counterpart – a Mexican national he was meeting for the first time – warm and open in their communication. The negotiation progressed over several days with frequent breaks and delays when the Mexican was called away on other business. The German was invited to the Mexicans home each evening, but no business was discussed. The German made a strong effort to gradually strengthen the personal and professional relationship with the Mexican so that they could begin their discussions on resolution of the quality control problem.

In many key world-wide negotiations with the American key account representatives, German account representatives were effectively applying high-level cross-cultural **core negotiating skills, bridging** both narrow and wide **cultural divides,** and leveraging the coordinated, consistent, and clear **strategic method of the marketing-sales-customer service team** for a triple-win for the company.

References

Hackman, J.R., Oldham, G.R. (1980) Work redesign. Reading, MA: Addison-Wesley

Hackman, J.R., Oldham, G.R. (1976) Motivation through the design of work: Test of a theory. Organizational Behavior and Human Performance, 16, 250– 279

Hall, Edward T. (1984) The Dance of Life. The Other Dimension of Time, 2nd ed., Garden City, NY: Anchor Press/Doubleday

Herzberg, F.I., One more time: How do you motivate employees? Harvard Business Review, Sep/Oct 87, Vol. 65, Issue 5

Hofbauer, G. / Hellwig, C. (2012) Professionelles Vetriebsmanagement – Der prozessorientierte Ansatz aus Anbieter- und Beschaffersicht, 3. Aufl., Erlangen

Hofmaier, R. (2011/2013) New Approaches, Methods and Implementation Options for Sales-Hit-Rate Optimization (B2B) – Emprical Studies, Munich

Hofmaier, R. (2011/2013) Vertriebliche "Hit Rate"-Optimierung im B2B Sales: Neue Ansätze, Methoden und Umsetzungsmöglichkeiten – Empirische Studie, München

Hofmaier, R. (1999) Systematische Marktsegmentierung und Hit Rate-Optimierung (im Business-to-Business-Marketing) in Pepels, W. (Hrsg.), Business to business Marketing, Neuwied, S. 130–139

Hofmaier, R. / Leutbecher, K. (1996) Investitionsgüter zeitgemäß vermarkten, in: Harvard Business Manager, Heft III, S. 106–110

Homburg, Ch. / Schäfer, H. / Schneider, J.(2012) Sales Excellence – Vertriebsmanagement mit System, 7. Aufl., Wiesbaden

Parson, T. (1949) Essays in sociological theory: pure and applied, The Free Press, Glencoe, IL, p. 8

See S. REP. NO. 95–114, at 1–3 (1977)

U.S.C. §§ 78dd-1(f)(1)(A), 78dd-2(h)(2)(A), 78dd-3(f)(2)(A) (2006)

U.S. Foreign Corrupt Practices Act, 15 U.S.C. §§ 78dd-l (c)(2), 7Bdd-2(c)(2), 7Bdd-3(c)(2)

v. Bischopink, Y. / Ceyp, M. (2009) Suchmaschinen-Marketing: Konzepte, Umsetzung und Controlling für SEO und SEM, 2. Aufl., Berlin

Weber, Max, The methodology of the social sciences, The Free Press, New York, 1949. p. 76

V Integrated customer loyalty, customer relations and customer retention management (CRM)

In today's B2B marketing management, there is now another area of programs and measures, which evolved in recent years from practical-operative application requirements for everyday business tasks and which is explicitly substantiated through the integrated marketing approach outlined in this book. By including such customer management "perspective" and its specific methods and tools, an independent mix of programs and instruments develops, namely that of **integrated customer satisfaction, customer loyalty, customer relations, customer retention and tool management as an integrated CRM** (customer relationship management) approach.

1 Holistic CRM – Customer Relationship Management-Approach

A **holistic-oriented customer relationship management or CRM-approach** is a component of holistic customer orientation (see Fig. 49a, interpretation see Fig. 49b) and consists of the following **five program and measure areas** (see Fig. 50) and thus includes both a corporation strategy and an operational management perspective:

Holistic (Marketing, Sales & Customer Mgmt.) CRM Orientation (B2B)

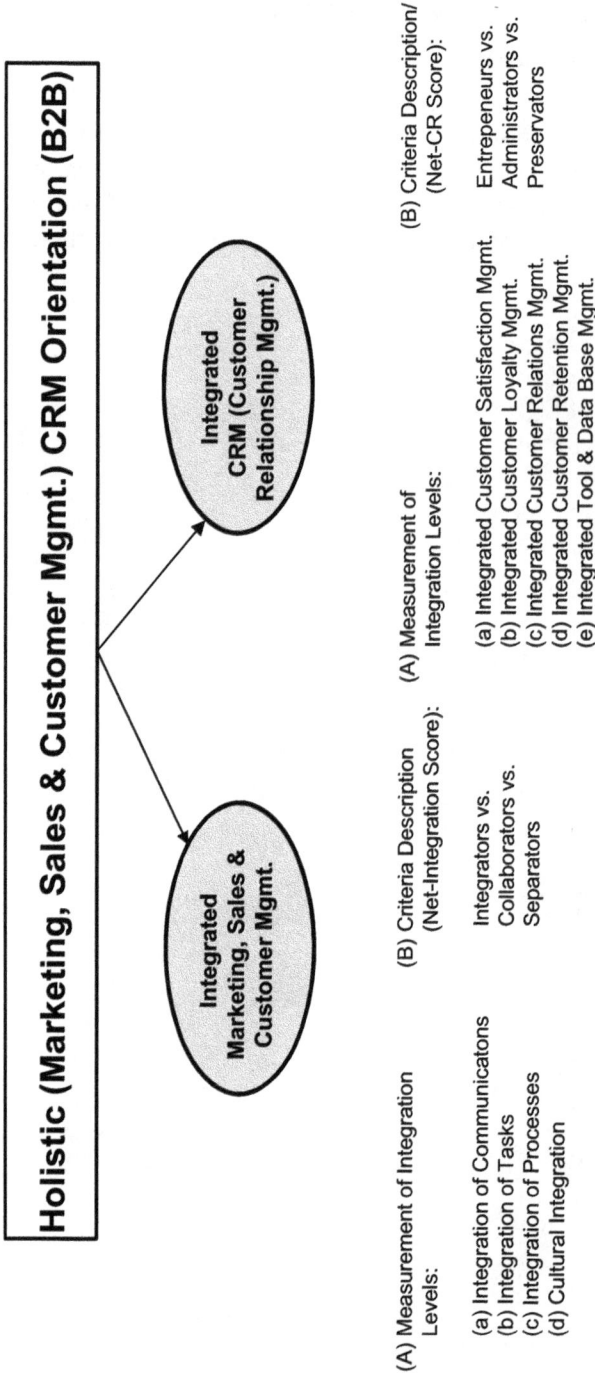

Integrated Marketing, Sales & Customer Mgmt.

Integrated CRM (Customer Relationship Mgmt.)

(A) Measurement of Integration Levels:

(a) Integration of Communicatons
(b) Integration of Tasks
(c) Integration of Processes
(d) Cultural Integration

(B) Criteria Description (Net-Integration Score):

Integrators vs.
Collaborators vs.
Separators

(A) Measurement of Integration Levels:

(a) Integrated Customer Satisfaction Mgmt.
(b) Integrated Customer Loyalty Mgmt.
(c) Integrated Customer Relations Mgmt.
(d) Integrated Customer Retention Mgmt.
(e) Integrated Tool & Data Base Mgmt.

(B) Criteria Description/ (Net-CR Score):

Entrepeneurs vs.
Administrators vs.
Preservators

Fig. 49a: Holistically integrated CRM as the main component of customer orientation (© Prof. Dr. R. Hofmaier).

Traditional Approach	New Approach
(1) Customer Satisfaction	(1) Customer Loyalty
(2) Customer Buying Support	(2) (a) Customer Relationship Mgmt. (b) Customer Retention Mgmt.
(3) Product Profitability	(3) Customer Profitability
(4) Current Sales	(4) Customer Life Time Value
(5) Brand Equity	(5) Customer Equity
(6) Market Share	(6) Customer's Share of Wallet/ Equity Share

Fig. 49b: CRM-related and modified approach definitions and measurement criteria
(© Prof. Dr. R. Hofmaier).

(I)   Customer satisfaction and customer loyalty management
(II) Customer relationship management
    in the form of
    a.   Business relationship management
    b.   Interpersonal relationship management, as well as
    c.   Customer recovery management
(III)   Customer relation management
    through
    a.   Ten dimensions of customer retention, and
    b.   Programs and measures of customer retention
(IV) Tool and database (DB) integration management
    through
    a.   (CRM) tool selection and implementation/optimization
    b.   Integrative database management
    c.   Tool-supported integration of sales, customer management, marketing and
      services
(V) (Complementary) Customer development management (KAM/see Part VI).

2 Integrated customer satisfaction and customer loyalty management

A holistic and integrative understanding of CRM is important, because often in business practice, CRM only "narrowly" refers to the selection and use of a suitable CRM tool, but this does not meet the current needs of a substantial CRM. Therefore, CRM first and foremost involves **strategic business and marketing alignment**, which focuses on comprehensive customer involvement, customer development and decision-maker "focusing" ("single decision-maker management;" see also the approach of Focus Group Management (FGM)) (Part VII). Operationally, it includes not only **customer satisfaction**, but also longer-term development and stabilization of **customer loyalty** (this includes far more than merely a customer satisfaction approach), as well as the explicit consideration of **business relationship and interpersonal relationship approaches**, and finally corresponding continuous **customer retention programs**, complemented by an **appropriate tool and database (DB) management approach**, and the necessary **customer development** perspective.

For the basic CRM approach, it is important, first of all, to know how much customer orientation is realized (especially with bigger customers) through corresponding customer feedback and integration management. The main focus here is on the integration of CRM in five stages, (a) customer satisfaction, (b) customer loyalty, (c) customer relation, (d) customer retention, and (e) tool and database management (see Fig. 50), which can be **measured** in terms of pronunciation (net-CR-score) and can successively be improved. Thus, the focus at first is not only to achieve or improve customer satisfaction, but develop and improve customer loyalty and customer retention. (Fig. 51 shows this as an "idealized" form).

According to Fig. 51, in the case of customer dissatisfaction, the reason for it should first be quickly detected and corrected, based on causes (not symptoms), and should be communicated to the relevant decision-makers and users. Only after achieving so-called "non-dissatisfaction" can and should the status of viable customer satisfaction (and, accordingly, further improvement measures) be realized. The next step for developing customer relationship is reaching "select" "commitments" and ultimately achieving a "convinced status" with respect to one's products, services, care measures, etc., until long-term cooperative business development (see Part II and VII) is achieved through a deep manifestation of **customer loyalty** (see Part VI).

Thus, the mere focus on primarily customer satisfaction-related inquiry and support measures is no longer enough. A variety of real-life projects and studies have shown that "classic" **customer satisfaction** analyses need to be **expanded** and **updated**. The implied connection that sufficient business success is possible purely with customer satisfaction-based feedback and design measures (see Fig. 52), can no longer be justified today or in the future.

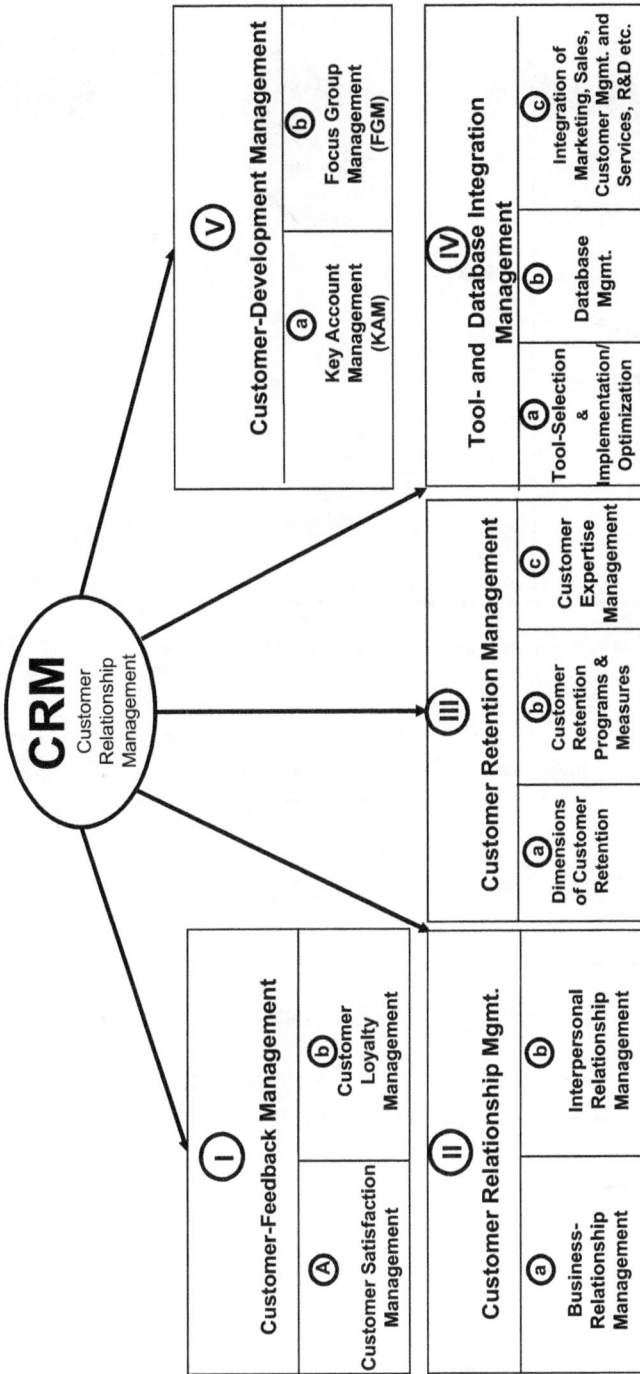

Fig. 50: CRM as holistically integrated customer management approach
(© Prof. Dr. R. Hofmaier).

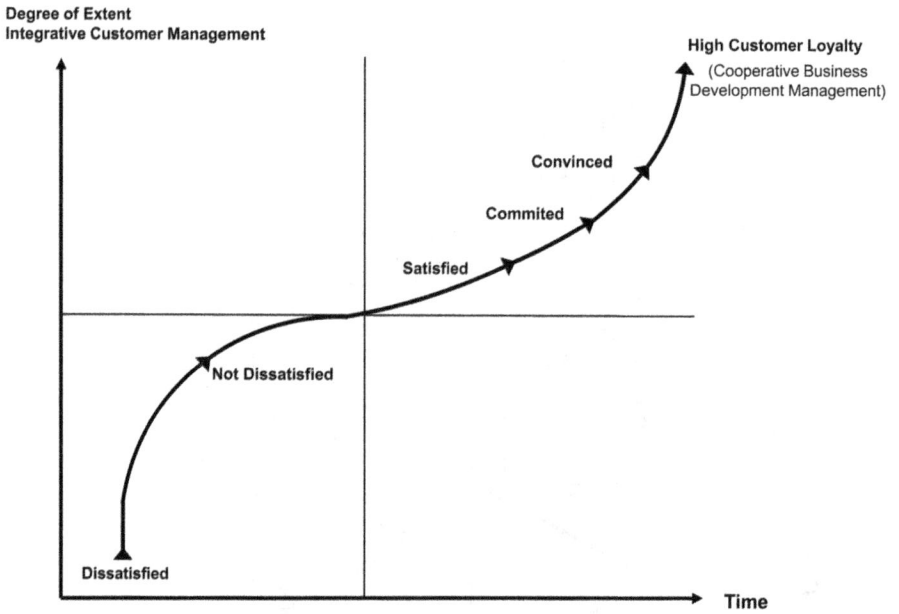

Fig. 51: "Idealized" manifestations of customer feedback and integration management (© Prof. Dr. R. Hofmaier).

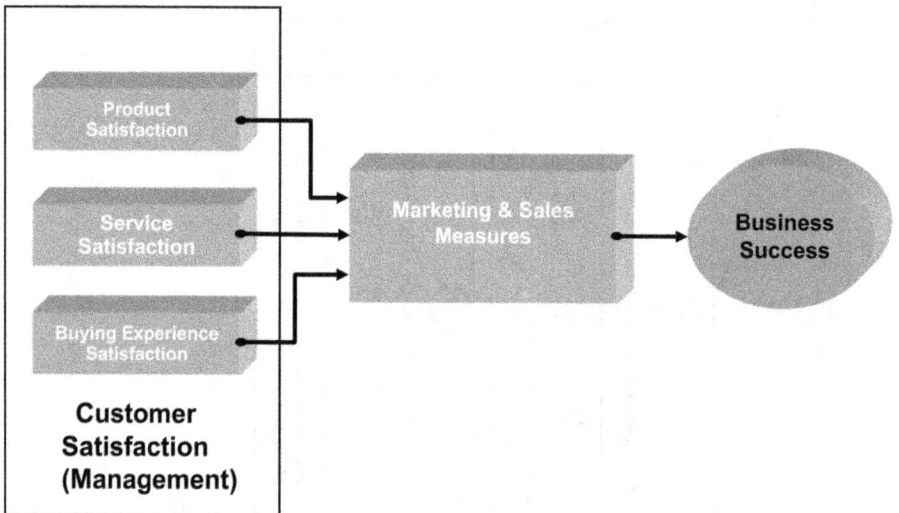

Fig. 52: "Mono-Causal" relationship between customer satisfaction management and business success (© Prof. Dr. R. Hofmaier).

Therefore, there needs to be advanced and longer-term potential-focused customer development (customer integration). These days, this usually means that the necessary **preferred supplier position** (via an appropriate needs analysis and corresponding MSC activities) should be achieved, developed and improved (since this can also extend one's own "leeways") on top of prior satisfaction management. In a further step (and thus supporting), necessary **customer relationship and retention** measures and also **customer loyalty** measures need to be identified and implemented in a targeted manner. In turn, this can improve overall customer loyalty, and with appropriate **customer development** management, further business development and thus a cooperative "**business partnership**" (for further business development measures) can continuously be sought and implemented (win-win partnership, especially with larger customers and key accounts; see Fig. 53).

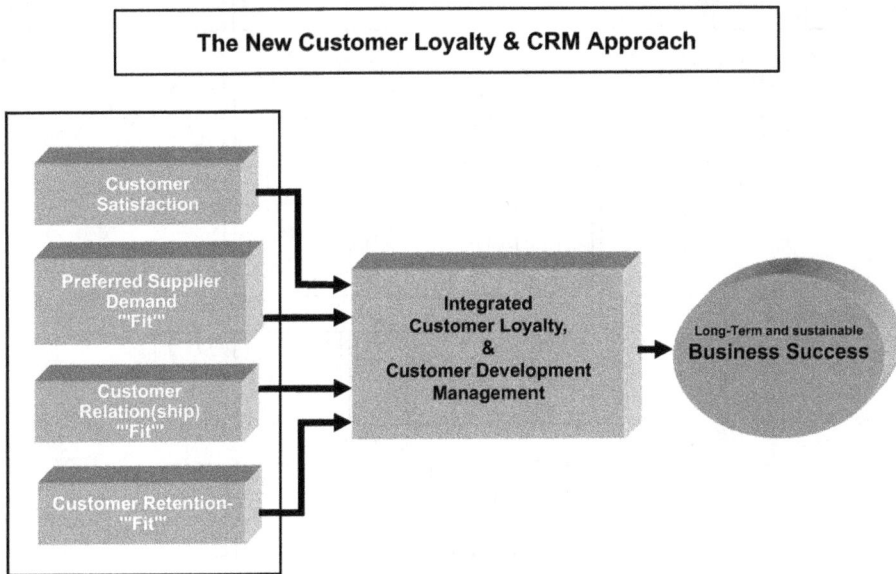

Fig. 53: "Multi-Causal" relationship between customer satisfaction, customer fit, customer loyalty and customer development management and business success (© Prof. Dr. R. Hofmaier).

Longer-term customer and business development at select (big) customers is therefore justified, because business opportunities with existing and new customers can be exponentially analysed and developed more deeply based on existing customer contacts, customer relationships and bonds, which can be beneficial for both sides. This also often presents the possibility of continuous **profitability improvement** (see also the systematic summary of profitability potentials depending on time-based customer retention in Fig. 54).

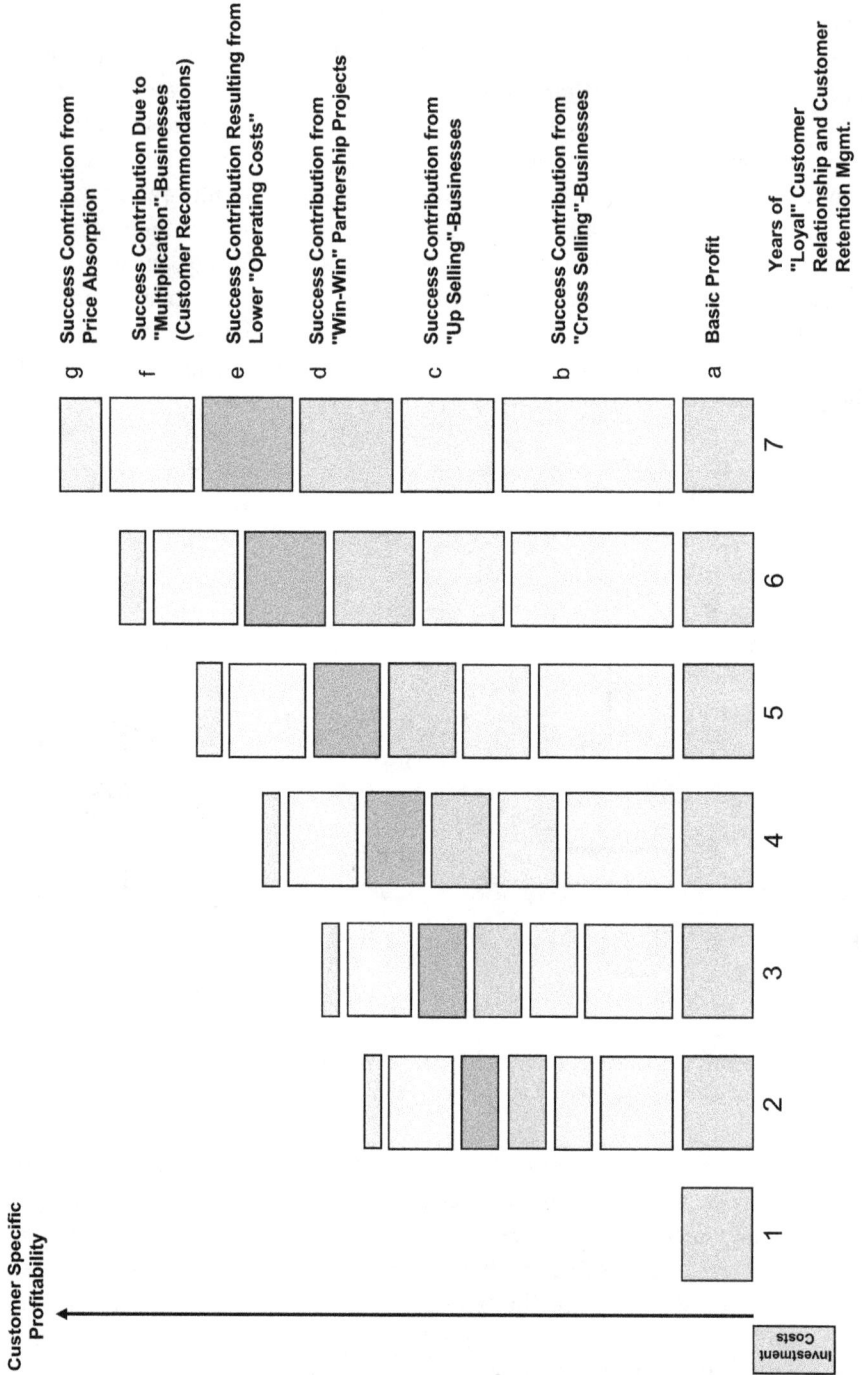

Fig. 54: Systematization of customer profitability depending on loyalty-focused business development (© Prof. Dr. R. Hofmaier).

Thus, for sustainable and long-term customer development, it is also important to consider attainable **different customer value and customer potential factors**. Especially for (large) customer and key account penetration, relevant possibilities present analysis and objective criteria (see Fig. 55). Thus, key figures of category I

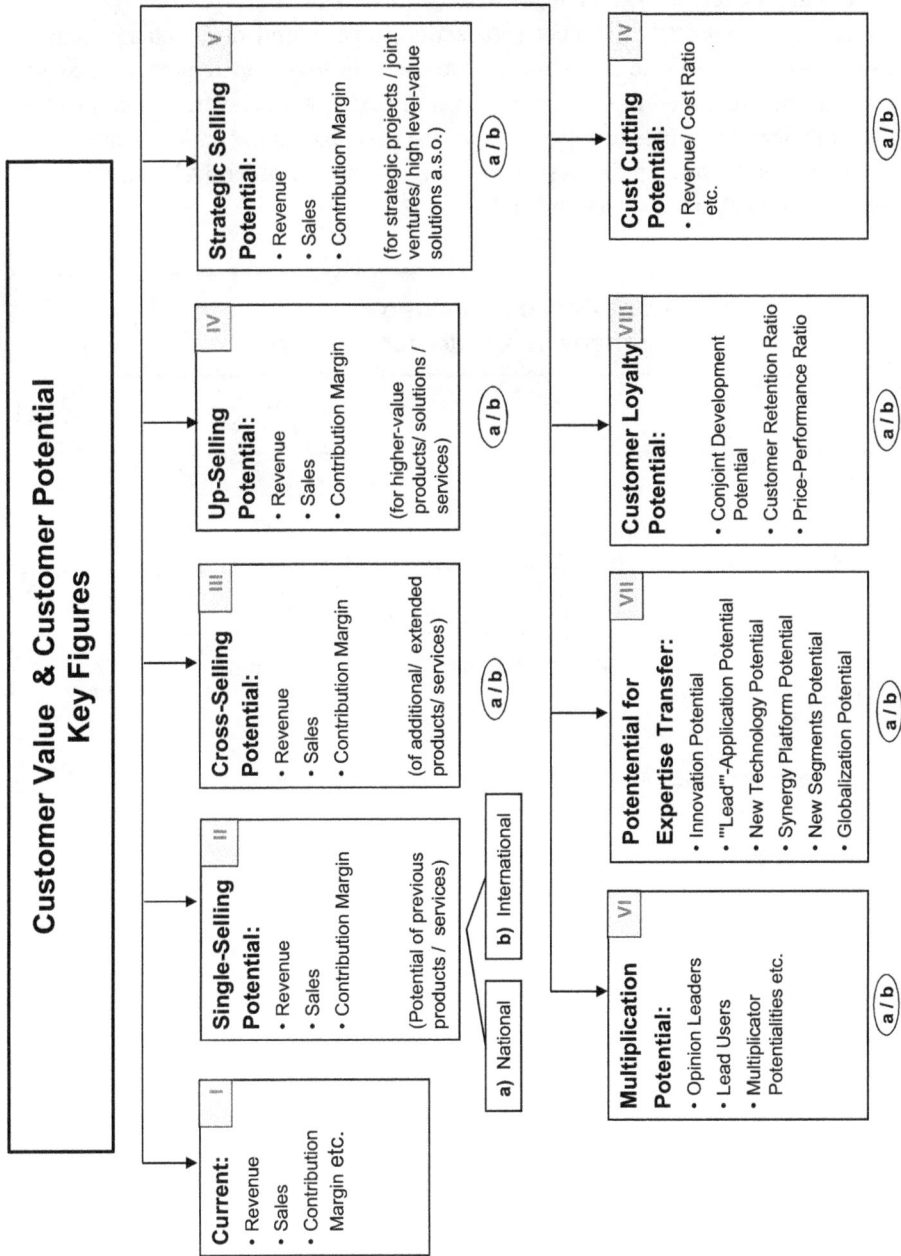

Customer Value & Customer Potential Key Figures

Current: I
- Revenue
- Sales
- Contribution Margin etc.

Single-Selling II
Potential:
- Revenue
- Sales
- Contribution Margin

(Potential of previous products / services)

a) National   b) International

Cross-Selling III
Potential:
- Revenue
- Sales
- Contribution Margin

(of additional/ extended products/ services)

a/b

Up-Selling IV
Potential:
- Revenue
- Sales
- Contribution Margin

(for higher-value products/ solutions / services)

a/b

Strategic Selling V
Potential:
- Revenue
- Sales
- Contribution Margin

(for strategic projects / joint ventures/ high level-value solutions a.s.o.)

a/b

Multiplication VI
Potential:
- Opinion Leaders
- Lead Users
- Multiplicator Potentialities etc.

a/b

Potentential for Expertise Transfer: VII
- Innovation Potential
- "'Lead'"-Application Potential
- New Technology Potential
- Synergy Platform Potential
- New Segments Potential
- Globalization Potential

a/b

Customer Loyalty VIII
Potential:
- Conjoint Development Potential
- Customer Retention Ratio
- Price-Performance Ratio

a/b

Cust Cutting IV
Potential:
- Revenue/ Cost Ratio
etc.

a/b

Fig. 55: Customer value and customer potential indicators (© Prof. Dr. R. Hofmaier).

(revenue, sales, margin) and category II (single-sell indicators, improving previous actual sales to customers) carry a certain primary importance in "traditional" customer support. However, for longer-term and loyalty-oriented customer development, key figures III, IV and V (cross-, up- and strategic selling), as well as key figures VI, VII, VIII and IX can be of great importance (see Part VI/KAM).

To implement such customer satisfaction, loyalty and development management, there now need to be relevant **customer surveys and feedback analyses**. They can be integrated into an annual overall customer survey, which can include further analysis priorities (e.g., select potential and positioning analyses) and can be supplemented by interim detail surveys.[34] All the **survey objectives** and the necessary **survey design** are shown in Fig. 56 and 57.

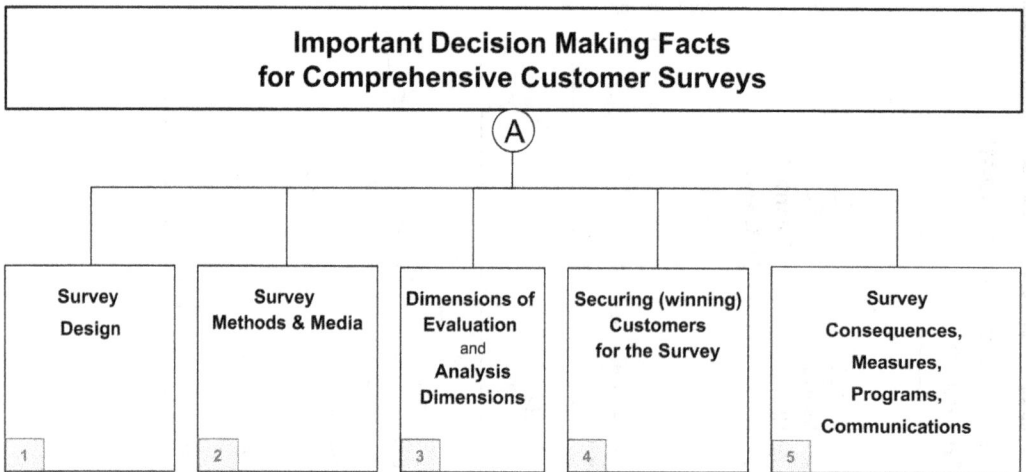

Fig. 56: Important decision making criteria for comprehensive customer surveys (© Prof. Dr. R. Hofmaier).

---

34 For different ways of customer surveys, see also Hofmaier, 1995, pp. 55–58.

Survey Design & Survey Media

(B)

Survey Goals (Main Criteria):

- Meaningful of Market Segments, Applications and Product Demands
- Meaningful and "Customer-Objectified" Overall Positioning
- Detection of Key Success Factors (KSF) / Critical Success Factors (CSF) & resulting Market- / Customers Segmentations
- Customer Satisfaction/ Satisfaction Positioning
- Customer Loyalty Positioning
- Customer Relationship Positioning (Relations Positioning)
- Customer Retention Positioning, (Incl. Customer Retention Measures)
- Customer Development Positioning (Incl. Customer Development Profiles)
- Specific Marketing, Sales, Customer Management, & Service Positioning
- Detailed Positioning of MSC Management Mix
- Detailed Information about Market, Application, Technology, Product Developments, etc.
- Detailed Information about Acquisition & Communications Practices / Behavior
- Information about (Conjoint) Business Development & Cooperation Possibilities
- Possibilities to Improve the Customers Collaboration
- Determination of Price Acceptance Levels
- Positioning of Supply and Logistics
- Etc.

Survey Levels:

- Selection of the Relevant Key Success Factors (KSF/KPI) & Required Criteria / Profiles
- Weighting of the Factors
- Evaluation of the Factors
- Causaling-Guided Revisions & Detailing
- Validity & Reliability Check
- Etc.

Survey Media:

- Face-to-Face:
  - Personal Conversations with Customers
  - Focus Groups/ Discussions
  - Selected Group Workshops
  - Event Based Discussions
- Written
- By Phone
- Online
- Combination based on the "T-Principle"-Survey (Large Customers Face-to-Face and More In-Depth, Small Customers via Media and More Standardized)

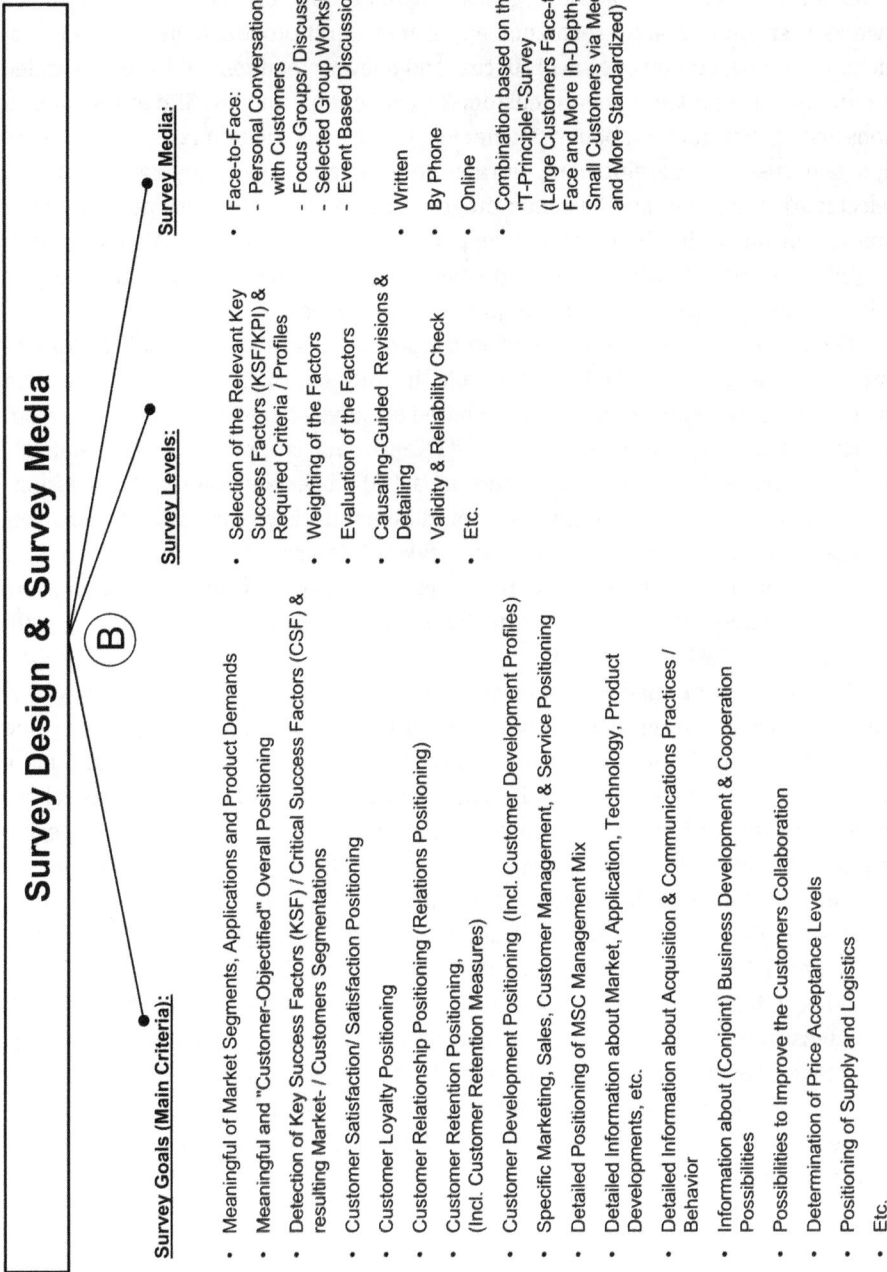

Fig. 57: Selected survey objectives, stages and media (survey design) (© Prof. Dr. R. Hofmaier).

By establishing the survey design, a **variety of survey objectives and related main criteria** can be taken into account, starting with introductory questions about one's own assessment of market segments, applications and product demands (developments), to consideration of critical success and relevant requirement factors, detailed positioning criteria and reviews (customer satisfaction), and specific indirect questions and criteria queries about customer loyalty, customer relations, customer retention and customer development. Furthermore, detailed questions can ask about select marketing, sales and customer programs as well as cooperative product development, business development and cooperation opportunities, etc. Also, questions on (informal/formal) information and communication behavior, willingness to pay, price-value prioritization, delivery requirements, and more.

Besides these survey objectives and assessment levels, the **combination of survey media** also plays an important role. In addition, the four areas of collection media can be combined with each other based on survey target, type of customer and content design. Sometimes, the so-called **"T" approach** is appropriate. The relatively few, but important and major customers are asked on deeper topics and discussions in personal and/or group talks, while their different decision-makers are intensively engaged and differentiated, analysed and taken into account with respect to their personal attitudes, evaluation, experience, etc. Mid-sized and smaller customers are surveyed in larger numbers via writing, by phone and electronically (online) or with a combination of different media.

In order to **gain survey customers** (see Fig. 58), it is important that they also gain "added value" from such a survey (and survey "relationship"). This added value can refer to added information value, where, for example, a management summary can provide the evaluated, summarized and analyzed "introductory questions" about market and application developments, or – after appropriate consultation – a specific evaluation of improved joint cooperation, (product) development, business development and marketing opportunities are identified, discussed and implemented. Also, the targeted improvement and application of key marketing programs and activities can be derived and offered to customers and implemented (see Fig. 58).

What is important in this context is that the derived **survey "consequences" and measures** (Fig. 59) are not only implemented in time with the customers, but are also actively communicated in advance, and that the corresponding "added value" is comprehensible and transparent. In turn, this can be the basis for cooperation that can be further developed, and thus such a customer survey itself becomes an important marketing MSC tool.

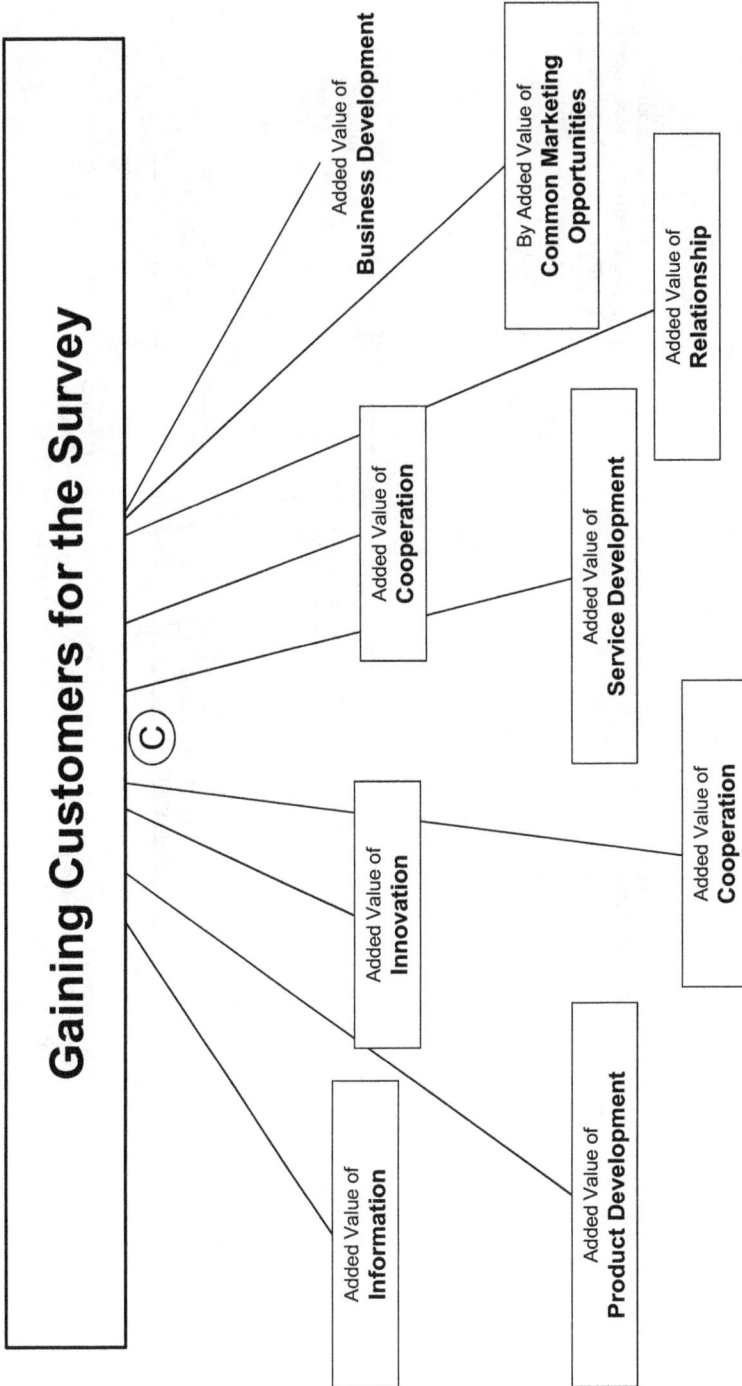

Fig. 58: Possibilities for collecting customer (survey) acquisition (© Prof. Dr. R. Hofmaier).

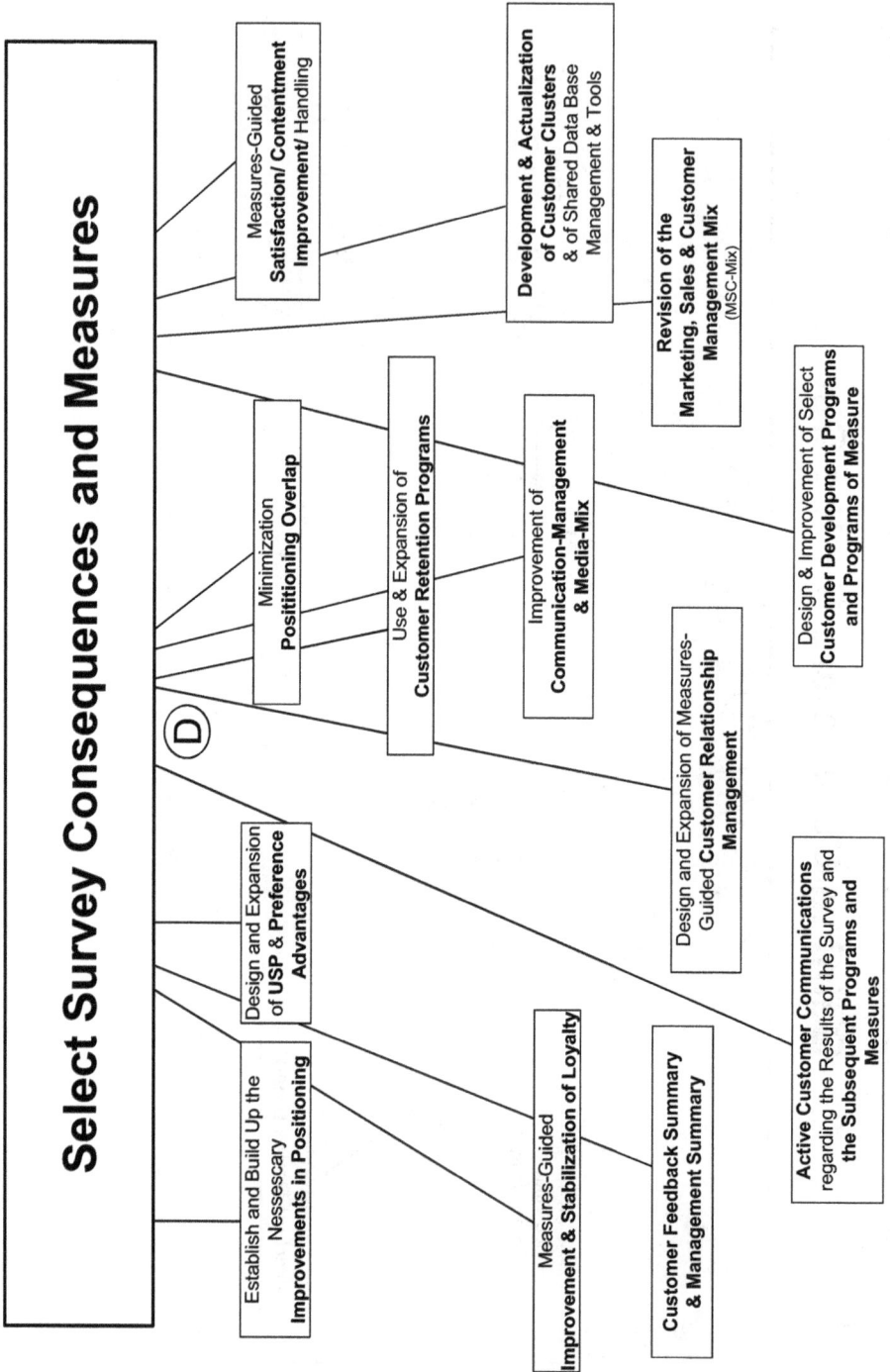

Select Survey Consequences and Measures

- Measures-Guided Satisfaction/ Contentment Improvement/ Handling
- Development & Actualization of Customer Clusters & of Shared Data Base Management & Tools
- Revision of the Marketing, Sales & Customer Management Mix (MSC-Mix)
- Minimization Postitioning Overlap
- Use & Expansion of Customer Retention Programs
- Improvement of Communication-Management & Media-Mix
- Design & Improvement of Select Customer Development Programs and Programs of Measure
- Design and Expansion of Measures-Guided Customer Relationship Management
- Active Customer Communications regarding the Results of the Survey and the Subsequent Programs and Measures
- Establish and Build Up the Nessescary Improvements in Positioning
- Design and Expansion of USP & Preference Advantages
- Measures-Guided Improvement & Stabilization of Loyalty
- Customer Feedback Summary & Management Summary

Ⓓ

Fig. 59: Survey consequences and measure programs (© Prof. Dr. R. Hofmaier).

To evaluate such a customer survey, it is primarily important to address some important perspectives. A central focus of evaluation comes from the juxtaposition of prioritized survey characteristics (e.g., critical success factors and requirements according to their weighting) and the assessment and evaluation of these characteristics by the customer. This then results **in different needs for action,** which need to be implemented through respective marketing, sales and customer management programs and activities (see Fig. 60).

3 Business Relationship Management and Interpersonal Relationship Management (CRM)

The summarizing **comparison of customer loyalty and satisfaction evaluations** is now important for the basic derivation and **accentuation** of **programs and measures of relationship and customer retention management.** Their basic options are the results of the customer clustering shown in Fig. 61. We can distinguish between **"regular" customers** (with a high percentage of viable key accounts), potential **"switch" customers** (with a strong overall satisfaction and relatively low loyalty), so-called **"risk" customers** (with strong loyalty and low satisfaction) and potential **"migration" customers.** It becomes apparent that the exclusive satisfaction orientation in such surveys is no longer the only thing that is meaningful, since there are also customers who are relatively satisfied, but have low customer loyalty and thus usually a high willingness to switch and vice versa. (The "assumption" that the expression of satisfaction corresponds to that of loyalty, i.e. that customer groups alone are positioned along the "image diagonals" from top right to bottom left, is not a sufficient explanation, as is shown by the verified customer clusters of exchange and risk clients.) Especially the switch and partly the migration customers require different specific MSC programs and activities. However, it is important in this case that customer clusters (see Fig. 34) be labeled with appropriate customer typologies (i.e., based on information from the customer database, which part and how much of that distribution of A, B, C and D customers is in the respective clusters). Thus, targeted marketing as well as specific customer relation and customer retention tools can be applied.

For **"regular" customers** with a relatively high A- and B-customer share, the (survey-based) gradual development and customer-differentiated accentuation of the marketing mix often applies, while taking into account **select relationship and customer retention measures** (Fig. 62 and 63). Thus, the focus especially for larger customers and key accounts can be on (further) development of win-win partnerships (e.g., coordinated or joint product development projects, internationalization, etc.) and on expansion of directly addressing decision-makers and integration as starting points of business and interpersonal relationship management. This can be supplemented and structured with specific measures of customer retention management, such as concrete innovation partnerships, best expertise sharing, etc. (see especially Fig. 62).

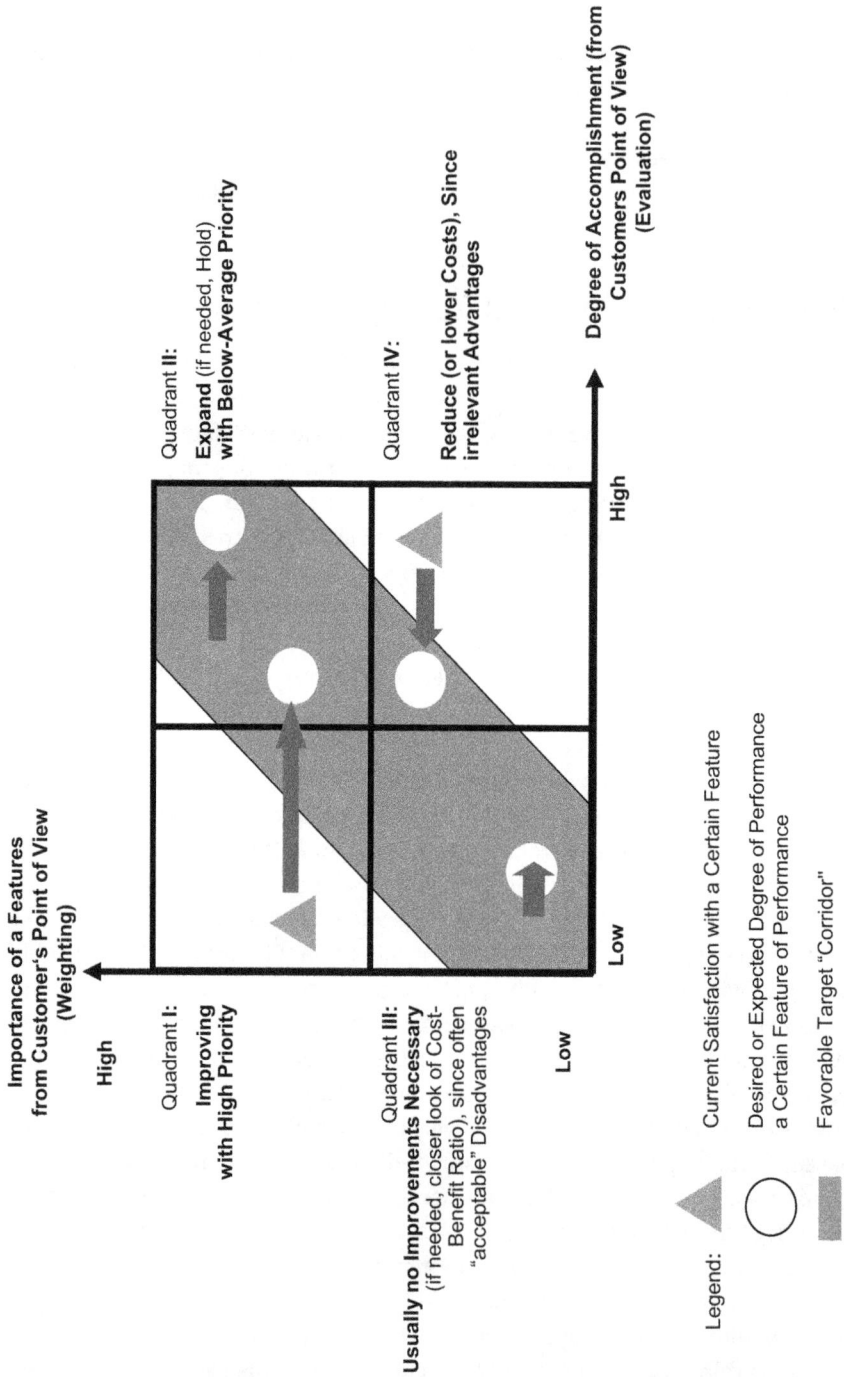

Fig. 60: Customer analysis portfolio and need for actions (MSC programs and implementation) (© Prof. Dr. R. Hofmaier).

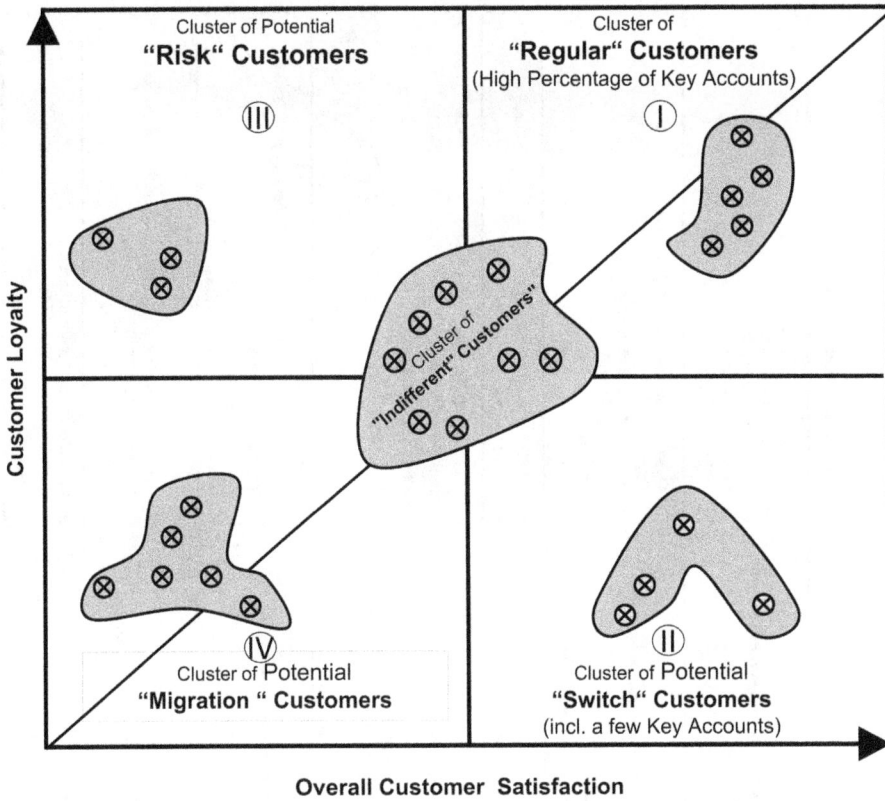

Fig. 61: Customer satisfaction and customer loyalty portfolio (© Prof. Dr. R. Hofmaier).

Special attention should be paid to **"switch" customers,** so that, for example, better **reach of decision-makers** can be achieved with a focus on generating **"commit- ments"** and persuasion efforts regarding possible product placement, development and integration projects, etc., for A- and B-customers (beyond classic marketing mea- sures). Similar to regular customers, this can be accompanied by **select** expertise- sharing, tech days, product clinics as customer retention measures.

For **"risk" customers, problems** arising from certain non-satisfaction results must be quickly **resolved** and a **corresponding satisfaction** must be **achieved** again and stabilized through concerted actions. This can be supplemented by more active communication of improvement measures, more targeted outreach to decision- makers, and "involvements" for further measures and select customer retention mea- sures (such as the integration of tech days and special events, etc.).

Customer Programs (Opportunities) / Customer Cluster	Customer Relationship Programs	Customer Retention Programs
"Regular" Customers (High A-/B-Customer Share) — **I**	❶ A/B- Customers (Accounts): (Further) Development of Win-Win Partnerships & Involvements	a) Innovation Partnerships b) Best Expertise Sharing c) News-Groups / Events d) Integrated Consulting Teams e) Tech-Days & Workshops & Special Events
"Switching" Customers — **II**	❶ A-B- Customers: Improved Approach of Decision Makers and "Generation" of: • Commitments • Win-Win Partnership (Added Value) ❷ D- Customers: 3rd Partly Retention/ Adressing	• Optimized/ Broader Product-/Performance Differentiation • Increasing Solutions-Business • Increasing Added Services • (Ia... e) • Selected Warranty Measures • Bonus/ Conditions Programs
"Risk" Customers — **III**	❶ A/B- Customers: • Targeted Approach of Decision-Makers & Involvements • Active Implementation of Respective Communication Programs and Imporovement Measures • Active Implementation of Respective ❷ D- Customers: Selected Improvement of Communication and Implementation	• Dissatisfaction Reduction • Consolidate Satisfaction • "Attractivate" Incentives • Programs to Reduce: Disappointment, Sullenness, Disgruntlement, Buying Fatigue • Programs to Increase: Customer Satisfaction/ Contentment • Broader Incentive Programs
"Migration" Customers — **IV**	❶ A/B- Customers: • Examine Select Communications and specific Customer Retention Programs and Measures (for specific Decision Makers) • Improving Feedback Management ❷ C-(D)- Customers: • Stay Connected via More Effective Sales & Communication Channels	• Implementation of Select Customer Retention Programs and Measures (See Above) • Check for More Effective (Cheaper) Sales Channels and/or Customer Support Channels • Allow / Accept Select Migration

Fig. 62: Select customer relationship and customer retention opportunities (based on customer cluster and customer types) (© Prof. Dr. R. Hofmaier).

For **"migration" customers**, there should be a test of improved ways of using the marketing mix for A- and B-customers, but **also select relationship and loyalty**

programs whose use makes sense. For very "critical" customer perspectives, an examination of other or "more favorable" **distribution channels** and bodies or possibly targeted **migration** (if there are sales, revenue and margin deficits, etc.) can be acceptable for existing C- and D-customers.

When applying ways and measures of relationship management, those for **business relationship management** are to be distinguished from those for **interpersonal relationship management** (see Fig. 63). With the former, this can mean company-specific and derived functionally relevant business objectives within the framework of customer-related product uses, solutions and/or projects, including their successful implementation, while for interpersonal relationship, it can also mean the consideration and integration of individual (personal) decision-maker goals and ambitions within the context of such projects and the associated personal professional success. Accordingly, personal "involvement", "commitment" and the conviction of these decision-makers can also be important for their job enrichment and thus also for their personal "win" (triple-win projects). In addition and in a broader sense, the CRM approach also helps the **recovery of lost customers** or customers who are maybe just "being lost" by using aligned measures and building an adequate relationship and bond.

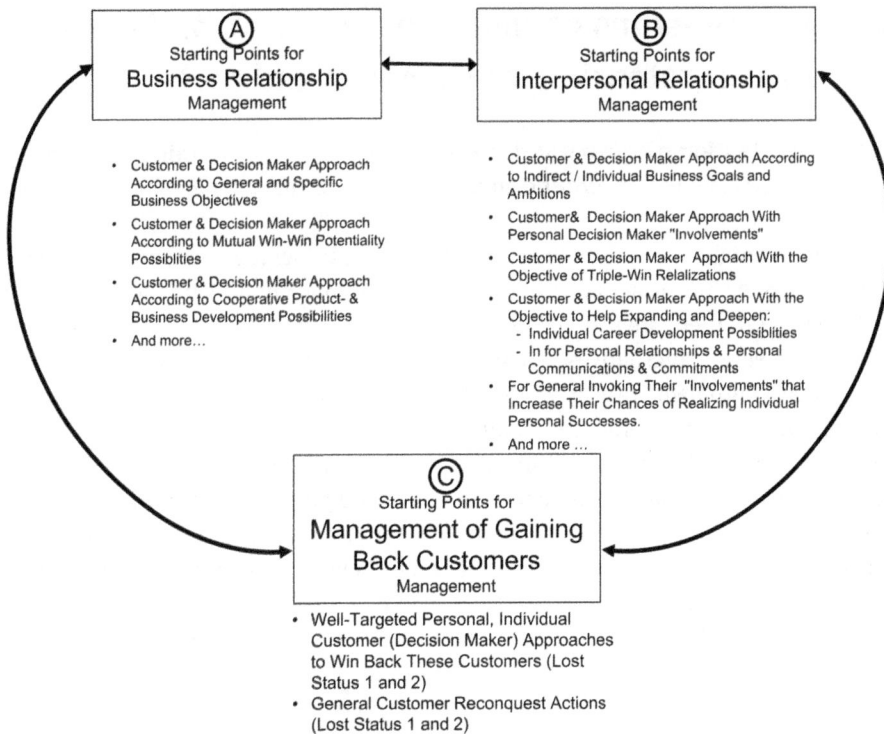

Fig. 63: Starting points of business relationship and interpersonal relationship management (CRM) (© Prof. Dr. R. Hofmaier).

Starting point for such an approach of defining decision-makers is the sufficient collection of relevant decision-maker data and profiles, without which professional customer data base management and thus CRM is not possible. (For this purpose, a decision-maker information matrix (see Fig. 88 and 89 in Part VII) can be used as basis in order to clarify appropriate tool-integrated relationship perspectives, criteria and information.)

Overall, it can be noted that not only can the existing product and service approach be systematically **expanded** for regular customers, as well as for switch and risk customers, but also that **broader value coverage** (which in turn supports customer retention (including higher switching costs)) can make deeper customer penetration and customer loyalty possible. This can be specifically used for **higher-value** product combinations, packages, added services, all the way to so-called partial solution or solution business (total solution business). Thus, the preferred supplier position can be improved, and the acceptance and cooperation basis for future **win-win partnerships** can be developed. Therefore, the consideration of select customer **relationship** and customer **retention** measures becomes increasingly **more important** (see Fig. 63, 64 and 65).

4 Ten Dimensions of customer retention and their customer retention instruments and tools

Customer retention programs and measures required for an overall CRM approach can be derived from the **different dimensions** of basic customer loyalty[35] and retention (see Fig. 64).

Fundamental customer retention dimensions first include need-optimized, purchase- and project-contractual customer retention opportunities with their respective obligations. But there are also technological, community-specific and psychological customer retention alternatives, where the former can, for example, refer to technology-related equipment, test and integration opportunities for customers (e.g., IT-, control- and application-focused manufacturer "alignment", providing certain test equipment and technical consulting expertise by the manufacturer). Other important customer dimensions can be psychological and personally "binding" customer loyalty options that may form through long-term, mutually fruitful and successful cooperation, but also "development-oriented" customer loyalty and retention in terms of product development and business cooperation, as well as subject- and interest-centered, event-specific, and institutional customer loyalty opportunities.

---

35 For dimensions and measures of customer loyalty and customer retention programs and measures, see also Hofmaier, 2012, pp. 6–13; for customer loyalty generally, see also Homburg / Bruhn, 2005.

Customer retention programs and measures that can be derived from this are generally particularly useful and helpful for **A- and B-customers**, but also for **A "potentials"**, for long-term customer development.

Regarding **individual programs and measures** that arise from the previously mentioned customer loyalty and retention dimensions (see Fig. 65), can be thematic workshops and events, win-win partnerships and work groups (e.g., focus groups and product clinics), project workshops and project groups (e.g., product development and "internationalization" workshops), best expertise and best practice measures, tech days (e.g., application-oriented illustration and communication of user-specific developments with pilot customers for select customers), special interest events and relevant (joint) publications should be particularly mentioned (see again Fig. 65). Furthermore, so-called innovation circles and innovation network communities, the customized knowledge extranet, as well as select partner events (for customer retention through joint pull and added value programs for end users), select technology installations and transfer measures, added service (development) workshops, and selective guaranteed performance, terms and/or bonus programs can be used.

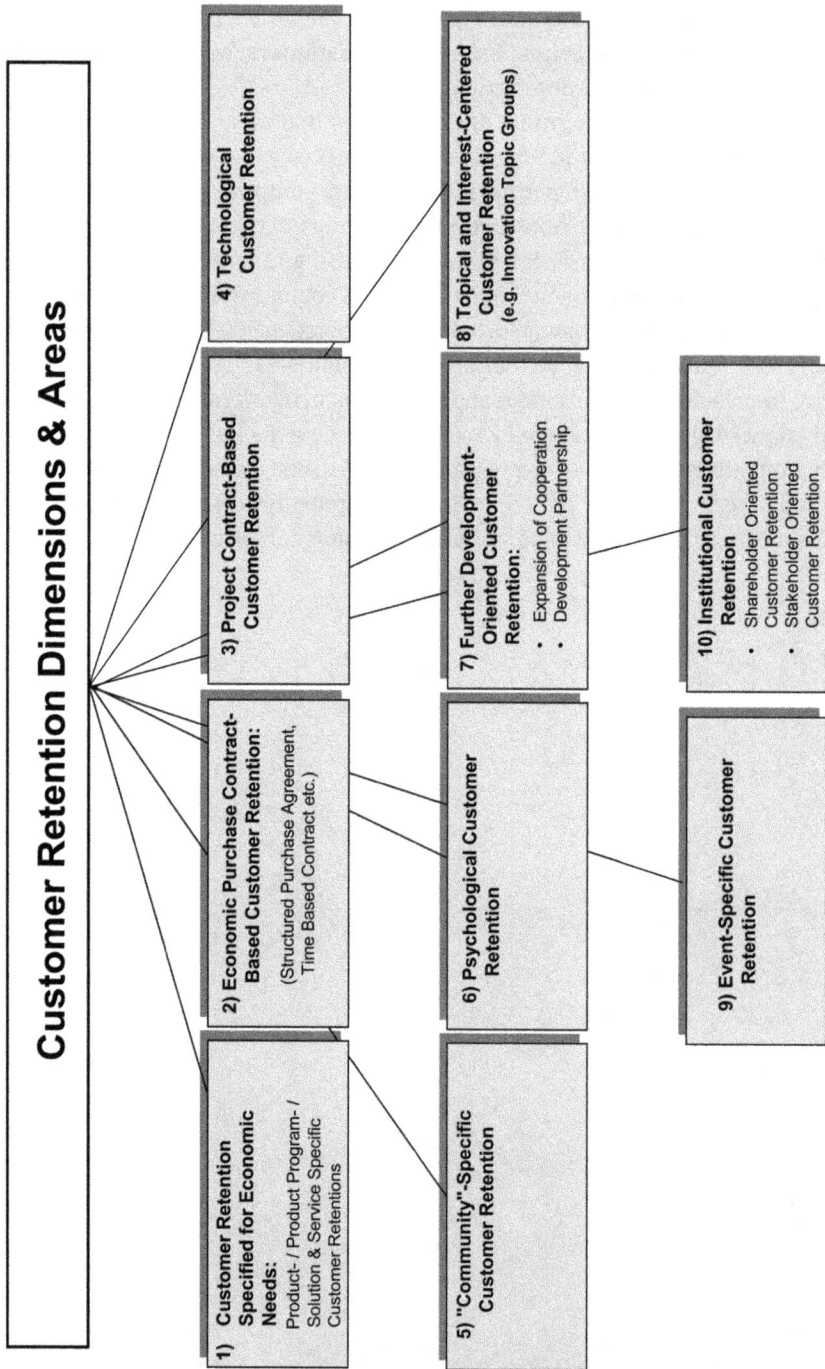

Customer Retention Dimensions & Areas

1) Customer Retention Specified for Economic Needs:
Product- / Product Program- / Solution & Service Specific Customer Retentions

2) Economic Purchase Contract-Based Customer Retention:
(Structured Purchase Agreement, Time Based Contract etc.)

3) Project Contract-Based Customer Retention

4) Technological Customer Retention

5) "Community"-Specific Customer Retention

6) Psychological Customer Retention

7) Further Development-Oriented Customer Retention:
• Expansion of Cooperation
• Development Partnership

8) Topical and Interest-Centered Customer Retention
(e.g. Innovation Topic Groups)

9) Event-Specific Customer Retention

10) Institutional Customer Retention
• Shareholder Oriented Customer Retention
• Stakeholder Oriented Customer Retention

Fig. 64: Dimensions of Customer Retention (© Prof. Dr. R. Hofmaier).

Select

Customer Retention Programs & Measures

a) Topic-Specific Workshops & Events

b) Win-Win Partnerships and Work Groups
(Incl. Focus-Groups, Product-Clinics, etc.)

c) Project Workshops & Project Groups
(E.g. Product Develeopment- / Internationalization Workshops, etc.)

d) Best Expertise Sharing and Best Practice Workshops / Events and Measures

e) Integrated
   · Consulting &
   · · Coaching &
   · Training- Teams

f) Tech Days
(Lead-User Oriented Pilot Applications and Information Days for Selected Customers)

g) Special Interest Events & Publishing

h) Innovation Circles & Innovation Network Communities

i) Customized Knowledge Extranet

j) Select "Partner Events" (e.g. Pull Programs & Workshops)

k) Select
   · Technology Installations
   · · Technology Transfer- &
   · Technology Support Measures

l) Added-Service- (Development) Workshops & Measures

m) Selective Warranty Performance, Conditions and/or Bonus Programs

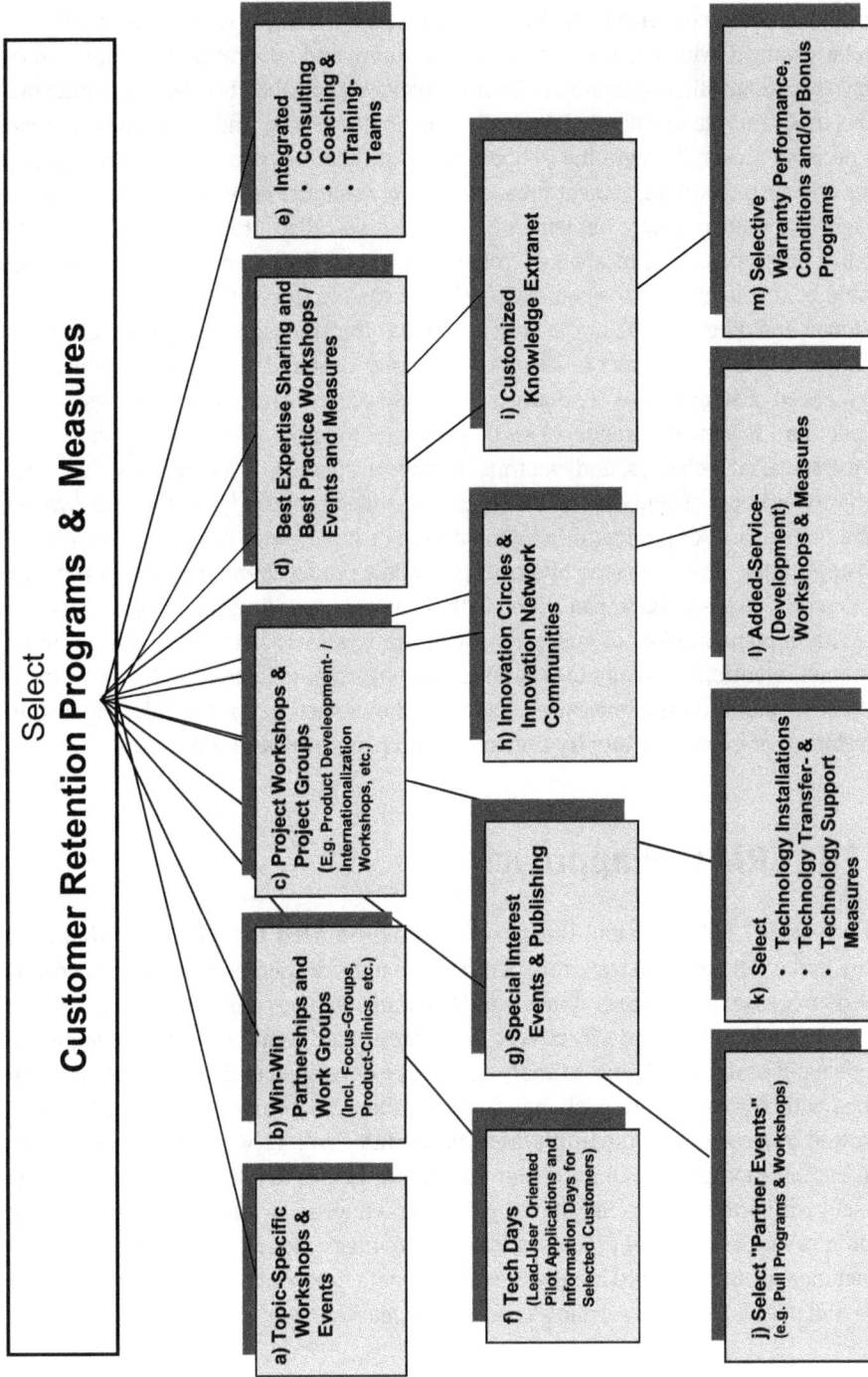

Fig. 65: Selected Customer Retention Programs and Measures (© Prof. Dr. R. Hofmaier).

For different large customers and their decision-makers, a corresponding set of methods can be arranged, which enjoys increasing importance and application intensity with its respective design and combination. (In this context, we can already reference the actions of Focus Group Management (FGM).) By further developing and integrating support for decision-makers, integrating actions, and coordinating with "current" marketing, sales and customer management measures, select customer development goals can be designed and successfully implemented (see also so-called product, application and product development "clinics"). Expertise sharing is another example of measures that should be highlighted. In the context of select workshop (possibly in combination with customer and other events), an "experience-based" transfer of know-how can take place for important topics, in order to allow for successive penetration, but also expansion of the targeted customer base. Similarly, specific project and application findings as well as pilot and reference customers can be presented to additional interested customers during so-called tech days, and can thus be made available to a broader customer base with varying depth of application. With help of so-called circles of innovation, innovation communities, and/or product development partnerships – with varying substantiation and application depth – new technology application, product trends or pilot projects can be prepared, tackled, and implemented in the context of specific customer solutions.

The implementation of customer loyalty programs is based on corresponding customer retention goals and tasks and can be implemented and established through different combinations of measures. Figure 66 shows such an approach for the **implementation of customer loyalty and retention programs and measures**.

5 The CRM tool approach

For a holistic CRM approach, the corresponding **required tools (CRM tools)**, their value and efficiency "shares", relevant requirements and implementation needs, as well as **necessary customer databases (DB)** must now be considered.

In order to **select and effectively implement** the **"right" CRM tools**, appropriate demand profiles and process analyses must be developed and determined in accordance with corresponding customer data and their cross-functional "links." This is followed by a corresponding **implementation plan**[36] with its various implementation and optimization phases. Of particular importance here is that the CRM tool that must be selected jointly and agreed upon by the marketing, sales and customer branches, should cover the essential processes for such an integrated marketing, sales and customer management, should handle the relevant data in an easily configurable, upgradable and updatable way, and allows continuous marketing-driven development.

---

36 To select and implement appropriate CRM tools (Tool project) and tool-related cost-benefit analyses, see also Hofmaier / Bauer, 2007/2012.

Customer Retention Goals	Customer Retention Proceeding	Customer Retention Target Groups & Programs	Customer Retention Measures & Tasks	Actions	Responsibilities	Supports	Implementation Phases & Measurement Criteria	Time Frame	Misc.
1									
2									
3									
. . . . .									
N									

Fig. 66: Implementation of customer loyalty and retention programs and measures (© Prof. Dr. R. Hofmaier).

The thus implementable **value-adding and efficiency goals** from such a **CRM tool in conjunction with holistic CRM** can also be seen in Fig. 67. Now, significant strategic and process-guided tool use objectives for tool selection and implementation are now (based on a previous requirement analysis) need to be derived and specified accordingly. Required cost-benefit analyses[37] for tool selection should be taken into account. Using the CRM system that needs to be selected, important sub-processes should also be systematically improved. It is also relevant to incorporate "affected" staff members and their training in a timely and comprehensive way. The targeted "incentivization" of customer management, sales and marketing staff members with respect to tool implementation and comprehensive personal use can be very important. Such a "CRM tool project" must be led by a competent sales or customer manager (not an IT manager!) and be supported by an appropriate work and control circle.

The **strategic customer, sales and marketing benefits** shown in Fig. 67 can be incorporated into and considered for individual tool project steps and CRM activities in a derived form. Only then the possibilities of a holistic approach will be realized.

In addition, listed and empirically investigated **cost advantages** regarding the selection, use and development of CRM tools can be specified and evaluated. Overall, this should help better systemize and evaluate the necessary marketing, sales and customer processes.

Figure 68 exemplifies **key areas of the design of the CRM approach**, including a CRM tool. It shows clearly how the different **processes** related to goals, tasks, content, responsibilities, times, individual measures, metrics and benchmarks should be defined and can be established, activated and controlled. This helps individual marketing, sales and customer managers with compressed and effective planning, management and evaluation of their own activities and measures and allows for an effective overview of strategic and operational relationships in the context of goal attainment and the possible need for additional measures and activities.

---

37 See ibid.

Value-Adding and Efficiency Benefits by Applying Holistic CRM- and Tool Management

Strategic Customer Management Benefits

- High Customer / Decision Maker Transparency
- Better Customer Satisfaction
- Improvement Customer Loyalty
- Improvement Customer Relationship
- Higher Customer Retention
- Improved Customer Development & Customer Penetration (Cross / Up / Strategic Selling)
- Higher Customer Value

Strategic Sales Benefits

- Optimzied Sales Processes
- More Time to Spend with/for Customer
- More Sales Enrichment
- Higher Motivation of Sales
- More Individual & Efficient Sales Planning
- Optimized Forecasting
- Optimized Reporting
- Improved Price Calculation
- Improved Tool Integration (Tool- & Use Efficiency)

Strategic Marketing Benefits

- Higher Market (Market Segment) Penetration
- Improved (Market / Market Segment) Expansion & Market Development
- More Comprehensive Customer Information
- Improved Customer Target Group Planning
- More Detailed Market- & Customer Segmentation
- More Exact Prognoses of Demand Development
- Improved Product Development- & Innovation Management

Cost Advantages

- Reduced Presentation- & Offer Process (e.g. 40%–60%)
- Reduced Customer Acquisition Process (e.g. 40%–60%)
- Reduced Reporting Efforts (Meeting Reporting) (e.g. up to 70%)
- Reduced Customer Meeting Preparation (e.g. 40%–60%)
- Faster Complaint Management (e.g. 30%–50%)
- Faster Partner Communication (e.g. up to 50%)
- Shorter Delivery Time Information to Customers (e.g. 60%–80%)

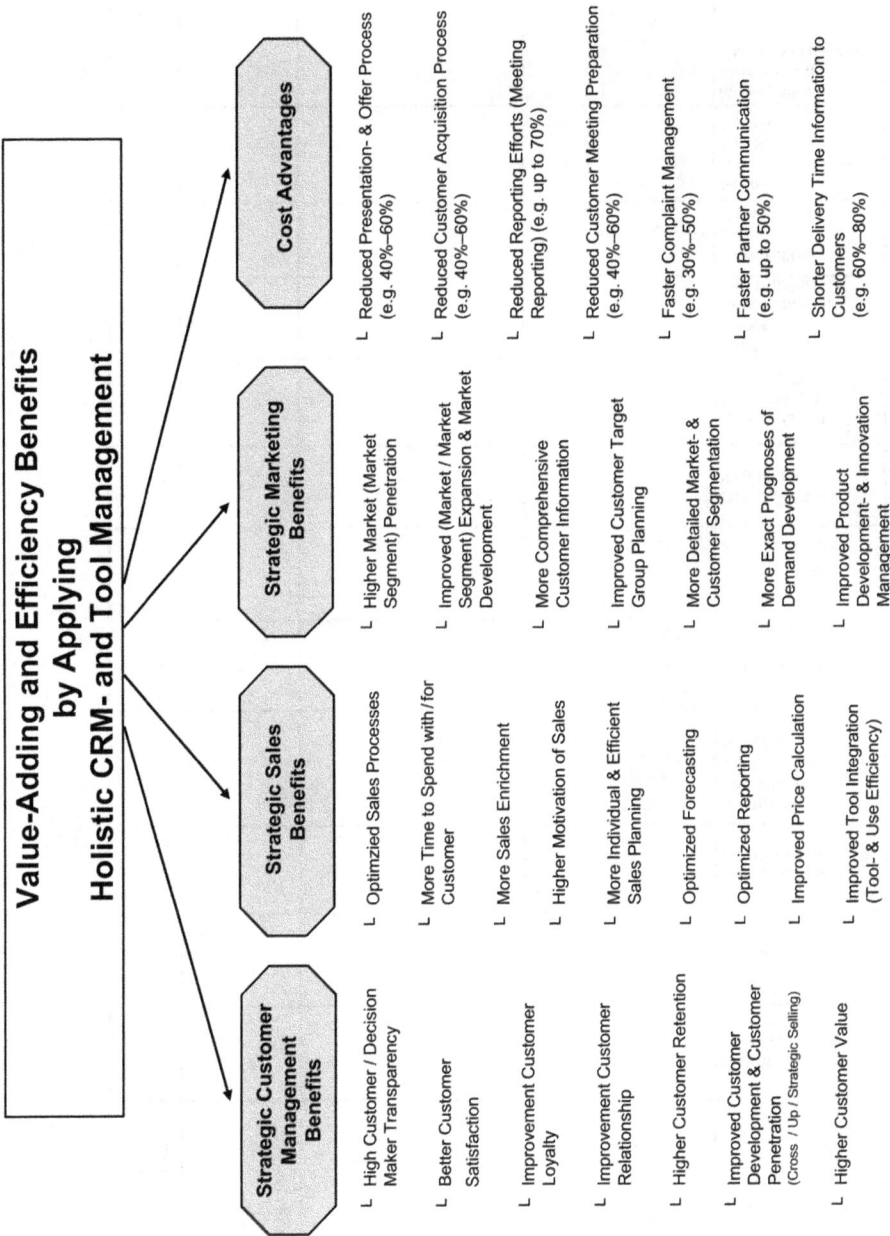

Fig. 67: Value-Adding and efficiency advantages through holistic CRM and tool management (© Prof. Dr. R. Hofmaier).[38]

---

38 Following Winkelmann (in a modified and empirical "substantialized" way), 2010.

CRM Processing Steps \ Targets, Tasks, Areas of Responsibility & Hit-Rate Figures	Identification of New Customers	Customer Qualification	Decision-Maker Qualification	Customer/ Decision-Maker Contact & Scheduling	Analysis Solution and · Solution and · Application Proposals	Achieve Win-Win Situations & Commitments	Generate Quote Requests	Qualify Quote Requestes & Compile Offers	Follow-Up on Offers, Renegotiation and Closing	Offer Billing and Managment	Accompanying Customer Relations and Retention Measures	Management of Subsequent Demand (if needed Gain Back Customers)
Targets, Tasks, Priorities, Time Frames and Other Requirements (e.g. Decision Maker Penetration ABCD Prioritizations Improvement Options)												
Mgmt. (Those in Charge/ Support) & Extend/ Coordination (Top Mgmt./ Marketing, International Sales/ Business Dev. / Customer Support / Technical Support / Hotline / Call Center s/ Sales Partners, etc.)												
Individual Measures/ Information/ Competences/ Qualification												
Hit-Rate Key Figures (and Measurement Criteria)												

Fig. 68: CRM process analysis and tool application matrix (© Prof. Dr. R. Hofmaier).[39]

39 For details, see also Winkelmann, 2012, and Winkelmann, 2008.

References

Bruhn, M. (2009) Relationship Marketing – Das Management von Kundenbeziehungen, 2. Aufl., München

Hofmaier, R. (2012) Möglichkeiten und Chancen einer konzeptionellen Fundierung und Weiterentwicklung des Key Account Management (B2B), in: FORUM Betriebswirtschaft München, Heft 01, S. 6–13

Hofmaier, R. / Bauer, H. (2007/2012) Status Quo and Opportunity Analysis of Optimized Selection and Implementation of CRM-Tool – A Research Study

Hofmaier, R. / Bauer, H. (2007/2012) Stand und Auswahlmöglichkeiten bezüglich der Implementierung von leistungsfähigen CRM-Tools – Empirische Studie, München

Hofmaier, R. (Hrsg.) (1995), Erfolgsstrategien in der Investitionsgüterindustrie, Landsberg a. Lech

Homburg, Ch. / Bruhn, M. (2005), Kundenbindungsmanagement – Eine Einführung in die theoretischen und praktischen Problemstellungen, in: Bruhn, M. / Homburg,C. (Hrsg.) Handbuch Kundenbindungsmanagement, Wiesbaden, S. 3–35

Reichheld, K. (1997) Lernen Sie von abtrünnigen Kunden, was Sie falsch machen, in: Harvard Business Manager, Heft 2, S.57–68

Winkelmann, P. (2008), Vertriebskonzeption und Vertriebssteuerung, 4. Auf., München

Winkelmann, P. (2010) Marketing und Vertrieb – Fundamente für die marktorientierte Unternehmensführung, 7. Aufl., München

Winkelmann, P. (2012) Integriertes und fachgestütztes CRM – Vortragsmanuskript

VI Integrated Customer Development and Key Account Management (KAM)

Sustainable **customer development management** includes not only the features of customer relations, but also **modern** and **conceptually** sound B2B **Key Account Management (KAM)**. Therefore, methodically stringent, long-term KAM is important for integrated MSC management for continuous, mostly disproportionate growth in the strategically important major customer market and allows the company to develop "distinctive" positioning, differentiation and **penetration potential** within national and international major customer and key account competition. This is especially important for B2B sectors, since truly profitable and long-term customer development can only be developed through customer processing, customer loyalty and customer penetration based on key accounts when available resources are limited. This distinguishes empirically sound and **advanced** key account management (B2B) as it is shown here from "classic wholesale resp. major account management" through a much more sophisticated conceptual and methodological approach.[40]

Classic major account management in B2B sectors with the traditional focus on "pure" single-selling is no longer enough, and there needs to be a more extensive, **value-oriented holistic approach** that includes so-called **single-, cross-, up-** and **strategic selling** strategies within the general CRM context. It focuses mainly on major customers or defined key accounts as well as potential, "developable" (not-yet) key accounts. The focus is on **partnership-based business development** that can be developed further or multiplied, starting from classic product or service business to partial solution or **"solution" business** and all the way to **strategic business or development partnership**. Properly applied, a strategic, business-based "multiplier effect" and thus business potential development is possible, which can exceed traditional customer business many times and can enable an effective knowledge partnership. In many cases, long-term successful product and market development is no longer possible without such a win-win partnership. Defined by the so-called value chain, the supplier, usually the **preferred supplier**, covers an increasingly large part of the value chain for customers, so the customer can concentrate on his/her own core competencies without neglecting outsourcing areas. Knowledge- and expertise-sharing is especially used here successfully in order to develop and implement a common win-win strategy.

---

40 For this KAM approach and its methods, see also Hofmaier, 2008, pp. 42–45, and Hofmaier, 2012, pp. 6–13; also further detailed empirical studies by Hofmaier, 2010/2013.

1 Modern and sustainable customer development and Key Account Management (KAM)

The KAM "business model" has evolved from earlier, purely transactional selling into consultative selling and later enterprise management, and finally value-oriented, multi-dimensional KAM.

A characteristic of the value-oriented, multi-dimensional KAM approach is that the various possibilities of the **"arena"** with respect to **"shared value development"** and win-win cooperation with the key account can be extended by multiple layers (see Fig. 69). By actively involving personal (provider) expertise, the customer has the opportunity to anticipate and cover early future application and development options and thus areas of need, which would often not be visible without such (provider) expertise integration and would not be implementable to the extent necessary (**"customer's blind spot"**).

Likewise, specified customer feedback and, for example, joint cooperation and/or development partnerships allow for new solutions and products to be developable, which were so far not implementable or hidden based on one's own view (**"my blind spot"**). (For example, for the former, there would be the development of a new flow meter with advanced technology and main value-adding benefits by the provider for a chemical client company, while for the latter, there would be the required product profile with new performance features and prototype-tested by the customer.)

For the outlined customer development and penetration, it may therefore be necessary to eventually **extend this actual arena** in three directions. With appropriate customer care, relation and loyalty measures, the customer can get "conveyed", through our expertise, important new applications and their solutions that are important to him in the future (e.g., additional/extended benefits of use and added value of his/her equipment/systems), and even we or our company can, based on the customer's application know-how, develop new products and application (parts) solutions, which can eventually lead to new application solutions and value-added benefits for our clients and for our new solutions (win-win advantage) in the context of joint projects (see Fig. 70). Thus, the actual arena (quadrant I/previous joint business and MSC field) can be systematically expanded into areas II, III and finally IV (joint development, application and marketing of new application/system solutions). Thus, **both sides can benefit from business opportunities** that can be **developed** and **expanded** for both parties and from **new joint business potential**. (Initially targeted development of know-how and transfer design in both "vertical" and "horizontal" directions though appropriate, integrated MSC measures is important!)

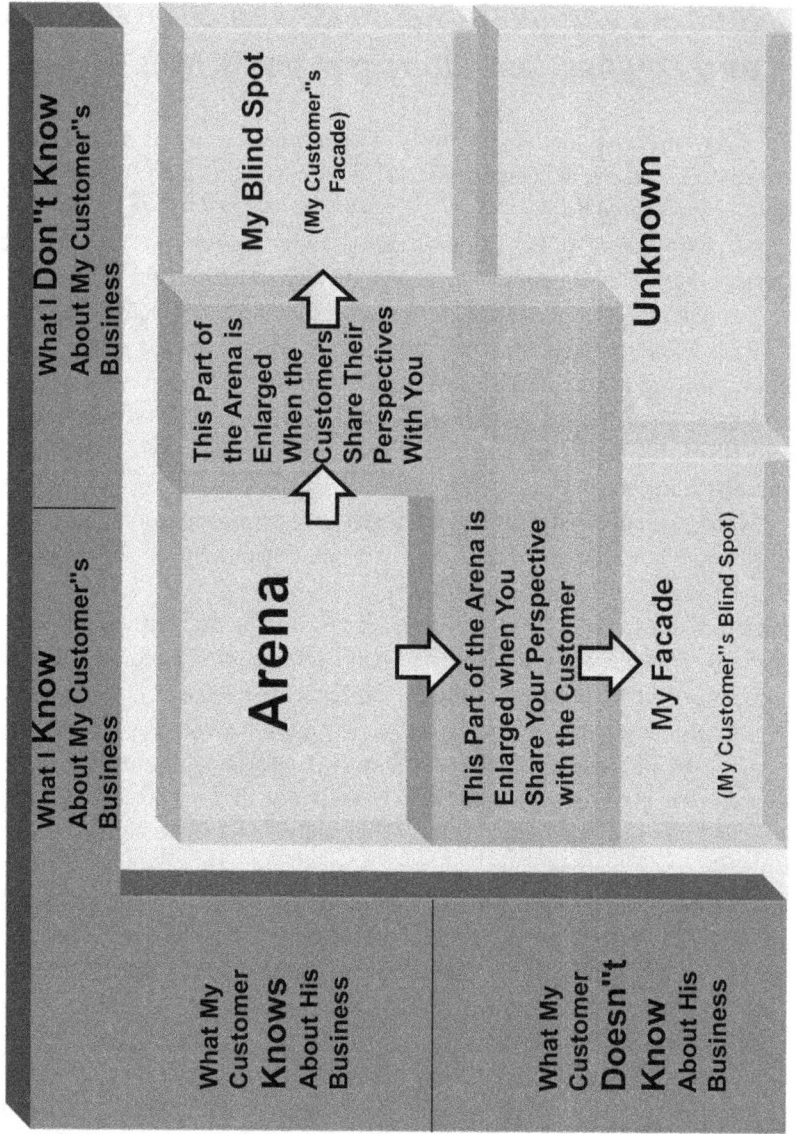

Fig. 69: Development of the common win-win arena with key accounts (© Prof. Dr. R. Hofmaier).[41]

---

41 For this "arena" illustration, see also Bacon, 1999.

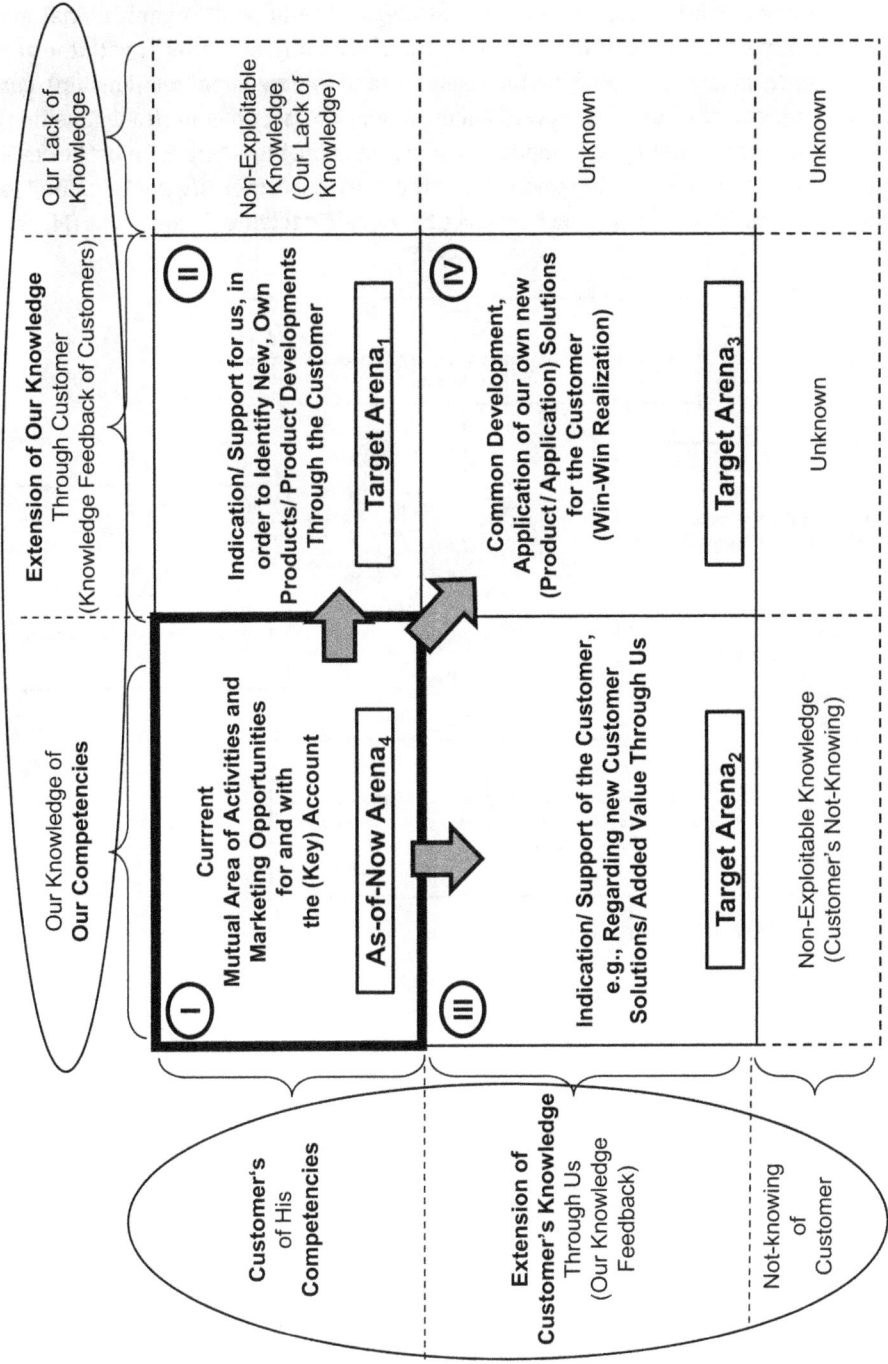

Fig. 70: Existing and potential "exploitable" knowledge- and MSC opportunities together with key accounts (© Prof. Dr. R. Hofmaier).

Value-oriented KAM first involves the strategic, operational, organizational and individual-personal care of the customer and his/her buying center[42], with the goal of a **long-term** customer relationship (business and interpersonal relationship), customer retention and customer development (single-, cross-, up- and strategic selling). Key accounts are thus key customers, whose common business "arena" must be developed in order to thus develop and expand the **"key customer life cycle/value"** for the long term. This KAM approach involves **four basic decision dimensions** (Fig. 71).

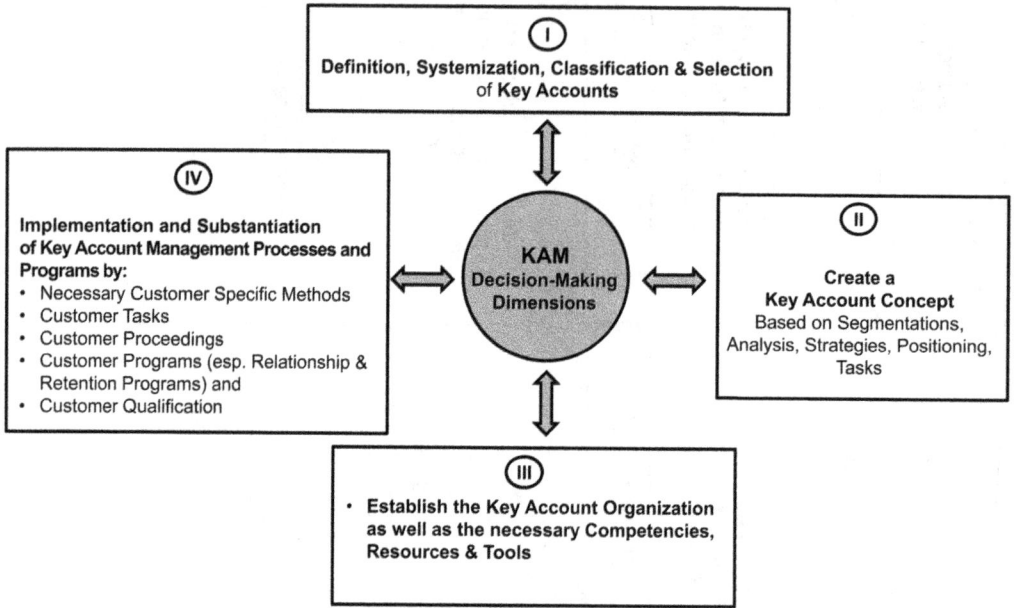

Fig. 71: Decision making dimensions of advanced key account management (KAM) (© Prof. Dr. R. Hofmaier).

---

42 A buying center can be composed of technical decision-makers (research and development, production, product management, sales, quality management, etc.), commercial trade decision-makers (e.g., procurement: centralized/decentralized), business and marketing managers, top management, users, influencers, and so-called gatekeepers.

2 Systematization, classification and selection of key accounts

Basically, **key account analysis** first involves the **systematization** and **classification** of key accounts and their potentials. Here, the following **four criteria** are mainly important:
- actual sales (of the key account)
- strategic potential (revenue potential, but also lead user-/opinion leader and know-how transfer potential)
- the actual margin or the customer contribution margin (and his "shaping" potential), and
- customer growth (and potential; in addition, national and international market coverage of the customer can be included).

For **international and globally operating key accounts**, there can thus also be the **categorization** (see Fig. 72) of
- corporate strategic key accounts,
- country key accounts,
- industry key accounts,
- potential key accounts.

The first represent client companies that must be supported, advised and supplied globally (with local support), the next represent those companies that – not only, but also – need to be mainly supported and supplied nationally; then there are key accounts assigned to industry segments (national), and the final ones are those companies that do not yet fulfill the necessary key account categories, but generally have potential for this. Here, basic "business opportunities", "responsibilities", "programs and tasks" are included in initial considerations.

For meaningful KA-systematization and classification, the establishment of a comprehensive **key account database** is useful, where criteria need to be updated continuously and in greater depth in order to ensure adequate KA-processing. (Corresponding requirements for CRM processes and their tool-supported database must be considered.)

Account Categories Based on Importance / Factors	Corporate Stragegic Key Account (CSKA) (A₁ Accounts)	Country Key Account (CKA) (A₂ Accounts)	Industry Key Account (IKA) (A₃ Accounts)	Potential Key Accounts (KA) (A₄ Accounts)
Sales Potential:				
• Actual Sales (in K $)	> 3.000	> 500	> 100	
• Estimated Value Potential (in 3–5 Years K $) (+ Strategic Potential)	> 30.000	> 2.500	> 500	
• Customer Market Share & Positioning (Today/Tomorrow)				
Margin:				
• Actual Margin	> 450	> 100	> 25	
• Estimated Margin (3–5 Years)	> 4.500	> 500	> 125	
Company Growth (Ø)	High	Medium–High	Medium–High	High
Business Opportunities: • Business Potential (incl. Strategic Potential/SWOT-Analysis) • Business Development Partnerships • Targets & Programs • Impacts & Soft Facts	L Potential for Joint Venture/Strategic Partnership/Joint Technol. (Development) L Cross, Up & Strategic Selling Opportunities	L Single Source Supplier L Joint Business Solutions L Cross & Up Selling Opportunities	L Significant Value Growth L Cross Selling Opportunities	L Significant Sales, Potential Value Development
Proposal & Responsibilities/ Reporting & Supports/ Structure / Duties	L Strategic Key Account Mgr. L Regional Key Account Mgr. L Divisional Key Account Mgr.	L Country Key Account Mgr. (Regional KAMgr.)	L Regional Key Account Mgr. L Sales Mgr. (Divisional KAMgr.)	L Sales Mgr L Key Acct. Mgr.
KA Hit-Rate Optimization (incl. HR Improvements)	Yes (High)	Yes	Yes	Yes

Fig. 72: Key account classification categories and criteria (example) (© Prof. Dr. R. Hofmaier).

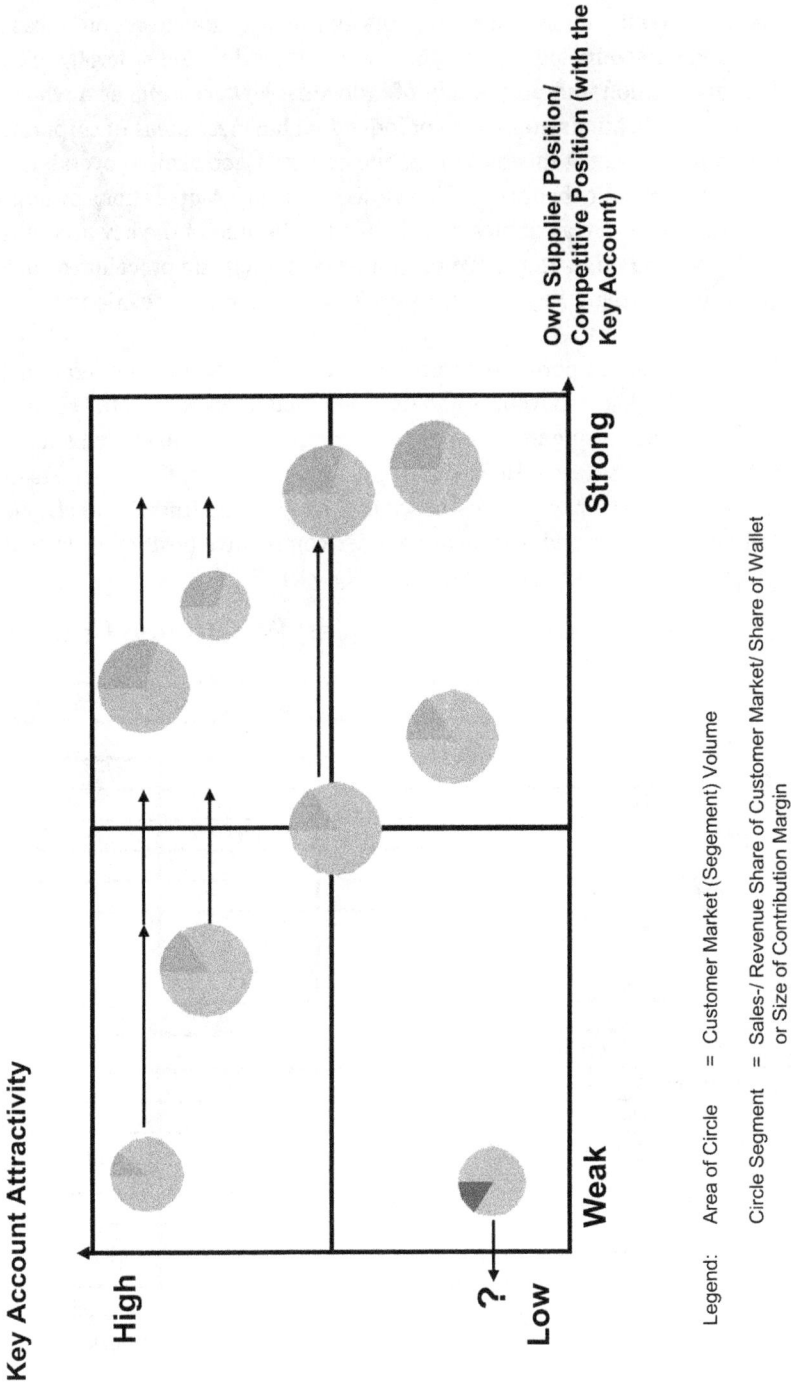

Fig. 73: Strategic key account portfolio (© Prof. Dr. R. Hofmaier).

For a more detailed classification of key accounts and their actual selection, please refer to so-called **key account portfolios** (Fig. 73) and their detailed criteria, which allow the clear distribution and positioning of individual key accounts as a whole, but also by region, applications areas, etc., or individual business areas of corporate strategic key accounts. Against this backdrop, one can get a good initial overview – according to general portfolio theory – which key accounts (or KA-operations by large KAs) possess which attractive attributes, which own positioning of the key accounts is effective, and which **basic strategic targets** (target positions) and procedures must be derived from the **strategic key account portfolio**. Basic target positioning can thus be compared and prioritized.

According to the general portfolio approach[43], key accounts (or KA-operations) that have a relatively high attractiveness and thus potential for growth in the coming years and where provider or preferred supplier positioning can be extended should be **developed** and infiltrated first. However, this requires an in-depth single-, cross- and up-selling analysis, which will be discussed in the following. (Individual criteria of key account attractiveness and their own provider/competitive position as well as their weighting and rating can be seen in detail in Fig. 74.)

Key Account Attractiveness & (Supplier) Positioning Criteria

Criteria	Weight	Score
Key Account Attractivity		
Current Key Account Revenue	(High)	
Strategic Potential of Key Account	(High)	
Profitablity of Key Account	(High)	
Key Account Growth		
Key Account, Credit Rating		
Lead-User Function / Lead User Image (of Key Account)		
Price Sensivity		
Intensity of Returns and Processing		
Sum (Key Account Attractiveness)		
Supplier Positioning for Key Account		
Own Supplier/ KA Market Share (Share of Wallet), Single-Selling	(High)	
Own Supplier/ KA Market Share (Share of Wallet), Cross-Selling	(High)	
Own Supplier/ KA Market Share (Share of Wallet), Up-Selling	(High)	
Degree of Supplying Equipment With Own Products		
Specific Product/ Service/ Application Expertise regarding Key Account		
Geographical Proximity		
Price-Performance Positioning		
Sum (Supplier Positioning)		

Fig. 74: Criteria of key account attractiveness and provider (competitive) positioning (with key accounts) (© Prof. Dr. R. Hofmaier).

---

43 For possible applications of key account portfolio and their criteria, see also Sidow, 2002.

3 Key account concept development, key account strategies and tasks

The creation of the **overall KAM** concept and its substantiation with respect to individual key accounts can be done graphically using a **three-dimensional approach** (see the visual representation of the KAM approach in Fig. 75 a, b and c). This **key account pyramid** presentation allows a meaningful and practically applicable ("visualizable") approach.

Individual business segments of individual key accounts can initially be derived in a plausible way, and a related potential and positioning analysis (KA-SPOT/SPOS) can be clarified and detailed step by step in a clear and detailed way. **Key account levels (levels I–IV)** can now be divided respectively into individual product and service segments (customer partial markets/segments). Most of the time, the **product** (see Fig. 75a) **or component level** is the **first level**. It illustrates (from left) previously addressed customer market segments (actual segments) and allows for possibilities of **segment share expansion (single-selling potential/measures)** to be qualified and quantified. Not only should individual customer segment shares be determined or queried, but also the absolute size of customer segments and their development (customer market segment volume/potential/growth ratios). Thus, initial actual customer market coverage can be recorded, related share improvements/share gains can be developed and concretized, and corresponding measures or steps can be implemented **(single-selling strategies, programs and measures)**.

In a further step (on level I), so-called "neighboring product segments" or directly related "value adding segments" of the customer (customer market) can be illustrated in a transparent way and developed, and opportunities for their development and coverage with one's own products and services can be worked out and identified for mutual advantage (successive win-win generation). Such an opportunity analysis allows gaining further potential customers by marketing an **expanded range of offers** (other, modified or new products) at **level I (cross-selling strategies, programs and measures)**. Most of the time, several "neighboring" segments can be explored successively and key accounts can be afforded additional "synergy benefits." If subsidiaries or foreign companies of key accounts can now also be **internationally** be tapped, one gets to the third cross-selling dimension (international cross-selling segments of KAs; see Fig. 75a).

Vertical expansion of one's service offering includes so-called **up-selling**, which can take place in several stages. Often, the seller has the opportunity here to offer **additional services, product packaging, partial solutions**, special processing and deliveries, etc., and/or offer, for example, specific integration solutions. This leads to "higher quality" services for the customer **(level II)** with the benefit of decreasing the so-called coordination expense, etc. Beyond packaging products and partial solutions, **complete solutions** can also be (developed and) offered to the key account

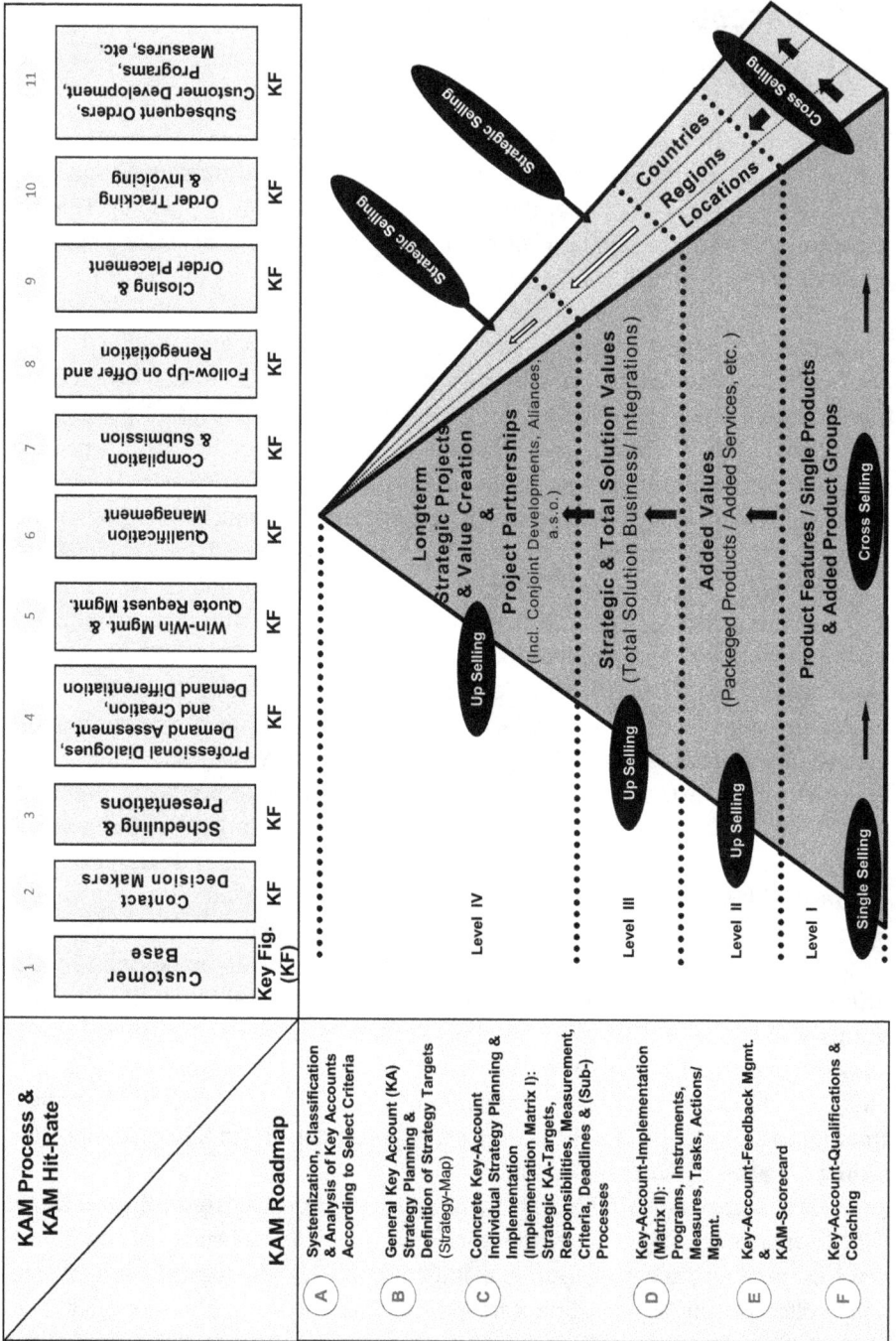

Fig. 75a: Holistic key account management (KAM) concept (I) (B2B) (© Prof. Dr. R. Hofmaier).

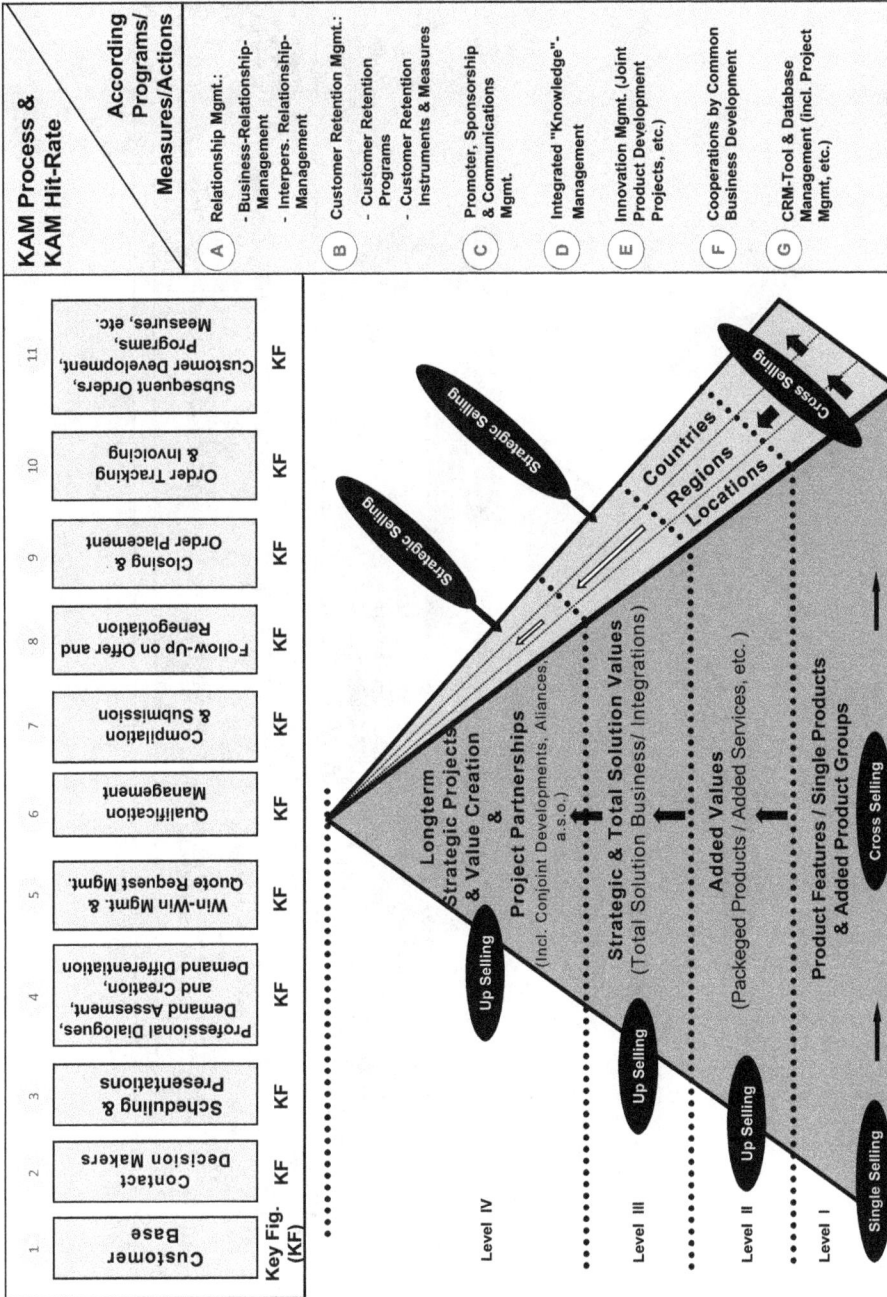

Fig. 75b: Holistic key account management (KAM) concept (II) (B2B) (© Prof. Dr. R. Hofmaier).

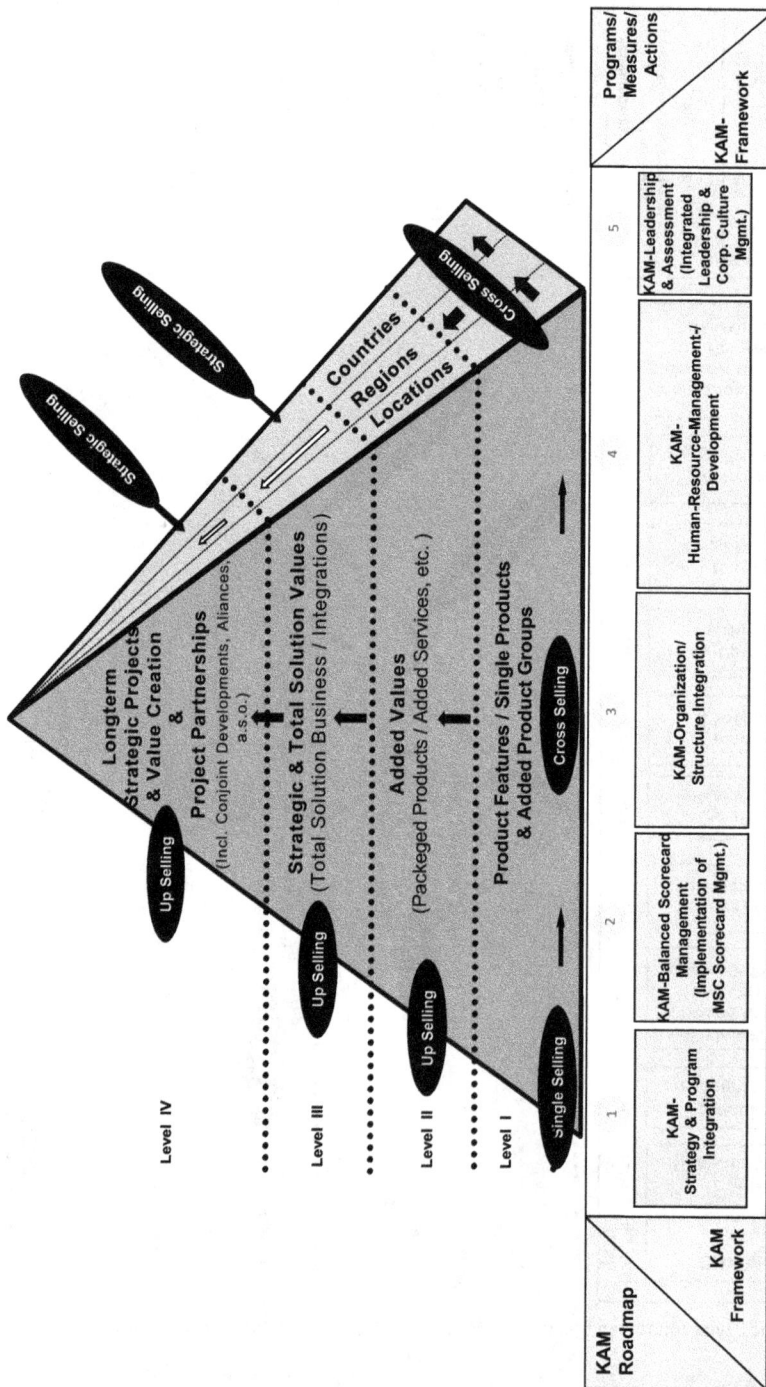

Fig. 75c: Holistic key account management (KAM) concept (III) (B2B)
(© Prof. Dr. R. Hofmaier).

(solution business). Thus, a manufacturer and supplier of control modules of product group 1 (see also Fig. 76a) can not only offer more control modules than product groups 2 and 3 (e.g., more PLC modules and AMD modules, etc.) (cross-selling), but can integrate them with other corresponding products for so-called sub-controllers (up-selling I) and market them with appropriate services (e.g., as engineering services) up to so-called **total solutions** or **overall control systems (upselling II/ level III)**. This way, advanced and higher-quality value-adding sectors (value chains) of the client or advanced/additional application areas can be integrated and covered. Another KAM **level (IV)** is the one of **strategic selling**. Here, **complete** (strategic) **projects** (prime contractor properties, strategic project management etc.) can be adopted and implemented for Key customers, which can include strategic management and project tasks (including the coordination of subcontractors).

The following **practical example** (see Fig. 76a) clearly shows that with respect to the initial situation, i.e. prior coverage of customer product market 1 (level I) of only US $ 0.2 million (with only 7% customer segment share), can be expanded up to US $ 1.5 million **(simple-selling)**, customer markets 2–4 can be addressed and covered step by step through cross-selling activities, and thus, for example, US $ 3.5 million instead of US $ 0.2 million can now can be specifically solicited for the medium term from the available cross-selling potential market of US $ 10 million. Moreover, the packaging level **(up-selling I/**value level II) can be acquired with US $ 2.5 million, the solution level **(up-selling II/**value level III) with US $ 1.0 million, and possibly the value level IV **(strategic-selling)** with US $ 1.25 million in the medium term thanks to conceptual KA-management. Thus, step by step, instead of the previous mere US $ 0.2 million of the addressable customer potential of US $ 17.5 million, a corresponding concept can, as this case illustrates, allow for US $ 7.0 million to be strategically and operationally approached and potentially developed in the medium term.

The reason why such an approach did not take place beyond existing product market approach 1 is often that the previous "classic" distribution was driven by daily business, that the responsible sales person was controlled and provisioned **only through product group 1**, and above all, that a detailed KAM methodology and procedure (from KA-analysis to conceptual KAM implementation) was **not known**, practiced or promoted until now. In addition to the methodological requirement, corresponding KAM qualifications and relevant assistance from associated sales, marketing and service personnel must be taken into consideration. Also, all KAM-parties must be compensated **("incentivized")** materially, i.e. variably. Holistic KA analysis and procedure and decision integration designed for the medium term are thus an essential prerequisite to develop potential business opportunities (opportunity management) in a focused way for **mutual benefit**.

Required are appropriate KAM-task objectives (see also preferred supplier targets), which reflect the imposed marketing, sales and customer management integration approach.

General Supplier Level

Value-Level IV

General Entrepreneur – Customer (KA) Market Segment: $2.5 Mio.
(Company X, Present Share of Wallet: $0 Mio./ Company X Target Share of Wallet: $1.25 Mio.) (Strategic-Selling)

Engineering & Consulting Level, (Incl. Installation, Maintenance, etc.; Total Solutions)

Value-Level III

Engineering & Consulting Customer Market Segment: $2.5 Mio.
(Company X Present Share of Wallet: $0 Mio./ Company X Target Share of Wallet: $1.0 Mio.) (Up-Selling II)

Packaged Products & Services Level

Value-Level II

Packaged Product Customer Market Segment: $2.5 Mio.
(Company X Present Share of Wallet: $0 Mio./ Company X Target Share of Wallet: $1.25 Mio.) (Up-Selling I)

Single Product & Component Level

Value-Level I

Customer Market (CM) = $10 Mio.
(Co. X Present Share 1: $0.2 Mio.)
(Co. X Target Share 1: $3.5 Mio.)

Prod. Group 1: (Cust. Mark. Seg. 1) Vol. $3 Mio. (Single-Selling) Comp. X Share of Wallet: $0.2 Mio. Comp. X Target Share of Wallet: $1.5 Mio.	Prod. Group 2: (Cust. Mark. Seg. 2) Vol. $3 Mio. (30%) (Cross-Selling) Comp. X Share of Wallet: $0 Mio. Comp. X Target Share of Wallet: 1.0 Mio.$	Prod. Group 3: (Cust. Mark. Seg. 3) Vol. $2 Mio. (30%) (Cross-Selling) Comp. X Share of Wallet: $0 Mio. Comp. X Target Share of Wallet: $0.75 Mio.	Prod. Group 4: (Cust. Mark. Seg. 4) Vol. $1 Mio. (Cross-Selling) Comp. X Share of Wallet: $0 Mio. Comp. X Target Share of Wallet: $0.25 Mio.	Prod. Group 5: (Cust. Mark. Seg. 5) Vol. $0.5 Mio. (Cross-Selling) Comp. X Share of Wallet: $0 Mio. Our Comp. X Target Share of Wallet: $0.25 Mio.	Prod. Group N: (Cust. Mark. N Seg.) N Vol. $0.5 Mio. (Cross-Selling) Comp. X Share of Wallet: $0 Mio. Comp. X Target Share of Wallet: $0.25Mio.

⇧ Potential Total Cust. (KA) Market (I-IV) Today: ≈ $17.5 Mio.
Mio $ (Total Cust. Market (I-IV) Near Future: ≈ **$20 Mio.**)
⇧ So Far No Strategic KAM (No Opportunity Mgmt. & No Strategic KAM) by Comp. X

Our Company X Present Share of Customer/ KA Market: $0.2 Mio.
≈ 7% Share of Customer Market I/1
≈ 2% Share of Component Customer Market I/1-N
≈ 1% Share of Potential Total Customer Market I-IV

Our Company X Target Share of Whole Cutomer Market (I-IV) $7.0 Mio.
≈ 40% Share of Total Cust. Market (I-IV)

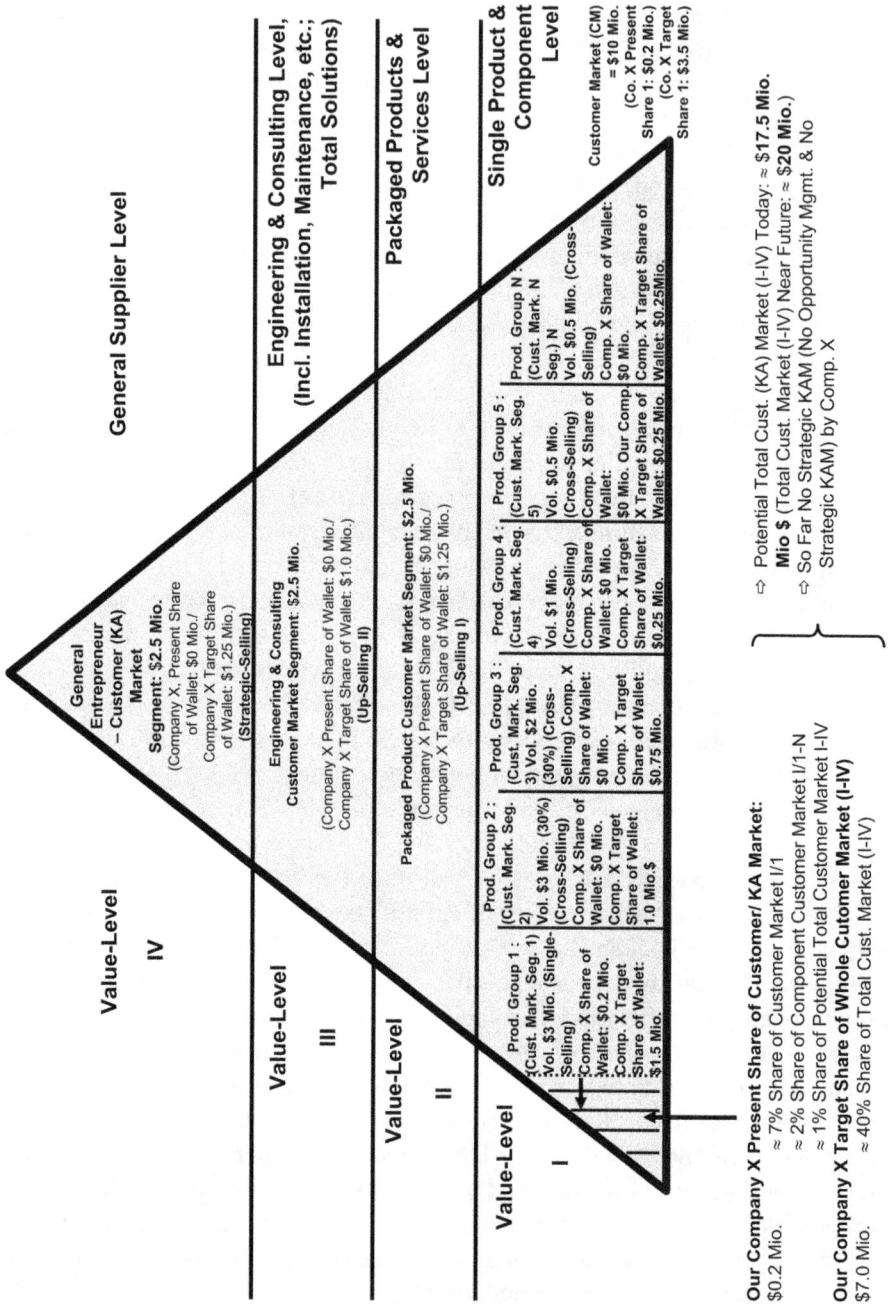

Fig. 76a: Key account management (KAM) approach by segmentation, quantification and infiltration based on a practical example (© Prof. Dr. R. Hofmaier).

Behind on that is a kind of general modification of the basic KAM process: the KA- and decision maker-specific demand and problem analysis, problem solving and modified/new demand creation, demand profiling, solution integration and decision-maker involvement, added value generation and win-win proposition improvement and last but mot least sustainable mutual business development (see Fig. 76b).

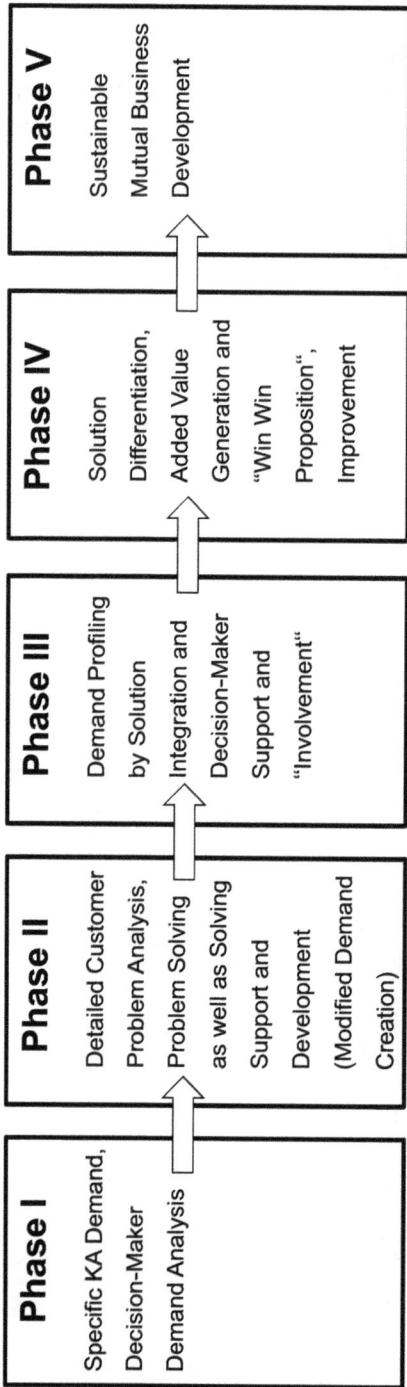

Phase I

Specific KA Demand, Decision-Maker Demand Analysis

Phase II

Detailed Customer Problem Analysis, Problem Solving as well as Solving Support and Development (Modified Demand Creation)

Phase III

Demand Profiling by Solution Integration and Decision-Maker Support and "Involvement"

Phase IV

Solution Differentiation, Added Value Generation and "Win Win Proposition", Improvement

Phase V

Sustainable Mutual Business Development

Fig. 76b: Modification of basic key account management (KAM) Process (B2B) (© Prof. Dr. R. Hofmaier).

Key account management tasks

On one hand, the **KAM roadmap (left column)** shown in the KAM design (see Fig. 75a) shows both the **prerequisite** for such a KAM, such as the systematization and fundamental **analysis capabilities** of key accounts (see corresponding analysis tasks in the next section), as well as the **integration of all KA-planning** into the basic MSC strategy (see strategy map/Part II) and corresponding strategy-led **implementation** and KA-**feedback** (see the implementation matrix in Fig. 82a and b), and the necessary **skills** management (see Fig. 84–86). The **top row** in Fig. 75a shows the **KAM process** in compressed form (by respecting the big points of modification of the Key account process (see Fig. 76b), while the **right column** in Fig. 75b shows the accompanying (CRM) **programs and measures** that need to be integrated, and finally, the bottom line in Fig. 75c shows **KAM-Framework** (incl. conditions and measures) that need to be taken into consideration.

Important KAM methods in addition to the methods already mentioned include (so far) KA-systematization, KA-analysis (especially segmentation and opportunity analysis methods), strategy, positioning and implementation planning (selling strategies), KA-scorecard and KA-qualification methods, and in particular KAM implementation measures and procedures. As part of KA-analysis, **opportunity management** methods particularly gain importance, because they allow for systematic tapping into current and future KA-market segment and value-adding potentials.

Some of the main methods here can be split into so-called **"cross" methods** and **"detailed" methods** (see Fig. 77). With them, "new" business opportunities can be identified and related value-adding stages can be worked out, covered and integrated into an overall solution.

The emphasis here is on the KA-funnel method, the KA-potential matrix, the KA-SWOT analysis, KA-demand mapping and the KA value chain analysis[44]. While the **funnel method** is a top-down approach based on select and derivable customer investments that need to be captured (for example, investments in production facility improvements, new investments, etc.), which in turn are proportionately "broken down" in production and application segments (e.g., amount of automation technology) and in a further step in appropriate automation solutions (direction solution) and product groups (control modules, etc.), the **KA potential matrix** is based on customer, application and product segments that are from the past, new or need to be modified, that are juxtaposed with prior, modified and new products and services (of/ for the customer) and that are determined and detailed systematically in select development and plausibility analyses. The KA-SWOT matrix is based on a classic SWOT analysis in terms of select KA-segments and analysis areas.

---

[44] For details on these methods, see also Hofmaier, 2010/2013.

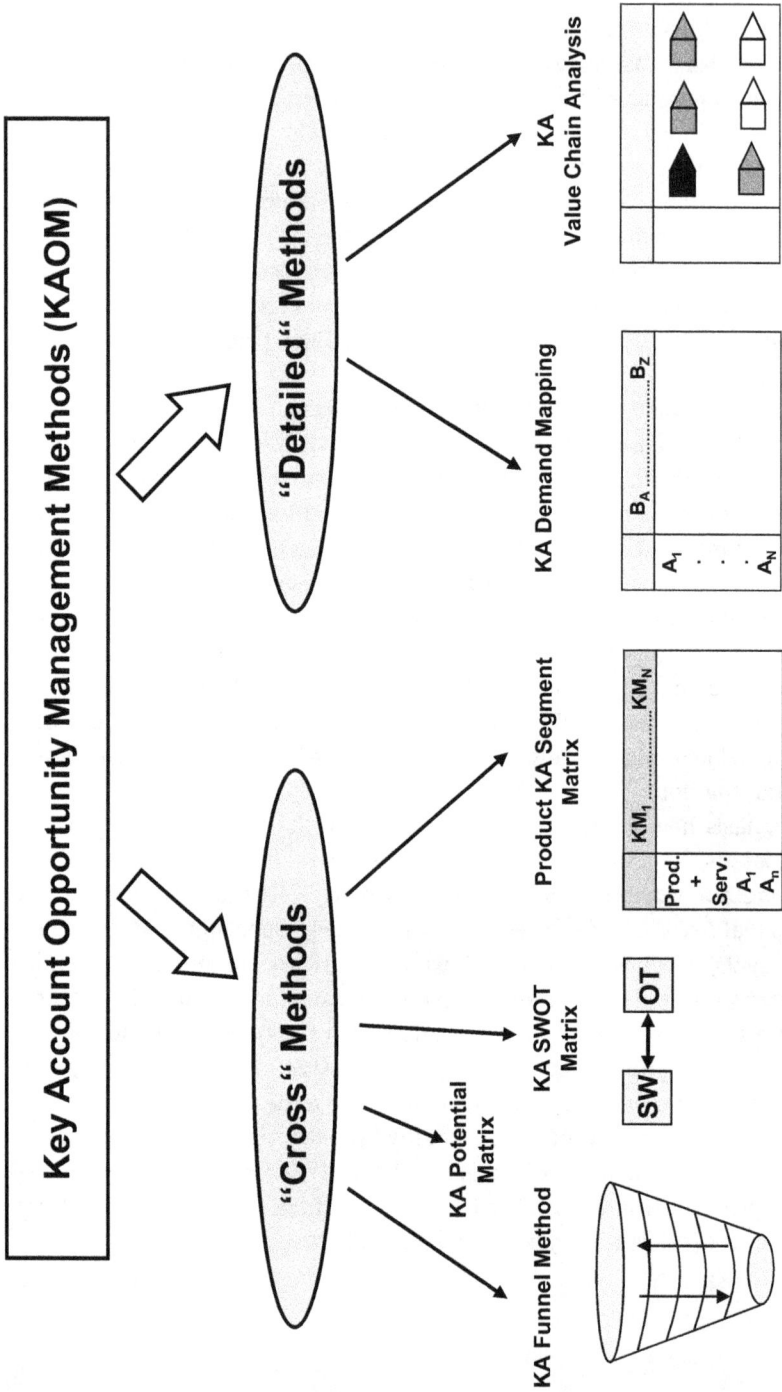

Fig. 77: Selected methods for key account opportunity management (KAOM) (© Prof. Dr. R. Hofmaier).

KA demand mapping includes "functionally analytical" segmentation and differentiation of products and applications with the customer against the backdrop of corresponding actual or optional coverage through own products, product development, services, and other adaptation measures. **KA value chain analysis** (see Fig. 78) can focus on showing the fine segmentation of customer-specific applications substituted specifically with own products across multiple value-adding stages, which had so far been covered by competitive products, and can specifically lay out added values and competitive advantages to be developed for one's own positioning and competitive share gains/ousting. One's own products and solutions need to be developed and offered, so that favorable (overall) solutions and clear competitive advantages can be shown for both sides. Through systematic extension, for example, of an integrated control solution for all paper machine along the immediate value chain, control system, unit control and drive technology can be integrated and optimized as **(total) solution** for the customer (i.e., total one-stop solution for improved "performance features" and reduced coordination, interface and coordination costs, etc.).

Primary responsibilities of KAMs can be summarized as follows (refer to the implementation matrix in Fig. 82a and b as a guide) with the following tasks:

Strategic tasks:
– Derivation and coordination of key account strategy from the general marketing strategy
– Determination of the KA-roadmap
– Coordination and "match" of one's own account strategy and approach with the standardized implementation matrix
– Establishment and development of strategic customer relation, retention and development management
– Strategy support by integrating a "sponsor" from one's own top management and from corresponding customer management
– Implementation of key account strategy and its programs, measures and methods inward (within the company; groundwork areas) and outward (in the client company).

Operational tasks:
– Inbound/outbound coordination of all relevant key account programs and measures
– Targeting, participation and organization of groundwork (including incentives) for all internal and external key account tasks, programs and measures
– Project, contract, information and communication management, both internal and external
– Management and implementation of relevant customer relation, retention and development programs and activities with specified tasks and actions

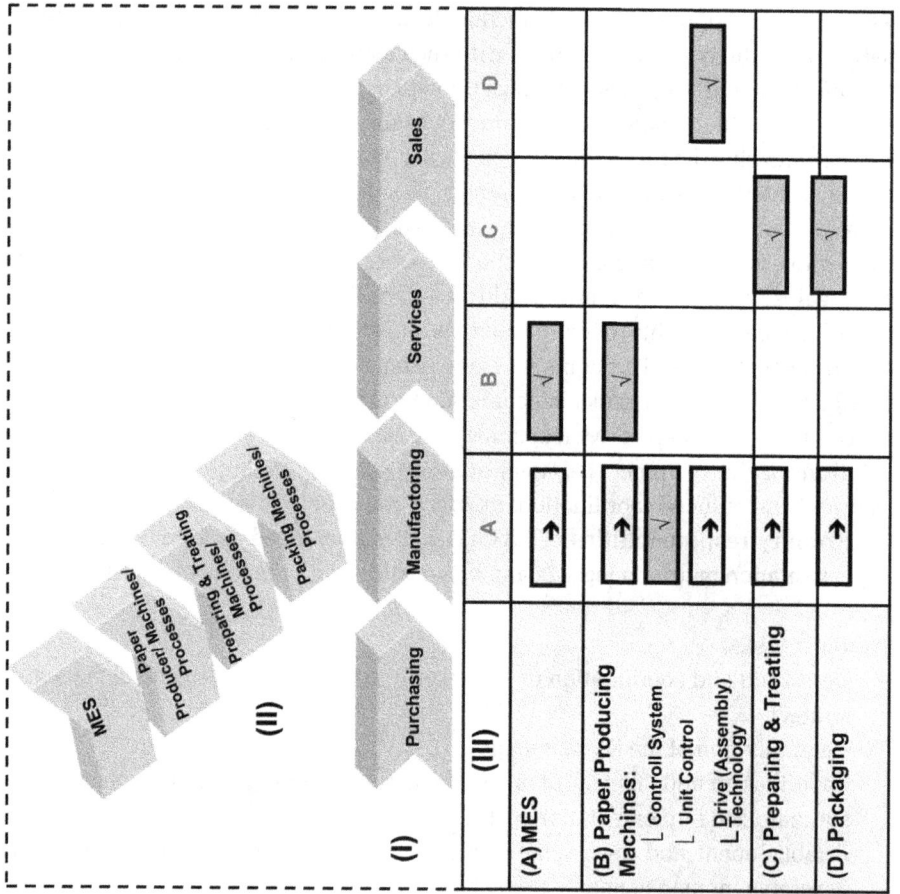

Fig. 78: Example of key account value chain analysis and planning (© Prof. Dr. R. Hofmaier).

-   Development and implementation of (strategic and operational) customer, product development and marketing partnerships
-   Implementation of KA-feedback and scorecard management
-   Optimization of internal and external key account processes
-   Implementation of relevant complaint, customer satisfaction, loyalty and customer experience management
-   Implementation of relevant own and employee-related training and coaching courses and so on.

In connection with the complexity of the task area of key account management (national and international), the key account manager often leads a **cross-functional own and client team**, which is (case by case) comprised of (country-specific) sales, customer, marketing and service staff members as well as possibly additional "interface managers" (see next section).

Here, the **main supporters (locally)** are sales or field sales representatives, possibly supplemented by other direct sales, inside sales, or e-sales managers and technical services. It is important to pay special attention to "KA-specific" marketing **(KA marketing)**. The tasks of KA marketing increase in content and intensity from "value-level to value-level" (see Fig. 79), so that "traditional product marketing" with existing knowledge and methods is no longer sufficient and specific KA-marketing management is required. This KA-marketing also needs to address KA-relevant opportunity, SPOT- and SPOS-analyses, packaging and solution, as well as value-adding and detailed up-selling analyses and needs to support the KA-manager. Furthermore, partial and total solution profiles, win-win simulations, best practice and value-chain scenarios and calculations, etc., can become necessary.

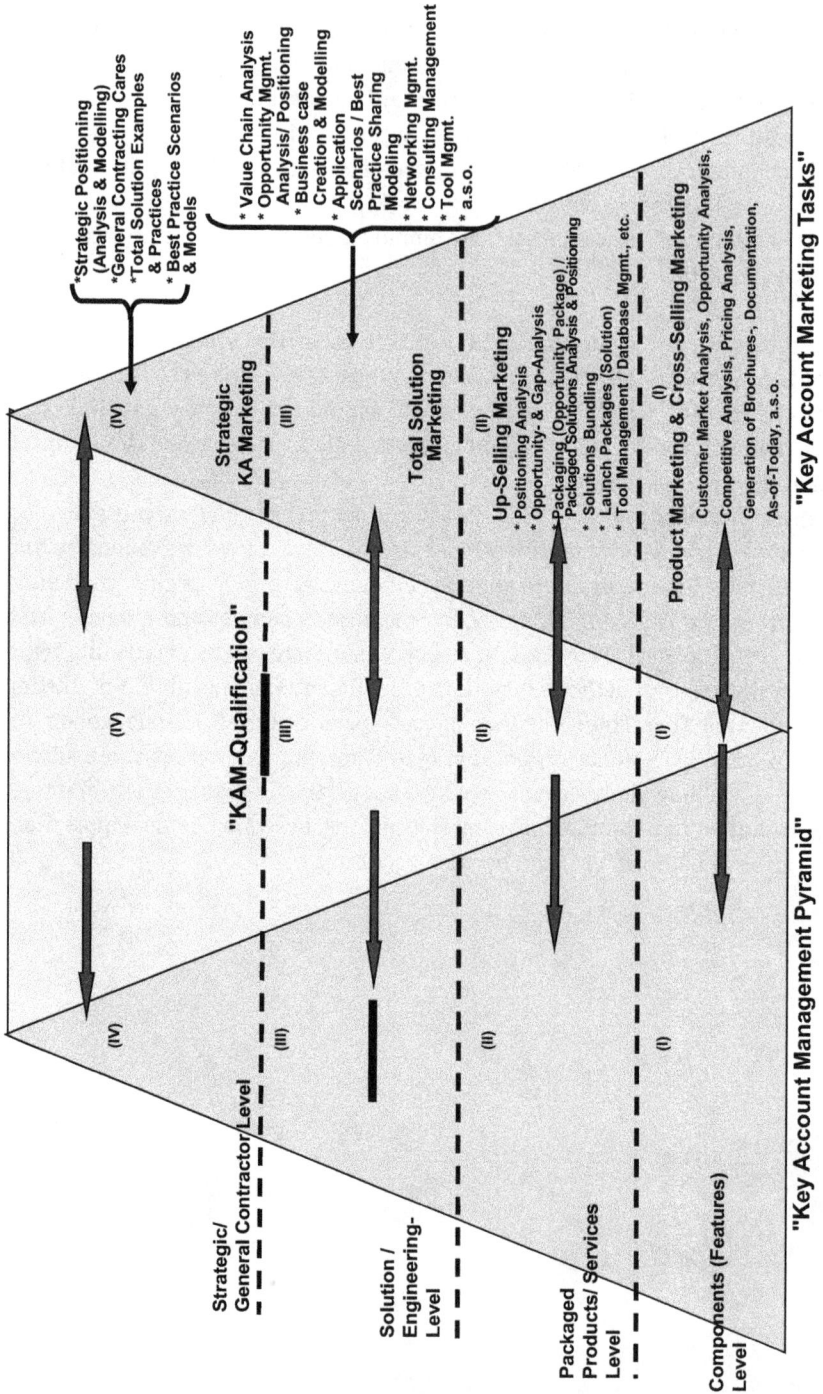

Fig. 79: Potential key account marketing tasks (© Prof. Dr. R. Hofmaier).

4 Key account management organization, structure, implementation and processes

For the organizational structure of key account management (KAM) in your own business, it is important that the KA Manager **is not assigned** to a sales manager from a particular company or business section, but votes **independently and KA-based**, and thus cross-sectionally in a **team approach** with the necessary marketing, sales, service, R&D and production staff members, etc., and purports related objectives and measures (see Fig. 80). The KA-manager or KA-leader should him- or herself be subordinate to KA-managers from the **executive ranks** or the (KA) board. This should ensure that the KAM can operate independently from "division-driven" product objectives and sales and a holistic customer and KA approach is guaranteed considering all possible (actual and to-be-developed) products and solutions (including services).

The definition of **key account organization** should be marked by **cross-functional KAM** (see Fig. 80), in which the key account manager (KA Mgr.) works directly with respective sales, marketing, account, service, R&D, quality, production and logistics managers, etc., and in which the respective decision-making authority, responsibility and support function (content- and time-wise) must be specifically defined and laid down for relevant **"cooperation junctions."** Thus, the **development and obligation of the junctions is crucial for the success** of such a matrix structure. It should also be determined which participant is "incentivized" and how and to what extent (e.g., variable participation in product/customer sales and margin) and which KAM goal achievement is to be integrated, and how, into the MBO (management by objectives) goal agreement (including skills training, development and career goals). In accordance with flexible corporate control, the key account manager usually reports directly to the KAM-leader or overall manager, who should be a member of company management or the board. He/she is thus **independent** from individual product lines, business divisions and business units independently, and can thus be available for comprehensive customer control and penetration! The responsibility for all key account management is thus anchored in top management (through a general key account manager and/or an explicit executive/board member for KAM). The role and responsibilities of a key account manager **distinguish** themselves significantly, for example, from those of a sales manager, who is purely oriented and aligned with matters of divisions, business units, product divisions or regions. The KA manager should especially have many years of professional experience and have polyvalent technical, sales, marketing, customer management, leadership, team development, social and methodological competences (see also Fig. 84). To support his/her activities, a KAM-specific CRM tool is of great importance.

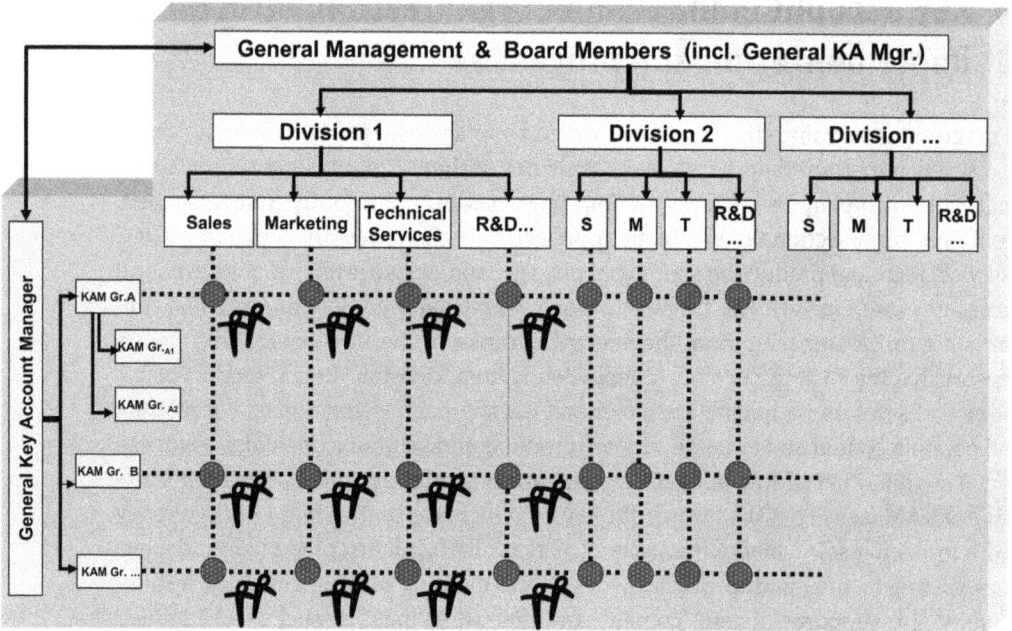

Legend: ⬤ **Points of Interaction & Coordination**

Fig. 80: KAM organizational structure (© Prof. Dr. R. Hofmaier).

For very **large and global companies** with a strong KAM structure and different international KAM functions, it can be quite advantageous to divide one's own KA-management features into **three different forms of organization**, namely a global KAM that is in charge overall, a **regional** and a **divisional KAM** (see Fig. 81).

The **global KA Manager** (KA Mgr.) is responsible worldwide for a globally strategic key account, to him/her can be assigned a regional KA manager and/or a divisional KA manager. The **regional KA Manager** is then responsible for a region (e.g., Asia) for all activities that need to be coordinated across all products and services relating to a global key account (if necessary, other key accounts) (e.g., a regional KAM of an electric company for Coca-Cola in Asia) and reports to the "Global Key Account Manager." The **divisional KA Manager** is responsible worldwide (across all regions) for select products and services (division-related) for a key account with a comparable reporting structure. This allows for relevant coordination, development, control and feedback functions of the global KA manager to be significantly supported and compressed.

Corporate / Global KA Mgr..

- Overall Decision-Making Powers & Responsibility for One Worldwide KAM (Including all Reporting and Regional & Divisional KAMgrs.)

- Overall Decision-Making Powers For all Regions

- Overall Competence for all Products & Services

Divisional Key Account Management / KA Mgr.

- **D-KAM** Decision-Making Powers for one International KA (Multi-Regional)

- In Respect to specific (divisional) all Products and Services of the Division

- Support Corp. KA Mgr.

all KA Mgr.s

Corporate / Global Key Account Management / Mgr.

All Products & Services (All Divisions)

All Regions

Corp. KAM
- All regions
- All products and services
- All KA Mgrs.

Regional Key Account Management / KA Mgr.

- Decision-Making Powers & Responsibility for Regional Area

- In Respect to all Products and Services

- Support Corp. KA Mgr.

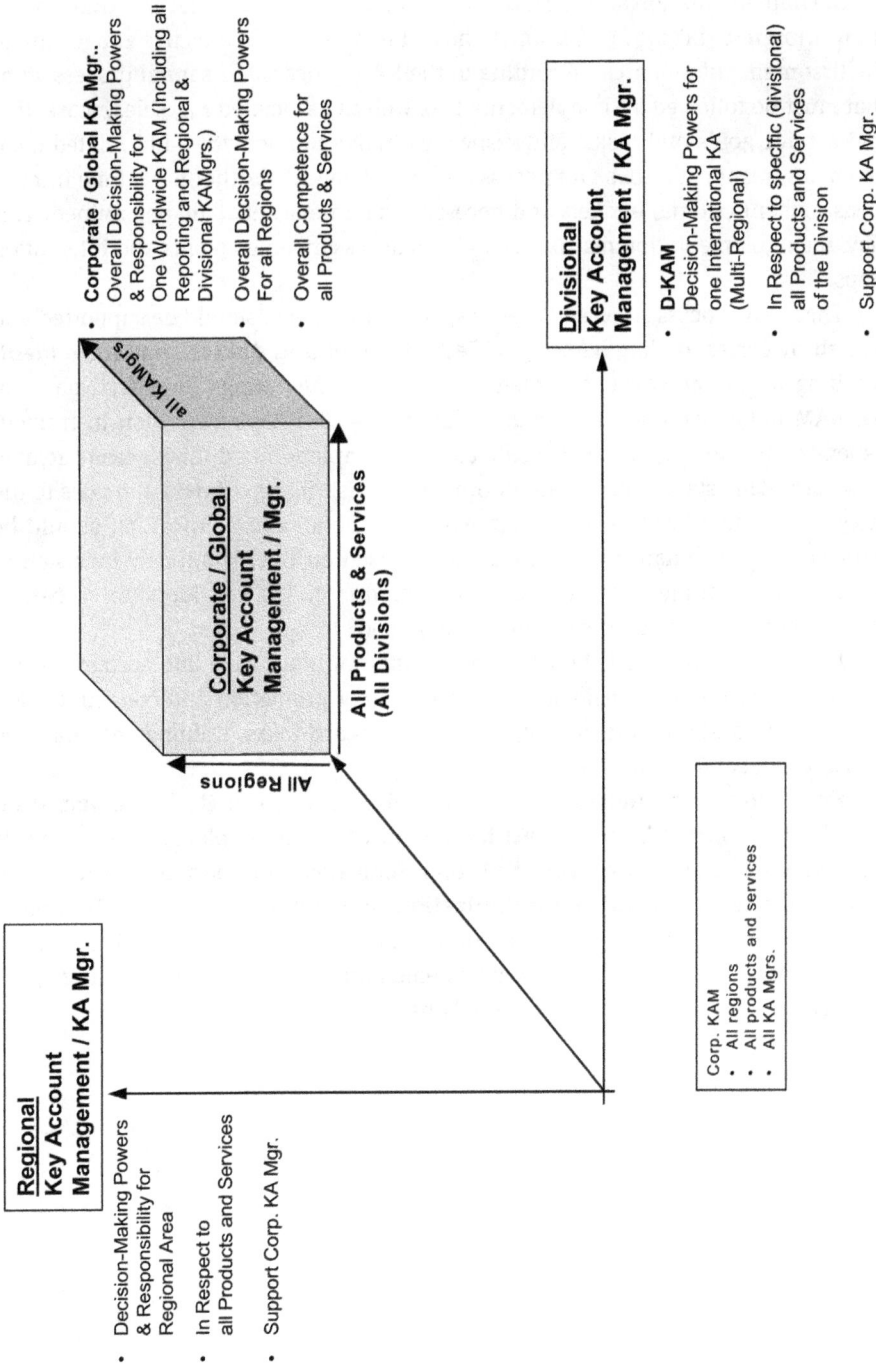

Fig. 81: Global, regional and divisional key account management structure (© Prof. Dr. R. Hofmaier).

For the implementation and execution of the company KAM, a relevant **KAM implementation matrix** (see Fig. 82a and b) has often proven to be effective and useful. In the first main column are – according to the KAM process – essential process steps that must be followed and implemented, as well as associated KA, sales, marketing and service goals and tasks, and respective individual activities and related competencies, responsibilities and necessary "board votes." Furthermore, time frames, measurement criteria, budgets and necessary data items, etc., are determined. This way, the implementation matrix also defines necessary adjustments and integration steps.

These KA process steps and their respective roles, etc., should be supported and backed by corresponding **KAM-specified CRM tool and data base management**, resulting in a more effective implementation and fine-tuning. The effectiveness of the KAM implementation matrix as a fine-tuning and implementation instrument depends considerably on the specific content completion and timeliness of related KAM data. This starts with the input of relevant visiting report data and goes to the integration and consideration of strategic and operational metrics that should be pursued and the balanced scorecard that is based on this. The timely inclusion of those involved in the KAM process is very important. The consideration of benchmark-oriented hit rate improvement is understood.

It must be added that the KAM implementation must take into account necessary customer relation, customer loyalty, customer promotion and communication measures. In addition, the **accompanying scorecard** tasks, training and coaching measures must be included and observed.

KAM should be **analysed** and **reviewed** in regards to its **implementation status and progress** in the context KAM application and implementation analysis and review every one to two years. Key application areas must be subjected to critical reflection to determine **further optimization opportunities** (see Fig. 83) in order to ensure the continued development of this approach. (This approach is also to be recommended for the first systematic implementation of KAM by **prioritizing** application areas based on specific situational analysis.)

Key Account: ....
Decison Makers (KA): ....
Selling Strategy: ....
State: ....

KAM Proceedings & Activities / KAM Phases and Modules	Individual Targets, Tasks and Priorities	Sub-Steps and Single Activities (Inbound / Outbound)	Responibility (Internal / External)	Supports & Additional Tasks, Coordinate with Board Members (Internal / External)	Time Frame	Mile Stones & Measurement Criteria	Budgets	Data Base / CRM / Interrupting Factors & Handling	Miscell.
1. KA Status, Potentialities and Oportunities Analysis									
1.1 KA Classification and Status (Today / Future)	Definition and Assignment for Global Strategic, National & Industry Key Accounts etc.	KA Segmentation and Sub-Tasks	KAMgr.	Field Sales, Product Mgmt., Inside Sales	Q_1	Segment-Criteria / Ssaignments / Portfolios	KA Specific Budget per FY/Q_1-Q_4	Common Key Account Data Base; Varying, Alternating Key Account Priorities	
1.2 KA Situation Analysis (Customer Market Segments, Positioning, Competitive Differentiation, Decision Maker- and Sales Analysis and Appoaches, a.s.o.)	KA Analysis / Positioning per Customer Market Segments- / Applications-/ Product- and Services Segments	Specific Analysis- and Positioning Survey	KAMgr.	Field Sales, Product Mgmt., Inside Sales	Q_1	Customer Market Developmen / Requirements/ Determine Voluminas & Potentialities	KA Specific Budget per FY/Q_1-Q_4	Interface Problems	
1.3 KA Potentialities Analysis (KA SPOT / SPOS / Share of Wallet Opportunity- Analysis)									
a) Current-Business Analysis / Potentialities / Demand Analysis (Incl. Single-Selling Analysis)	Share-of-Wallets / Single-Selling Analysis / Hit-Rate Optimization Analysis (National / International)	Analysis Specific Conversations & Workshops; Determine Potentialities Exactly	KAMgr.	Field Sales, Product Mgmt., Inside Sales, R&D	Q_2	Detailing the Volumina	KA Specific Budget per FY/Q_1-Q_4	Inbound-/ Outbound- Coordination- Challenges & Smoothing	
b) Cross-Selling-Analysis / (Potentials / Demands / Exploiting Opportunities)									
c) Up-Selling Analysis / (Potentials / Demands / Exploiting Opportunities)		Detailed Win Win Potentialities	KAMgr.	Field Sales, Product Mgmt., Inside Sales	Q_2; Q_3	Detailing the Volumina	KA Specific Budget per FY/Q_1-Q_4	Get Support by KA Sponsors	
d) Strategic-Selling Analysis (Potentials / Demands / Exploiting Opportunities)									
1.4 Comprehent Customer Market-/ Product-/ Performance Analysis" and Positioning Targets									
1.5 KA SWOT Analysis (& Business Modelling)									
2. KA Business-, Sales-, Marketing- Project Targets									

Fig. 82a: KAM implementation matrix (A) (© Prof. Dr. R. Hofmaier).

Key Account: ....
Decison Makers (KA): ....
Selling Strategy: ....
State: ....

KAM Proceedings & Activities / KAM Phases and Modules	Individual Targets, Tasks and Priorities	Sub-Steps and Single Activities (Inbound / Outbound)	Responibility (Internal / External)	Supports & Additional Tasks, Coordinate with Board Members (Internal / External)	Time Frame	Mile Stones & Measurement Criteria	Budgets	Data Base / CRM / Interrupting Factors & Handling	Misc.
2.1 KA Targets, Forecasts, Programs, Measures, Effort, Resources, etc. (incl. Single-, Cross-, Up- & Strategic-Selling)	KA Overall-, Segment-, Positioning Goals; Customer Retention Goals	KA Scorecard and Tasks; Definition and Customer Retention Measures	KAM,; KAM, and PM/MarCom	Segment Mgmt./ PM / Finance; Event Marketing		Operative Goals; Achieving Retention Goals / Success Criteria	(See Above)	Missing CRM Data base	
2.2 KA Roadmap & Process Plan									
a) Inquiry Contact, Decision-Maker, Discussion and Presentation									
b) Demand Analysis & Demand Creation, Generating Added Values, Positioning and Top-Down Support									
c) Win-Win Generation & Value Proposition and Generating of Quote Request and Qualification									
d) Offer Preparation									
e) Offer Follow-Up & Renegotiation									
f) Closing / Order Acquisition)									
g) Order Execution & Invoicing Mgmt.									
h) Order Management/ Project Management (Order Execution)/ Management of Subsequent Orders									
3. Accompanying KA Relationship Mgmt. and Retention Mgmt.									
3.1 Planning of Measures									
3.2 Realization									
3.3 Feedback & Optimization									
4. KA Scorecard Qualification, KA Scorecard Mgmt. and Coaching-Management									

Fig. 82b: KAM implementation matrix (B) (© Prof. Dr. R. Hofmaier).

KAM Optimization Opportunities / KAM Application Areas	Actual Need for Action			Room for Improvement			No Potential for Optimization		
	Top Mgmt.	KA Mgmt.	Participants (Involved Staff Members etc.)	Top Mgmt.	KA Mgmt.	Participants (Involved Staff Members etc.)	Top Mgmt.	KA Mgmt.	Participants (Involved Staff Members etc.)
Systemizing and Selecting Key Accounts									
KAM Strategy Determination									
KAM Instruments for Analysis									
KAM Data Base and Timelines									
KAM Programs and Measures/ Activities									
KAM Implementation, Coordination & Support									
KAM (Organization) Structure									
KAM Board Coordination and Reviews									
KAM Top Mgmt. Support and KAM Culture (Development)									
KAM Qualification and Coaching									
KAM Tool Efficiency									
Misc.									

Fig. 83: KAM status and optimization matrix (© Prof. Dr. R. Hofmaier).

5 KAM qualification, coaching, assessment and leadership programs

For KAM employees and especially for the KA manager, **a polyvalent qualification profile and appropriate skills** are important (see Fig. 84). Since he/she has to cover a widely structured, comprehensive task area that coordinates the most diverse internal and external employees, the KA manager must unite both diverse MSC, project management and methodological, social, technological, and sound tool-related knowledge, experience and skills.

At first, the focus is on customer care, sales, marketing, method-specific and corresponding strategy-relevant skills and competencies, which must be supplemented by relevant project and process methodological knowledge and application experience. Furthermore, various interdisciplinary qualifications, social, personal and leadership-related qualifications (such as coordination, integration, communication, motivation, conflict resolution skills and commitment competencies, etc.) are important, which, in turn, require specific skills training. Furthermore, foreign language and intercultural skills are needed to meet today's KAM requirements. To prepare for the first KA-related tasks and their accompanying development, corresponding **KAM-assessment**[45] can be considered and applied by the participants (see Fig. 85, as well as the example of a **KAM-assessment questionnaire** in the appendix). It is integrated into an on-the-job multi-level skills, motivation, coaching and career program. The latter can be passed after the KAM-relevant requirements and task areas and in accordance with respective KAM implementation. Ongoing and coordinated situational **KAM coaching measures** have proved successful (see an example in Fig. 86). This supports the transfer of necessary KAM know-how with tasks for its application-specific implementation and provides it with a feedback process.

For the **selection of future and the development of today's KA-managers** and KA participants, a so-called **KAM potential and performance analysis** (KAM potential and performance portfolio; see Fig. 87) can be used with the two dimensions (1) KAM individual potential and (2) KAM job performance. On the basis of this, it can be deduced, among other things, who is eligible for a particular KA-sector or will be developed for it and who brings the required potential (e.g., sector 7–9). Furthermore, it can be deduced who should generally be considered and can be trained more for KAM-support functions and tasks, for example (sectors 4–6) and who should not be involved (sectors 1–3).

---

45 See also Hofmaier, 2010/2013.

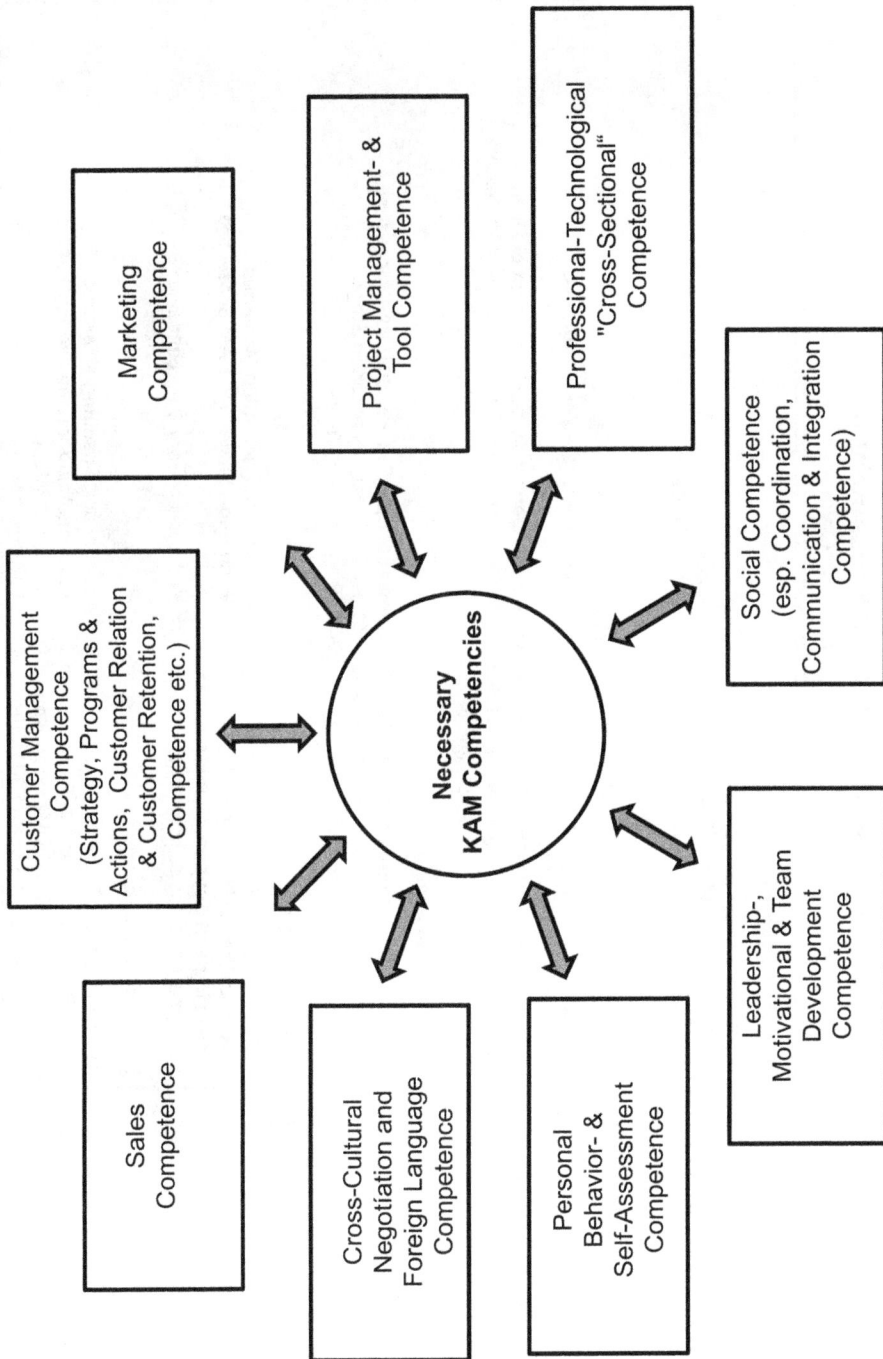

Fig. 84: Areas of competence (qualification requirements) of holistic key account management (© Prof. Dr. R. Hofmaier).

KAM Assessment:
Topics and Options

1. Area of Concern:

a) **Functional and Process-Related** Assignment
b) **Content-Based** and Temporal **KA Task Assignment**
c) **Bonitary and Monetary Compensation Options / Goal Achievement**

2. Area of Concern :

a) **Application, Scope** and **Result** Related of **KA Analysis Methods**
b) **Application, Scope** and **Result** Related of **Applying KA Strategies, Programs, Methods** and **Proceedings**
c) **Way, Scope** and **Result** of Related **KA Demand Developments** and **Fulfillment of Demand**
d) **Way, Scope** and **Target Related** of Specific **KA Decision Maker "Involvements"** and **Results**
e) Important **"Success Stories"** (so Far)

3. Area of Concern :

a) **Presentation, Compliance** and **Goal Achievment** of Specific **Individual KA Processes**
b) **Execution, Compliance** to and **Success** of Specific **KA Implementation Steps**
c) **Status** and **Goal Achievment** of **KA Support Resources and Tasks**

4. Area of Concern :

a) **Way, Scope** and **Result** of Targeted **KA Relationsship** and **Retention Measures**
b) **Application** and **Putting into Practice** of the **Marketing-, Sales-** and **KAM Scorecard**
c) **Backing and Support** of Top Management
d) **Support** and **Scope** of an **CRM-System** with all the Necessary Capabilites

5. Area of Concern :

a) **Execution** and **Result** of Specific **KAM Qualification-** and **Coaching-Measures**
b) **Job Potentiality** and **Job Performance Development, Assignments** and **Further Career Planning**
c) Prospective / Future **KAM Priorities** and **Development Profiles**
d) **KAM Attitude, Motivation, Identification** and **Integrated Work-Life-Balance**

Fig. 85: Summary of the main points of KAM assessments (© Prof. Dr. R. Hofmaier).

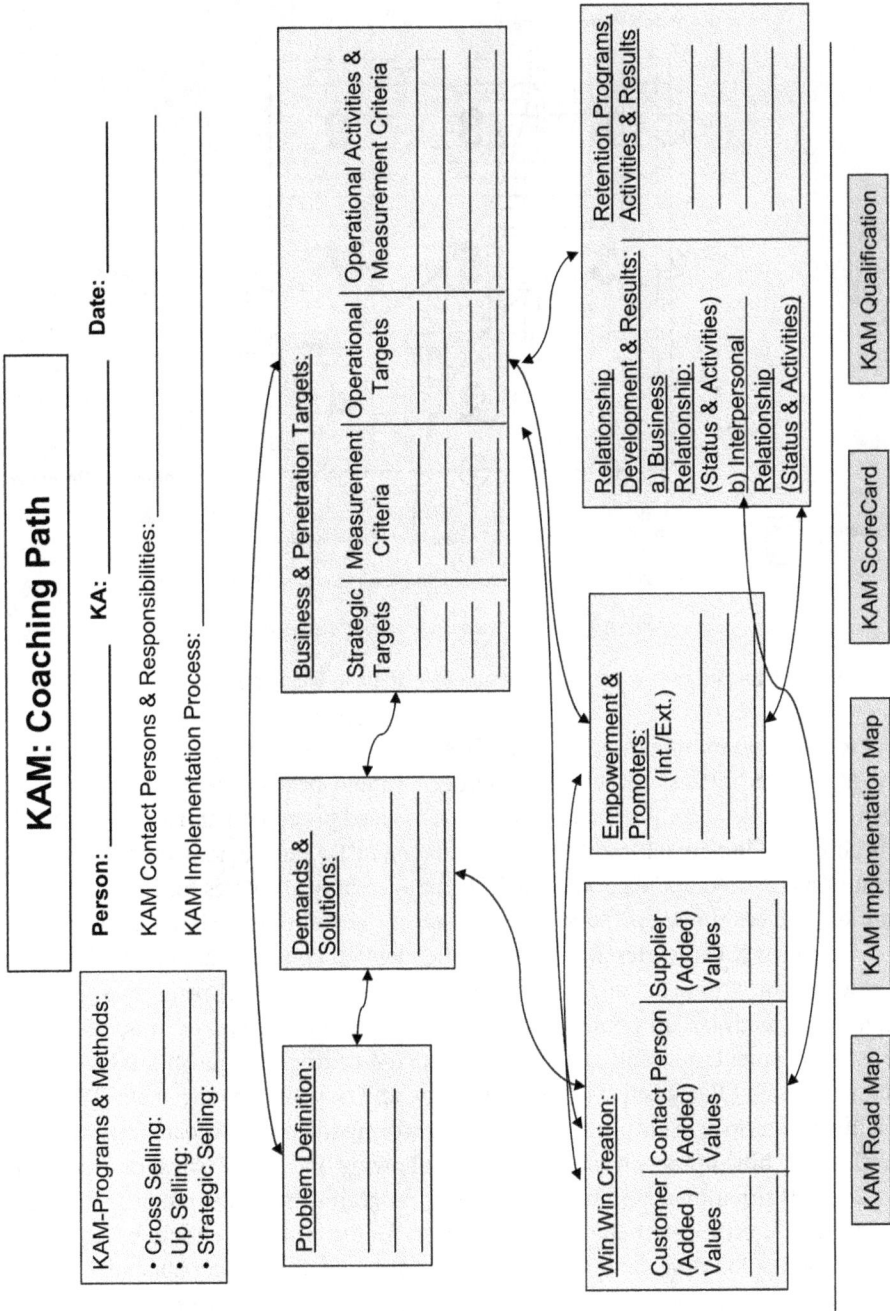

Fig. 86: Possible KAM coaching measures (© Prof. Dr. R. Hofmaier).

KAM Job Performance

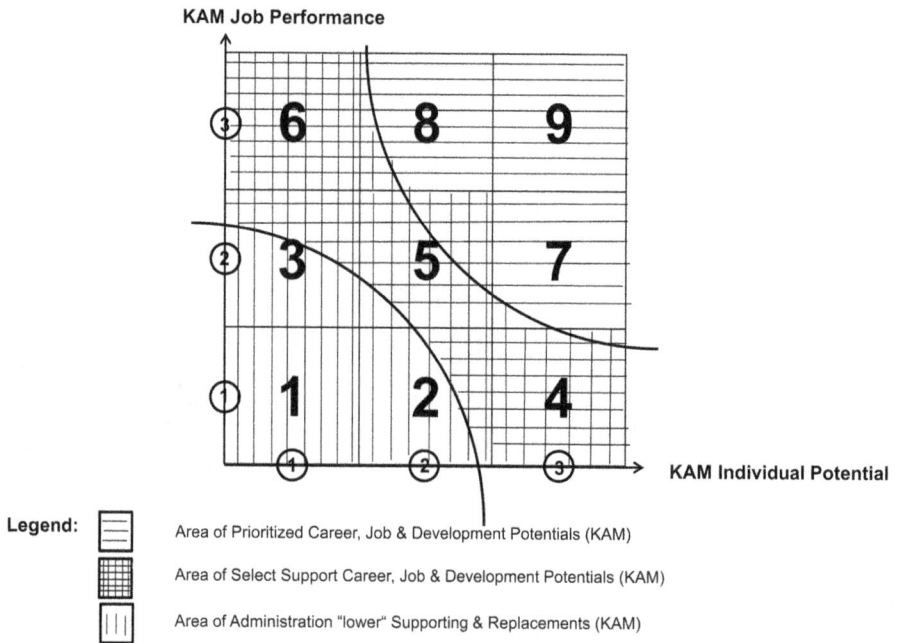

Legend:

Area of Prioritized Career, Job & Development Potentials (KAM)

Area of Select Support Career, Job & Development Potentials (KAM)

Area of Administration "lower" Supporting & Replacements (KAM)

Fig. 87: KAM potential and performance portfolio (© Prof. Dr. R. Hofmaier).

For **motivation management** as part of KAMs, essential tools of a coordinated extrinsic as well as intrinsic motivation approach should be considered. An interesting motivational basis for KA-participants is the focused promotion and support towards specific **KAM job enrichment** (not job enlargement!), where, among other things, relevant "success stories" can be identified and necessary measures for further success stories ("success journeys") and adequate job enrichment can be implemented.

So-called **KAM leadership** includes a leadership approach mainly based on the following three dimensions: situational support regarding (1) respective management-by-objectives, job performance, and job enrichment requirements, (2) appropriate implementation and application of a (KAM-centric) relationship management approach, and (3) respective proactive training and coaching management. The latter mainly means to actively provide and enable accompanying KAM coaching measures. Such a coaching approach can include the following objectives: based on a concrete initial KAM situation determination (strategy, programs, implementation status, decision maker profiles, etc.), the problem analysis for the customer should be developed for the derivation of a convincing win-win solution, should be implemented "on the job" while taking into account strategic and operational objectives, tasks and procedures, and should be trained. Measurable KAM objectives are to be defined and gradually reached. (Added) values are to be developed, profiled and "documented" concomitantly and thus customer decision-based. The necessary support through an internal and external "promoter" who is settled with the key account is also desirable, as well as the consideration and application of select customer relation and customer retention tasks (see Fig. 86).

In addition, we should refer to a **KAM-specified scorecard** at this point (see Part VII), which represents a necessary planning, control, feedback and optimization methodology for a successful KAM. Using this instrument, KA-specific strategic and operational objectives, actions, and tasks as well as their gradual evaluation can be illustrated in a stringent and communicative way and can be coordinated and pragmatically implemented with other relevant metrics in marketing and sales, but also from financial, process and human resource areas.

Finally, **possible benefits and opportunities of modern key account management** can be summarized as follows:

Strategic advantages and opportunities:
- Development not only of single-selling potential, but also cross-, up- and strategic selling potentials
- Establishment of long-term win-win partnerships with key accounts and thus use of necessary know-how transfer, decision maker, product and business development benefits
- Targeted development of a preferred supplier position (and the possibility to multiply markets)
- Use of synergy, but also cost reduction effects through intensive cooperation
- "Disproportionate" extraction and skimming off market and customer potential.

Operational Benefits and Opportunities:
- Better mutual understanding and thus agreed-on and improved coordination, internally and externally (performance improvement and cost reduction)
- Timely phasing-in and aligning of market- and customer-oriented product development programs
- Improvement of customer loyalty, customer relationship and customer retention
- Shortening and making more effective customer care and the sales process
- Timely and concrete coverage of current and future customer requirements (possibly relevant "pilot" requirements for more marketing activities)
- Reduction of time and cost that don't add value.

It should be noted that such a KAM represents a **longer-term, method- and competence-based concept**, which first requires appropriate investments in training, coaching, application of methods, tools, time, resources, assessments, etc., and should be applied to several key accounts and multiplied (based on experience). This will lead to further development of so-called **key-account-centric disciplines** and areas of expertise in the near future, such as so-called key account marketing (B2B), key account organization and process management, and key account resource management, etc.

References

Bacon, T.R. (1999) Selling to Major Accounts: Tools, Techniques an Practical Solutions for the Sales Management, New York

Belz, C. / Müller, M. / Zupancik, D. (2008) Spitzenleistungen im Key Account Management, 2. Aufl., München

Biesel, H. (2007) Key Account Management erfolgreich planen und umsetzen, 2. Aufl., Wiesbaden

Hofmaier, R. (2012) Grundlagen des Key Account Management, in: Hofbauer, G. / Hellwig, C.: Professionelles Vertriebsmanagement, 3. Auflage, Erlangen, S. 103–114

Hofmaier, R. (2012) Möglichkeiten und Chancen einer konzeptionellen Fundierung und Weiterentwicklung des Key Account Management (B2B), in: FORUM Betriebswirtschaft München, Heft 01, S. 6–13

Hofmaier, R. (2011/2014) Efficient Modelling and Application of Professional Key Account Management (B2B) – Empirical Studies, Munich

Hofmaier, R. (2010/2013) Empirische Studien zur Anwendung des Key Account Management, ITM-Institut, München

Hofmaier, R. (2008) Verkaufen in drei Dimensionen, in: Sales Business, Heft 7/8, S. 42–45

Sidow, H.D. (2002) Key-Account-Management – Wettbewerbsvorteile durch kundenbezogene Strategien, 7. Aufl., München

Sieck, M. (2011) Der strategische (Key) Account Plan, 2. Aufl., Norderstedt

A progressive and more in-depth methodology of marketing, sales and customer management is the advanced approach of **Focus Group Management (FGM)**. As it is presented here, it includes an independent approach to integration and includes select customer relation, inclusion, development, KAM and innovation measures. For this, important special topics can explicitly be considered (e.g., lead user-focused product development measures). Thus, FGM presents an essential **integrative program and measures approach**, especially in the context of KAM and product management (PM).

This book concludes by summarizing the presented strategies, programs and measures and illustrating them with user-friendly methodology for planning, managing, monitoring and systematic improvement of MSC processes. This is done using a specified balanced scorecard, namely the **focused marketing, sales and customer management scorecard (MSC scorecard management)**. Such a scorecard can be applied at different aggregation levels within the company for select areas of application (e.g., the KAM scorecard) specified in the overall corporate scorecard.

1 Integrated Focus Group Management (FGM)

The following **focus group management approach (FGM)** is based on an approach that directly focuses on (customer) **decision-makers and target groups** and initially requires **exact knowledge** of KA-specific decision-making, influence, relationship, promoter and network structures. This is based on a customer-specific decision and information database, presented in a compressed way by using a **decision-maker matrix** (see Fig. 88) and a **decision-maker information matrix** (Fig. 89) and thus rounded out by initial support measures and options.

The **exact knowledge** of both national and international key customer decision makers, their organizational involvement and decision-making authority plays an essential role in selecting decision-makers. Furthermore, it is necessary to concretely confirm which decision-makers, co-decision-makers and recommenders possess **which decision and influence scopes**, which task-related and personal **goals** are important to them, what **attitudes** they have toward "us" and our products, services and business development objectives, how specific win-win **relationships** and goals can be developed and achieved, and how respective **"commitments"** and buy-ins are carried out and implemented, etc. (see Fig. 88, 89 90a and b). Supplier-internal opportunities for support, measures and procedures should be established accordingly.

The FGM approach thus supports the more effective and efficient development of personal positioning prospects and joint sustainable **business development options**. The focus for the general approach is on the **focus group conceptual framework**[46] (see Fig. 90a and b). Each key account resp. major customer team is to be installed for select (key) accounts within one's own company must first recognize customer-focused "key performance indicators or criteria" (**KPI**/KPC), which are those criteria that are of utmost priority for achieving the client's and his decision makers' objectives with respect to the object area to be marketed (e.g., launching a new application solution for one's own customers). In contrast, core competencies (**CC**) of one's own company (with respect to the corresponding object area) must now be developed and juxtaposed accordingly. Furthermore, specific marketing-relevant key or critical success factors (**KSFs**) are derived, discussed and prioritized from the client's perspective, so that in turn, one's own "corresponding" (MSC) strengths can be juxtaposed. For this purpose – as hereinafter – various internal team workshops and joint FGM workshops can be conducted with the customer's decision-makers. This can also be done at select product clinics or can be supplemented with application workshops, expertise sharing, tech days, innovation events, and/or integrated consulting teams.

---

46 See in detail Hofmaier, 2010/2013.

Typology / Sub-Functions	Expert Decision-Makers -Mgmt.-		Expert Decision-Makers -Specialist-		Purchasing Decision-Makers -Central Mgmt.-		Purchasing Decision Makers -Local Mgmt.-		Purchasing Decision Makers -Specialist-		Co-Decision-Makers (Committees / Round Tables/ Users, etc.)		Purchasing "Recommenders'/ Professional Users (Internal/External)	Stake-holder
	Central	Decentral	Central	Decentral	Central	Decentral	Central	Decentral	Central	Decentral	Central	Decentral		
Top Level Mgmt., Board Members, Directors	• Names* • History • Contacts • Win–Win Proceedings etc.													
Head of Divsion / Region														
Professional Decision-Maker a) Product Management														
Professional Decision-Maker b) Sales														
Professional Decision-Maker c) R&D														
Professional Decision-Maker d) Production Planning e) Quality Mgmt.														
Others														

Legend: * = Possible Matrix Field Contents

Fig. 88: Decision-maker matrix (© Prof. Dr. R. Hofmaier).

Name / Criteria							
1. Company/Company Branch/Region							
2. Function							
3. Level of Decision-Making Power (A-B-C-D)							
4. Level of Influence/ Connectedness							
5. Attitude Towards Supplier (For/Against/Neutral)							
6. Attitude Towards Project (For/Against/Neutral)							
7. Business Objectives/Business Models (generic/specific)							
8. Personal Objectives/Ambitions, etc.							
9. Win-Win Potential/Development Opportunities (Business Relationship)							
10. Personal "Relationship/Retention" Potential (Interpersonal Relationship)							
11. "Commitment" Steps/Opportunities							
12. Prerequisites for "Buying-In"							
13. Contextual Measures & Actions							
Roundup/ Summary etc.							
Person in Charge of Contact & Handling at (Responsible Suppliers)							
1. Target-Setting							
2. Tasks							
3. Steps of Proceeding							
4. Time Frame							
5. Support							
6. Misc.							

Fig. 89: Decision-maker information matrix (© Prof. Dr. R. Hofmaier).

Another main step deals with the specific development of the widest possible coordination and focused **coverage** of requirement profiles identified through KPI/KPC and KSF/CSF with their own CC and strengths **(KPC-CC/KSF strengths fit)**. It should be noted that specific competition-**differentiating** and customer-relevant **(added) values** should be identified, communicated, "committed" and documented, in order to develop and eventually (jointly) implement sufficiently qualified and – where possible – quantified **decision-making** and reasoning. This will also substantiate progressive win-win profiling.

To **implement** such intermediate steps, **"commitments"** and results, important **topics, targets** and **campaigns** should be **supplemented** by respective retention measures for each decision-maker (decision-making target groups) (see Fig. 90b).

For this, future strategy planning for the customer can be integrated and taken into account, and personal weaknesses can be specifically decreased and possibly important (insourcing) competencies can be recognized and developed. In the long term, **future business development opportunities** should thus be recognized and phased in.

Such an FGM approach is also feasible for a provider who, for example, does not directly deliver to (acquisition-specific) final producers (OEM), but to one of his "preliminaries" (system supplier or partial solution/sub-segment supplier). In the context of select FGM measures, important decision-makers for all preliminary marketing (MSC) stages can now also be selected and incorporated. This allows the achievement of so-called **pull effects**[47] (e.g., as compared to the OEM) (economic cross-stage or vertical FGM). The FGM concept can be applied long-term to different (Key) customers and further developed, and can thus be tested, developed and implemented in multiple ways. (Also, with the initial application and further development of FGM, a KAM approach based on that can be developed and implemented for specific key accounts.)

---

47 See also Hofmaier / Leutbecher, 1996, pp. 106–110.

To Does: ....
Resp.: ....
Deadline: ....

Focus Group Map (I)

KPI (Cust.)	Weight	CC (Own)	Eval. (H/F)	KSF (Cust.)	Weight (H/F)	Own Strenghts	KSF-F/T	Competition	Context	DIFF. Pot. (T/F)	ADD-VALUE (WIN-WIN) (Qual./Quant.)	COM MITM. (Buy In)	Decision Maker	
													Name	Function CA

Legend:

KPI = Key Performance Indicator
CC = Core Competencies
KSF= Key Success Factors
Diff. Pot. = Differentiation Potential
CA = Critical Assessmemts
T/F= Today/Near Future

Fig. 90a: Focus Group Conceptual Framework (FGM Map I) (© Prof. Dr. R. Hofmaier).

Focus Group Map (II)

To Does: ....
Resp.: ....
Deadline: ....

Decision Maker			COMMITM (Buy In) (ind. Sponsors/Allies)	Themes/ Topics (FGr)	Targetting	Activities	Proceedings				Remain Actions	Longterm Development Options (Programs/Actions)
Pro/Con	B-Pot	BRS Act.	PRS Act.					Who? In Prep	What? FGr.	When?	Supp		

Legend:
B-Pot. = Business Potential
BRS = Business Relationship
PRS = Inter-/ Personal Relationship
In Prep. = In Preparation

Fig. 90b: Focus Group Conceptual Framework (FGM Map II) (© Prof. Dr. R. Hofmaier).

2 Integrated marketing, sales and customer management scorecard (integrated MSC scorecard management)

The so-called **integrated marketing, sales and customer management scorecard (MSC scorecard)** [48] is a scorecard specified for an integrated MSC approach that can be integrated into the company's **overall** balanced scorecard and works well for "integrated" planning, control, feedback and optimization management of the company or its business areas. The **different strategies, programs and measures** and their **implementation** and verifiability can thereby be derived, supported, communicated and optimized well.

According to Fig. 91, the focus is on **financial, process and employee dimensions, and especially on strategy dimensions of the MSC scorecard** with the sub-areas of an integrated **marketing, sales** and **customer management** scorecard and its **strategic** marketing, sales and customer management objectives (see also Fig.92b and strategy map). These objectives that are coordinated with each other will now be **coordinated** with the corporate strategy objectives and strategic financial objectives of the **corporate and financial management scorecard** (e.g., with profitability, ROI and ROCE targets; see Fig. 92a), as well as with the **process and structure management scorecard** (Fig. 92c) and the **employee and executive/leadership management scorecard** and their respective strategic objectives (Fig. 92d). As part of their specification, these strategic objectives are "broken down" per scorecard step by step into strategy-oriented metrics for interim **review**, operational **programs, measures, tasks** and **implementation**, and those are then assigned operational **metrics.**

These can be prompted at short notice. Then, the program and measures objectives or acceleration measures are contrasted with **short-term implementation-relevant** metrics, and reasonable **operational planning** is developed. These individual programs, measures and activities can be coordinated progressively for **each dimension**, and their respective influence opportunities and **interdependencies** can be checked and determined accordingly. Thus, the necessary condition is given for a successful implementation of each integration and implementation step, and the necessary "loop" is closed with its respective interdependencies (see Fig. 91 and 93).

With such a scorecard approach, individual marketing, sales and customer management areas can be **coordinated** within each other from strategy to their concrete implementation and control, and can be specifically tied in with strategy objectives, programs and measures of other relevant dimensions. In addition, necessary detailing, communication and reflection of strategy statements are **necessary**, the individual departmental levels and professional decision-makers are **integrated,** and thus the "affected parties" turn into active **"participants"** of the overall strategy and implementation.

---

48 For balanced scorecard in general, see also the basic approach of Kaplan / Norton, 1997, and Horváth and partners, 2007.

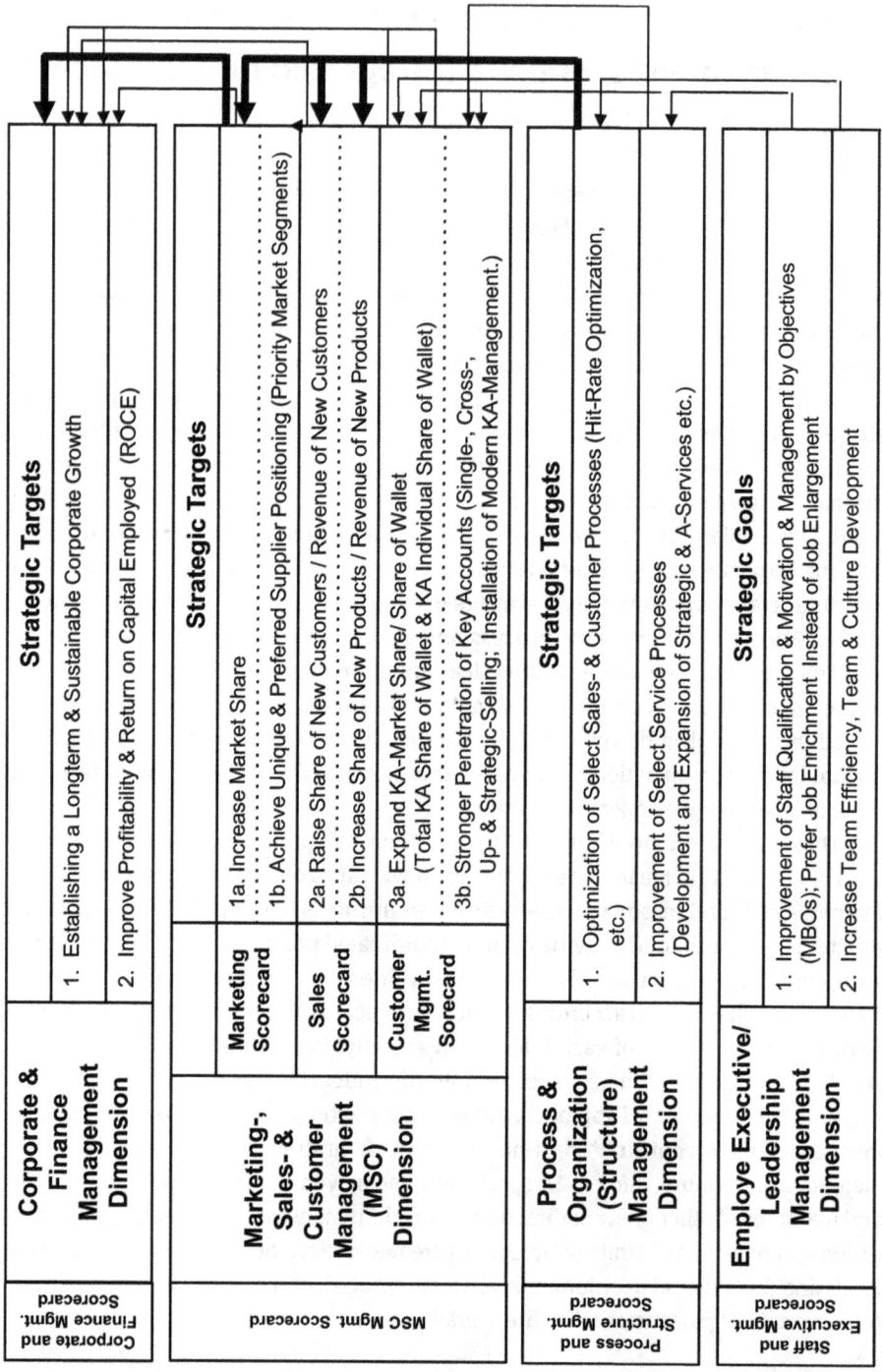

Fig. 91: Integrated marketing, sales and customer management scorecard (MSC management scorecard) overview (© Prof. Dr. R. Hofmaier).

It must be taken into account that comprehensive business or business segment and possibly corporate control (**"cockpit"** feature of the balanced scorecard) can be achieved with relatively **few key metrics** (e.g., overall a maximum of ten to 12 strategy objectives with their derived metrics). In addition, **specific** strategic goals and programs (for example, the integration and implementation of a modern KAM) can be integrated in such a scorecard and specified. The methodology of the integrated MSC scorecard is not just a perfectly appropriate and supportive strategy development and marketing tool for **major companies**, but especially also for **medium-sized companies**.

As already indicated, **"interdimensional" interdependencies** and influential or supportive effects must be taken into account, and the respective **synergies** must be considered (see Fig. 91). For example, certain strategic marketing, sales and customer management objectives can force select corporate and financial objectives, and certain process and employee goals **(endogenous targets)** can substantiate specific marketing and financial objectives **(exogenous targets)** accordingly. Thus, existing interactions can be used **cumulatively and multiplicatively** in a positive way. Especially the explicit consideration of employee and executive management objectives makes it possible to explicitly consider a hitherto rather "neglected" management area and thus to further cooperatively develop the existing "diversity" of the company's employees and managers, incorporate it as needed, and achieve necessary **job enrichment**.

Besides the integrated MSC scorecard (marketing, sales and customer management) and the initially explicit coordination with the corporate and financial management scorecard **(exogenous** scorecards), **both endogenous** scorecards must also always be integrated. Thus, the **process and structural management dimension** (Fig. 92c) applies to strategically important processes of customer acquisition, customer care, development and retention that usually **support** exogenous strategic objectives and actions, and to relevant service, delivery, logistics and possibly production processes. Select product development and innovation processes and resource transfer processes can also be considered here. The fourth and final dimension is that of **employee, human resource and executive management** goals and their measures (Fig. 92d). This often concerns important qualification, motivation, coaching and career goals and measures, but also the assignment of "right" incentives and cooperation objectives, as well as staff members for the **"right"** roles and tasks, and ultimately the development of an "active" corporate culture. Among other things, this is based on the continuous acquisition and development of employee skills, motivation and loyalty, but also necessary teamwork, team efficiency, and team and culture development can be part of the objectives and activities mentioned here.

A **specified application** of this scorecard approach can be the KAM implementation, as well as the **general implementation** of CRM, FGM, internationalization, innovation, online marketing and sales management.

Integrated MSC Scorecard focusing on Corporate and Financial Management

Strategic Targets	Strategy-Oriented Measurement Criteria	Operative Programs & Support/ Measures (Actions)	Operative Measurement Criteria
1. Establish a Longterm & Sustainable Corporate Growth	• Increase Corporate / Divisional Growth (by 15% within 3 Years)	• Top-Down Support of Releveant MSC Management Programs • Execute Specific Cost-Cutting and Synergy Programs • Differentiation of the Payment Model of Customers (Pay per use; Instead Purchase Price, etc.)	• Corporate / Divisional Growth by 5% Next Year in Respect to Operative Tasks • Corporate / Divisional Growth by 5% in the Year after Next • Corporate/ Divisional Growth by 5% again in the Following Year
2. Improve Profitability & Return on Capital Employed	• Raise Corporate / Divisional ROI by 5% within 3 Years • Increase ROCE by 10% within 3 Years	• Top-Down Support of all Releveant KAM Programs & Actions • Decrease Select Logistics Costs • Reduction of Strategic Manufacturing Lows • Improvement of Appropriate Margin & Resource Models (Margin & Transfer Resources Optimization)	• Increase Corporate / Divisional ROI by 2% Next Year • Increase Corporate-/ Divisional ROI by 2% two years from now • Increase Corporate-/ Divisional ROI by 1.5% three years from now • Increase ROCE by 3% Next Year • Increase ROCE by 3.5% two years from now • Increase ROCE by 3.5% three years from now

Fig. 92a: Integrated MSC scorecard focusing on corporate and financial management (© Prof. Dr. R. Hofmaier).

Integrated MSC Scorecard focusing on Marketing, Sales and Customer Management

Strategic Targets	Strategy-Oriented Measurement Criteria	Operative Programs & Measures (Actions)	Operative Measurement Criteria
Marketing Scorecard — 1a. Increase Market Share	• Increase Market Share in Select Market Segments over the next 3 Years by a total of 30%	• Acquisition of at least one New Market Segment per Main Region through Expanded Marketing & Product/ Service Programs • Stronger Penetration of Current Segments through Expanded Marketing & Acquisitions Programs • Improvement of Revenue Speed (Utilization of Volume Effect)	• Status of Implementation of Respective Marketing and Product/ Acquistion Plans and Processes • Increase Market Share by at least 10% per year through acquisition and Individual Process Optimization/ Key Performance Indicators
1b. Achieve Unique & Preferred Supplier Positioning	• Achieve Specific USP/ Preferred Supplier Positioning within the Next 3 Years	• Implementation of Newly Developed KAM & FGM Programs & Media and annual KA-Feedback Analysis	• Specific USP/ Preferred Supplier Positioning and respective KA Evaluation/ Verification (p.a.)
Sales Scorecard — 2a. Increase Share of New Customers/ Revenue of New Customers	• Increase the Share of New Customers by 5% over the next 3 years	• Implementing Measures of additional Acquisition & Media Actions • Hit-Rate Optimization	• Increase Sales of New Products by 3.5% per year • Improvement of Specific Hit-Rate Figures
2b. Increase Share/ Revenue of New Products	• Increase the share of New Products by 10% per year within next 3 years	• Revision of New Product Development & Marketing Process • Hit-Rate Optimization by Key Figures & Benachmarks	• Incrase Relevant New Product Share by 3.5% per year • Improvement by Specific Related Hit-Rate Figures
Customer Mgmt. Scorecard — 3a. Expansion of KA (Market) Share/ Share of Wallet (Improve Total KA Share of Wallet & KA Individual Share of Wallet)	• Expansion of Specific KA Market Shares to 20% over the next 3 years	• Improvement of KA Processes & Staff Qualifications/ Motivation • Implement targeted approaches of Decision-Makers and Commitments • Expansion of FGM Measures	• Increase of Specific KA Market Share by at least 7.5% per year • Implementation of respective expanded KA-CRM, Retention & FGM Measures with relevant Key Figures • Implementation of KAM-Assessments
3b. Stronger Penetration of KAs (by Specific Single-, Cross-, Up- and Strategic Selling & Installation of Modern KAM)	• Achieve Cross- & Up-Selling Customer Share of 15% over the next 3 years	• Improvement of KA Value Proposition • Implementing Optimized Cross- & Up-Selling Actions/ Measures • Expansion of KA Ressources, Supports & Tools	• Measurement of Improved KA Proposition • Measurement of specific Cross- & Up-Selling Key Figures (by at least 5% Improvement per year) • Naming of additional KA Managers per year

Fig. 92b: Integrated MSC scorecard focusing on marketing, sales and customer management (© Prof. Dr. R. Hofmaier).

Integrated MSC Scorecard focusing on Process and Structure Management

Strategic Targets	Strategy-Oriented Measurement Criteria	Operative Programs & Measures (Actions)	Operative Measurement Criteria
1. Optimization of Select Sales & Customer Processes (Hit-Rate Optimization)	• Achieve Improved (KA) Hit-Rate and Launch Integrated CRM-Programs & Actions • Achieve Higher Loyalty Score (by Prioritized Customers > 75% within 3 Years)	• Implement necessary CRM Tools & Customer Data Base (DB) Mgmt. (Joint DB) • Implement an Effective Sales Process & Hit-Rate Analysis/ Programs within KA Sales • Surveying, Analysing, Interpreting and Improving Relevant Benachmarks	• Improve Corresponding Hit-Rates by 10 % per year • Intensive Application & Utilization of Appropriate CRM-Tools • Introduce (at least) 3 Additional Incentive Programs (for Sales Processes) • Yearly Benchmark Activities & Consequences
2. Improvement of Selected Services Processes (e.g. Establish & Expand Strategic A-Services)	• Cut in half the return rate (within 3 Years) • Reduce Response Times by 50 % (Within 3 Years)	• Implement Relevant Complainment Processes & Customer Feedback Mgmt. • Develop Improvement Suggestions & Measures • Improve Resource Transfer Processes	• Decrease Complaint rates by at least 15% per year • Reduce Reaction Times by at least 15% per year • Improve Resource Implementation Times by at least 10% per year

Fig. 92c: Integrated MSC scorecard focusing on process and structure management (© Prof. Dr. R. Hofmaier).

Integrated MSC Scorecard focusing on Employee and Executive / Leadership Management			
Strategic Targets	**Strategy-Oriented Measurement Criteria**	**Operative Programs & Measures (Actions)**	**Operative Measurement Criteria**
1. Improve (MSC-) Staff / Employee & Executive Qualification & Motivation & Management by Objectives (MBOs); Prefer Job Enrichment Instead of Job Enlargement	• Deduction of Specific Benchmark Related Qualification Figures per Staff Member / Employee • Implement Select Job Enrichment Programs & Actions/Measures (for at least 20% of Relevant Tasks) • Remodel the MBO-System	• Select and Implement Relevant Qualification Programs • Explore & Detail Suitable (Fullfilling) Job Enrichment Programs & Actions • Implement these Programs and Actions effectively by Professionals • Implement an Improved Up-MBO System	• Prooving of Meeting / Reaching the Qualification Goals / Scores (through Programs, Contents, Realizations per Staff) • Verify the Accomplishment of the Relevant Motivations-, Satisfying- & Identifying Scores • Verify the Accomplishment of the Determined MBO Level
2. Increase Team Efficiency, Team- & Culture Development	• Implement Team Development Programs and Better Team Development & Team Efficiency Score (by 3 Years) • Improving Team Cohesion (by 3 Years) • Develop Corresponding Corporate Culture & Leadership	• Implement Individual Coaching & Incentive Programs with Extended MBOs for Target Groups • Implement Feedback-Coaching & Select Team Development Programs • Implement Specific Cultural & Leadership Development Programs (With Detailed Goals & Scores)	• Measurement & Verification of Improved Team Efficieny (by Qual. & Quant. Key Figures) • Implementation of relevant Assessments • Measure Cultural & Leadership-Specific Scores & Implement Consequences

Fig. 92d: Integrated MSC scorecard focusing on employee and executive management
(© Prof. Dr. R. Hofmaier).

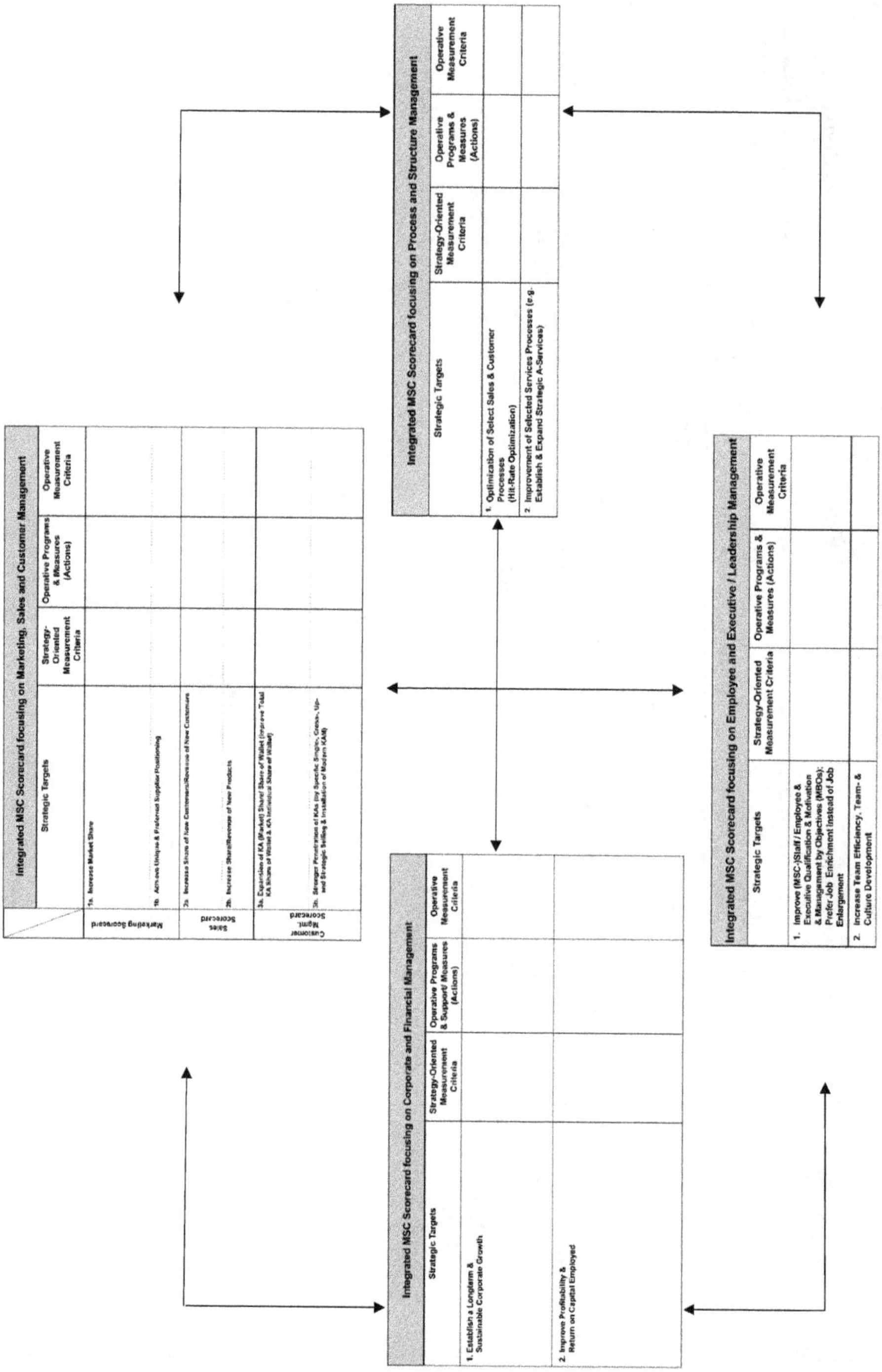

Fig. 93: Integrated marketing, sales and customer management Scorecard (MSC Scorecard) and their interdependencies (© Prof. Dr. R. Hofmaier).

References

Hofmaier, R. (2011/2013) Innovative Methoden und Instrumente des Kundenbeziehungs-, Bindungs- und Focus Management (FGM) in Industriegüter- und Dienstleistungsmärkten – Empirische Studie, München

Hofmaier R. / Leutbecher, K. (1996) Investitionsgüter zeitgemäß vermarkten, in: Harvard Business Manager, Heft 3, S.106–110

Horváth und Partner (2007) Balanced Scorecard umsetzen, 4. Aufl., Stuttgart

Kaplan, R. S. / Norton, D. P. (1997) Balanced Scorecard, Stuttgart

Steward, D. W. / Shamdasani, P. N. / Rook, D. W. (2007) Focus Groups: Theory and Practice, 2. Aufl., London

Appendix I: **Checklist for the Collaboration of Marketing, Sales and Customer Management**

- Checklist - **How Intensive Is the Cooperation Between** **Marketing, Sales & Customer Mgmt.? - 1 -**	Not Right 5	Mostly Not Right 4	More or Less 3	Mostly Right 2	Very Right 1
(1a) The **Priorities** of Total Marketing, Sales & Customer Mgmt. (MSC) Targets will be Mostly Defined by **Marketing**.					
(1b) The **Priorities** of Total Marketing, Sales & Customer Mgmt. (MSC) Targets will be Mostly Defined by **Sales**.					
(1c) The **Priorities** of Total Marketing, Sales & Customer Mgmt. (MSC) Targets will be Mostly Defined by **Customer Management (Especially KAM)**.					
(2a) The **Most Decision Competences** of Overall M, S & C will be Focused by **Marketing**.					
(2b) The **Most Decision Competences** of Overall M, S & C will be Focused by **Sales**.					
(2c) The **Most Decision Competences** of Overall M, S & C will be Focused by **Customer Management (Especially KAM)**.					
(3a) The **MSC- Targets, Proceedings & Structures** will be Defined by **Marketing**.					
(3b) The **MSC- Targets, Proceedings & Structures** will be Defined by **Sales**.					
(3c) The **MSC- Targets, Proceedings & Structures** will be Defined by **Customer Management (Especially KAM)**.					
(4a) The Most **Personel Human Ressources** (Professionals) will Belong to the **Marketing Department(s)**.					
(4b) The Most **Personel Human Ressources** (Professionals) will Belong to the **Sales**.					

(© Prof. Dr. R. Hofmaier)

- Checklist - **How Intensive Is the Cooperation Between** **Marketing, Sales & Customer Mgmt.? - 2 -**	Not Right 5	Mostly Not Right 4	More or Less 3	Mostly Right 2	Very Right 1
(4c) The Most **Personel Human Ressources** (Professionals) will Belong to the **Customer Management (Especially KAM)**.					
(5a) Most Qualification & Coaching Programs & Actions will be **executed in Marketing(Departments)**.					
(5b) Most Qualification & Coaching Programs & Actions will be executed in Sales.					
(5c) Most Qualification & Coaching Programs & Actions will be executed in C**ustomer Management (Especially KAM)**.					
(6a) The Broadest Range of **"Incentives"** will be offered from **Marketing**.					
(6b) The Broadest Range of **"Incentives"** will be offered from **Sales**.					
(6a) The Broadest Range of **"Incentives"** will be offered from **Customer Management (Especially KAM)**.					
(7a) At Minimum 1 **Board Member** belongs to **Marketing** (is a Markets Driven CEO or CMO).					
(7b) At Minimum 1 **Board Member** belongs to **Sales** (is a Markets Driven CEO or CSO).					
(7c) At Minimum 1 **Board Member** belongs to **Customer Management (Especially KAM)** (is a Markets Driven CEO or KAMO).					
(8a) **Marketing is Informing** and **Communicating** Intensively With **Sales**.					
(8b) **Marketing is Informing** and **Communicating** Intensively With **Customer Management (Especially KAM)**.					
(8c) **Sales is Informing** and **Communicating** Intensively With **Marketing**.					

(© Prof. Dr. R. Hofmaier)

- Checklist -
How Intensive Is the Cooperation Between
Marketing, Sales & Customer Mgmt.? - 3 -

	1	2	3	4	5
(8d) **Sales is Informing** and **Communicating** Intensively With **Customer Management (Especially KAM).**					
(8e) **Customer Management (Especially KAM) is Informing** and **Communicating** Intensively With **Marketing.**					
(8f) **Customer Management (Especially KAM) is Informing** and **Communicating** Intensively With **Sales.**					
(9a) **MSC-Analysis** are **Intensively** Coordinated and Adjusted Between **Marketing and Sales.**					
(9b) **MSC-Analysis** are **Intensively** Coordinated and Adjusted Between **Marketing and Customer Management (Especially KAM).**					
(9c) **MSC-Analysis** are **Intensively** Coordinated and Adjusted Between **Sales and Customer Management (Especially KAM).**.					
(10a) **MSC-Programs, Actions and Measures** are **Intensively** Coordinated and Adquired **between Marketing & Sales.**					
(10b) **MSC-Programs, Actions and Measures** are **Intensively** Coordinated and Adjusted **between Marketing & Customer Management (Especially KAM).**					
(10c)) **MSC-Programs, Actions and Measures** are **Intensively** Coordinated and Adjusted **between Sales & Customer Management (Especially KAM).**					
(11a) **MSC-Feedbacks** and **Balanced Scorecards** are Intensively **Coorinated and Adjusted** between **Marketing & Sales.**					
(11b) **MSC-Feedbacks** and **Balanced Scorecards** are Intensively **Coorinated and Adjusted** between **Marketing & Customer Management (Especially KAM).**					
(11c) **MSC-Feedbacks** and **Balanced Scorecards** are Intensively **Coorinated and Adjusted** between **Sales & Customer Management (Especially KAM).**					
(12a) **Marketing** is Supporting **Sales by Important Selected Sales Tasks & Actions** (so f.e. Product Flyers, Customer Acquisition, Special Events/Fairs).					

(© Prof. Dr. R. Hofmaier)

- Checklist -
How Intensive Is the Cooperation Between
Marketing, Sales & Customer Mgmt.? - 4 -

	Not Right	Mostly Not Right	More or Less	Mostly Right	Very Right
	5	4	3	2	1
(12b) **Marketing** is Supporting **Customer Management (Especially KAM) by Important Selected Customer Mgmt. Tasks & Actions** (f.e. Customer Analysis, Customer Information Mgmt., Product Clinics).					
(12c) **Sales** is Supporting **Marketing by Important Selected Marketing Tasks & Actions** (f.e. Profile Product, Pricing and Communications Mgmt.).					
(12d) **Sales** is Supporting **Customer Management (Especially KAM).by Important Selected Customer Mgmt. Tasks & Actions** (Customer Presentations Workshops, Handling Special Events, Relationship & Retention Programs)					
(12e) **Customer Management (Especially KAM) is** Supporting **Marketing by Important Selected Marketing Tasks & Actions** (f.e. KA Segment & Potential Analysis, Value Chain Analysis, Key Account Figures & Planings).					
(12f) **Customer Management (Especially KAM) is** Supporting **Sales by Important Selected Sales Tasks & Actions** (f.e. Market & Customer Segment Figures)					
(13) **Marketing, Sales & Customer Mgmt. Figures** can be **Used** from all **Efficiently** in Cause of a Common Used, Actualized & Integrated **Data Base (DB).**					
(14) The Implemented (or Planed) **CRM-Tool** is Efficiently Used Commonly by Marketing, Sales and Cust. Mgmt. and is **Covering** Efficiently Most Relevant **MSC Programs.**					
(15) **Marketing, Sales & Customer Mgmt.** is Working Together on the Basis of an **Integrated** MSC-Plan & Road Map.					
(16) **Marketing, Sales & Customer Mgmt.** is Working Together on the Basis of an **Integrated Approach/Plan.**					
(17)There Exists a a Corporate Wide **Career and Development Plan (between Marketing, Sales & Customer Mgmt).**					

(© Prof. Dr. R. Hofmaier)

Appendix II: **Example of a KAM Assessment Questionnaire**

Question Category I

1.
a) Do you **manage** a Business KA
(global/national) as a
KA executive?

Yes ☐   No ☐

or

b) are You involved in a **KA team?**

Yes ☐   No ☐

Comments (Role, etc.): ....

---

2. On average, how much time in work
days per month do you spend
on specific KAM Tasks?

more than 15 work days	11–15 work days	6–10 work days	1–5 work days	less than 1 work day

Comments: ....

---

3. Do you use specific methods **(KAM methods)**
for your **KA support?**

Yes ☐   No ☐

Comments: ....

4. So far, were you able to achieve specific **success with customers due to your KAM approach?**

Very Often	Often	Sometimes	Rarely	Never
←				→

Comments: ....

Question Category II

5. To what extent have you specifically implemented the **business opportunity analysis method** within your KAM?

Very Often	Often	Sometimes	Rarely	Never
←				→

Comments: ....

---

6. How many of the **opportunities** you've identified have you been able to **transfer** into a **sales project?**

Very Often	Often	Sometimes	Rarely	Never
←				→

Comments: ....

---

7. Have you been able to analyse **cross-, up-, and/or business potential** with your KAs?

Very Often	Often	Sometimes	Rarely	Never
←				→

Comments: ....

8. Where you able to **offer and provide** (new/modified **customer solutions** within your KA creating „**new**" customer demands?

Very Often	Often	Sometimes	Rarely	Never

Comments: ....

9. Did you encounter specific **issues** in connection with the **cross-, up-, strategie selling-analysis**?

Very Often	Often	Sometimes	Rarely	Never

If so, which ones? ....

10. Did you get **sufficient customer information** through your **CRM-system**?

Very Often	Often	Sometimes	Rarely	Never

If not, why not? ....

11. Have you prepared a mid- to long-term **customer (development) plan** for your KAs?

Very Often	Often	Sometimes	Rarely	Never

Comments: ....

12.

a) Have you conducted a
Customer classification

Very Often	Often	Sometimes	Rarely	Never
←				→

and

b) did you derive relevant
**Customer- or KA-specific
Measures from that?**

Very Often	Often	Sometimes	Rarely	Never
←				→

Comments: ....

13. Have you been able to
improve your corporate **KA
hit-rate?**

Very Often	Often	Sometimes	Rarely	Never
←				→

Comments: ....

14. Have you been able to design
**a value proposition for your
KA(s)?**

Very Often	Often	Sometimes	Rarely	Never
←				→

Comments: ....

15. Have you performed a
**value chain analysis for your
KA(s)?**

Very Often	Often	Sometimes	Rarely	Never
←				→

Comments: ....

16. Do you use detailed
decision maker profiles for
your KA support?

Very Often	Often	Sometimes	Rarely	Never
←				→

a) What **kind** of decision-
maker **profiles**?

Comments: ....

b) How many and what **kind of decision-makers**?

Comments: ....

---

17. Do you know your exact
supplier position for your KA(s)
in comparison to your
competitors?

Not at all	Barely	Partly	Mostly	Absolutely
←				→

Comments: ....

---

18. Have you been able to
exactly determine an **improvement**
of your **business relationship
mgmt.** over the past few years?

Very Often	Often	Sometimes	Rarely	Not Yet
←				→

Comments: ....

---

19. Have you been able to
exactly determine an **improvement**
of your **interpersonal relationship
mgmt.** over the past few years?

Very Often	Often	Sometimes	Rarely	Not Yet
←				→

Comments: ....

---

20. Have you been able to **implement** specific **customer retention measures** (what kind?) **within yoiur KAs and their decision-makers**?

Very Often	Often	Sometimes	Rarely	Not Yet

Comments: ....

---

21. When talking to your customers, would you **describe yourself** more as

a) **product-offering**

Very Often	Often	Sometimes	Rarely	Not Yet

b) or **problem-identifying**

Very Often	Often	Sometimes	Rarely	Not Yet

c) or **problem-solving**?

Very Often	Often	Sometimes	Rarely	Not Yet

Comments: ....

---

22. How often have you been able to increase your **single-selling value with** your KAs?

Never	Rarely	From Time to Time	Sometimes	Often

Comments: ....

---

23. How often have you been able to increase your **cross-selling value with** your KAs?

Never	Rarely	From time to time	Sometimes	Often

Comments: ....

---

24. Have you been able to
up-selling with your KA?

Never	Rarely	From Time to Time	Sometimes	Often

Comments: ....

---

25. Have you been able to do
**a strategic selling project
with** your KA(s)?

Never	Rarely	From Time to Time	Sometimes	Often

Comments: ....

---

26. Have you had a chance to
perform effectiv **solution selling
with** your KA(s)?

Never	Rarely	From Time to Time	Sometimes	Often

Comments: ....

---

27. Have you been
**utilizing your specific
implementation plan** for your KAM
process?

Never	Rarely	From Time to Time	Sometimes	Often

Comments: ....

28. Have you used the **balanced scorecard method for** your **KA** support so far?

Never	Rarely	From Time to Time	Sometimes	Often

Comments: ....

29. Have **innovative contributions** (projects, solution, etc.) supported your **KA in its product development** thanks to you or your KAM **approach**?

Never	Rarely	From Time to Time	Sometimes	Often

Comments: ....

30. Have you been able to or can your further **develop** a common **business ground with your KA(s) through your KAM**?

Never	Rarely	From Time to Time	Sometimes	Often

Comments: ....

Question Category III

31.

a) Have you been able to effectively combine your **KA plan & proceedings** with the **business plan** (roadmap) of your company division?

Never	Rarely	From Time to Time	Sometimes	Often

Comments: ....

b) and have you been **able** to **integratively coordinate** and **implement** it with **marketing and sales**?

Never	Rarely	From Time to Time	Sometimes	Often

Comments: ....

---

32. Can you use qualitive measurement **criteria for your** KA support and use them to **measure your KA contribution**?

Never	Rarely	From Time to Time	Sometimes	Often

If yes, which ones? ....

33.
a) Has **efficient** networking been possible within your KA(s)?

Never	Rarely	From Time to Time	Sometimes	Often

Comments: ....

b) Did your KA team work integraively and **efficiently**?

Never	Rarely	From Time to Time	Sometimes	Often

Comments: ....

Question Category IV

34. Did you get **recognition** and were you offered incentives for your **successful KAM** (what type/ frequency)?

Type \ Frequency	1 No, nothing	2	3	4	5

Comments: ....

31. Please list what you consider the **10 most important criteria and measures to specifically guide and measure the success** of your **KAM.** (Please use a weighting system of 1 to 5, 5 = highest weighting)

1	
2	
3	
4	
5	
6	
7	
8	
9	
10	

Comments: ....

36. Which **advanced structural, qualification, coaching** and other **improvement measures are important to you?** (Please list and weight it.)

Weight (Score)	Improvements (Programs & Actions)			
1				
2				
3				
4				
5				
6				
7				
8				
9				
10				

Comments: ....

Bibliography

Ansoff, J. (1966) Management-Strategien, München

Backhaus, K./Voeth, M. (2010) Industriegütermarketing, 9. Aufl., München

Bacon, T.R. (1999) Selling to Major Accounts: Tools, Techniques, and Practical Solutions for the Sales Management, New York

Barbour, R. (2007) Doing Focus Groups, London

Belz, C./Müller, M./Zupancik, D. (2008) Spitzenleistungen im Key Account Management, 2. Aufl., München

Biesel, H. (2007) Key Account Management erfolgreich planen und umsetzen, 2. Aufl., Wiesbaden

Bruhn, M. (2009) Relationship Marketing – Das Management von Kundenbeziehungen, 2. Aufl., München

Fiedler, R. (2010) Organisation kompakt, 2. Aufl., München

Gassmann, O./Sutter, P. (2011) Praxiswissen Innovationsmanagement, 2. Aufl., München

Greiner, O.: Das große Kräftemessen – Innovationsmanagement im Griff, in: The Performance Architect 2 (2008)

Grimm, U./Sommerlatte, T. (2003) Kreativität besser managen, in: Harvard Business Manager, Heft 2, S. 49–55

Haase, K. (2006) Koordination von Marketing und Vertrieb, Wiesbaden

Hackman, J.R., Oldham, G.R. (1976) Motivation through the design of work: Test of a theory. Organizational Behavior and Human Performance, 16, 250–279

Hackman, J.R., Oldham, G.R. (1980) Work redesign. Reading, MA: Addison-Wesley Hall

Edward T., The Dance of Life. The Other Dimension of Time, 2nd ed., Garden City, NY: Anchor Press/Doubleday

Herrmann, A./Huber, F. (2009) Produktmanagement: Grundlagen – Methoden – Beispiele, 2. Aufl., Wiesbaden

Herzberg, F.I., One more time: How do you motivate employees? Harvard Business Review, Sep/Oct87, Vol. 65, Issue 5

Hippner, H. (2006) Grundlagen des CRM: Konzepte und Gestaltung, 2. Aufl., Wiesbaden

Hofbauer, G./Hellwig, C. (2012) Professionelles Vetriebsmanagement – Der prozessorientierte Ansatz aus Anbieter- und Beschaffersicht, 3. Aufl., Erlangen

Hofbauer, G./Sangl,A. (2011) Professionelles Produktmanagement – Der prozessorientierte Ansatz, Rahmenbedingungen, Strategien, 2. Aufl., Erlangen

Hofmaier, R. (2014/2015): Empirical Studies of Marketing, Sales and Customer Management Integration in B2B Companies, Munich

Hofmaier, R. (2013): Product, Product Development and Innovation Management, Lecture Manuscript Munich

Hofmaier, R. (2013) Produkt-, Produktentwicklungs- und Innovationsmanagement, Vortragsmanuskript, München

Hofmaier, R. (2011/2014): Efficient Modelling and Application of Professional Key Account Management (B2B) – Empirical Studies, Munich

Hofmaier, R. (2011/2013) Innovative Methoden und Instrumente des Kundenbeziehungs-, Bindungs- und Focus Management (FGM) in Industriegüter- und Dienstleistungsmärkten – Empirische Studie, München

Hofmaier, R. (2011/2013) New Approaches, Methods and Implementation Options for Sales-Hit-Rate Optimization (B2B) – Emprical Studies, Munich

Hofmaier, R. (2011/2013) Vertriebliche „Hit Rate"-Optimierung im B2B Sales: Neue Ansätze, Methoden und Umsetzungsmöglichkeiten – Empirische Studie, München

Hofmaier, R. (2010/2013) Die Optimierung der Zusammenarbeit von Marketing und Vertrieb in Mittelstands- und Großunternehmen – Empirische Studien, München

Hofmaier, R. (2010/2013) Empirische Studien zur Anwendung des Key Account Management, ITM-Institut, München

Hofmaier, R. (2012) Grundlagen des Key Account Management, in: Hofbauer, G./Hellwig, C. Professionelles Vertriebsmanagement, 3. Aufl., Erlangen, S. 103–114

Hofmaier, R. (2012) Möglichkeiten und Chancen einer konzeptionellen Fundierung und Weiterentwicklung des Key Account Management (B2B), in: FORUM Betriebswirtschaft München, Heft 01, S. 6–13

Hofmaier, R./Bauer, H. (2007/2012) Status Quo and Opportunity Analysis of Optimized Selection and Implementation of CRM-Tools – A Research Study, Munich

Hofmaier, R./Bauer, H. (2007/2012) Stand und Auswahlmöglichkeiten bezüglich der Implementierung von leistungsfähigen CRM-Tools – Empirische Studien, München

Hofmaier, R. (2008) Verkaufen in drei Dimensionen, in: Sales Business, Heft 7/8

Hofmaier, R. (1999) Systematische Marktsegmentierung und Hit Rate-Optimierung (im Business-to-Business-Marketing), in Pepels, W. (Hrsg.) Business to business Marketing, Neuwied, S. 130–139

Hofmaier, R./Leutbecher, K. (1996) Investitionsgüter zeitgemäß vermarkten, in: Harvard Business Manager, Heft III, S. 106–110

Hofmaier, R. (Hrsg.) (1995) Erfolgsstrategien in der Investitionsgüterindustrie, 2. Aufl., Landsberg a. Lech

Hofmaier, R. (Hrsg.) (1993) Investitionsgüter- und High-Tech-Marketing (ITM), 2. Aufl., Landsberg a. Lech

Homburg, C. (2012) Marketingmanagement – Strategie, Instrumente, Umsetzung, Unternehmensführung, 4. Aufl., Wiesbaden

Homburg, Ch./Schäfer, H./Schneider, J. (2012) Sales Excellence – Vertriebsmanagement mit System, 7. Aufl., Wiesbaden

Homburg, C./Bruhn, M. (2005) Handbuch Kundenbindungsmanagement, 5. Aufl., Wiesbaden

Homburg, Ch./Bruhn, M., Kundenbindungsmanagement – Eine Einführung in die theoretischen und praktischen Problemstellungen, in: Bruhn, M./Homburg,C. (Hrsg.) (1998) Handbuch Kundenbindungsmanagement, Wiesbaden

Horváth und Partner (2007) Balanced Scorecard umsetzen, 4.Aufl., Stuttgart

Johnson, M.W./Christensen, C.M./Kagermann, H. (2008) Reinventing Your Business Model, Harvard Business Review, Vol. 6, pp. 51–59

Kaplan, R.S., Norton D.P. (1997) Balanced Scorecard, Stuttgart

Kleinaltenkamp, M./Plinke, W./Geiger, I. (2013) Auftrags- und Projektmanagement – Mastering Business Markets, 2. Aufl., Wiesbaden

Kleinaltenkamp, M./Plinke, W./Jacob, F./Söllner A. (2006) Markt- und Produktmanagement – Die Instrumente des Business-to-Business-Marketing, 2. Aufl., Wiesbaden

Kleinaltenkamp, M./Plinke, W. (2000) Technischer Vertrieb: Grundlagen des Business-to-Business Marketing, 2. Aufl., Berlin

Kostojohn, S./Paulen, B./Johnson, M. (2011) CRM Fundamentals, New York

Kotler, P./Keller, K.L./Bliemel F. (2007) Marketing Management – Strategien für wertschaffendes Handeln, 12. Aufl., München

Kotler,P./Cox, K.K. (1988) Marketing Management and Strategy, 4. Aufl., London

Kreutzer, R.T. (2012) Praxisorientiertes Online-Marketing: Konzepte – Instrumente – Checklisten, Wiesbaden

Kumar, V./Reinartz W. (2012) Customer Relationship Management: Concept, Strategy and Tools, 2. Aufl., Berlin

Lammenett, E. (2012) Praxiswissen Online-Marketing: Affiliate- und E-Mail-Marketing, Suchmas-
chinenmarketing, Online-Werbung, Social Media, Online-PR, 3. Aufl., Wiesbaden

Little, A.D./European Business School (2001), Innovation Scorecard, online unter URL: www.
innovation-scorecard.de (Stand: 26.06.2013)

Meffert, H./Burmann, Ch./Kirchgeorg, M. (2012) Marketing – Grundlagen marktorientierter Unternehmensführung, Wiesbaden

Parson, Talcott, Essays in sociological theory: pure and applied, The Free Press, Glencoe, IL, 1949.
p. 8

Pepels, W. (2006) Produktmanagement: Produktinnovation, Markenpolitik, Programmplanung,
Prozessorganisation, 5. Aufl., München

Pepels, W. (2004) Marketing: Lehr- und Handbuch, 4. Aufl., München

Porter, M. (1985) Competitive Advantage, New York

Porter, M. (1984) Wettbewerbsstrategie, 2. Aufl., Frankfurt

Reichheld, K. (1997) Lernen Sie von abtrünnigen Kunden, was Sie falsch machen, in: Harvard
Business Manager, Heft 2, S.57–68

Sidow, H.D. (2002) Key-Account-Management – Wettbewerbsvorteile durch kundenbezogene
Strategien, 7. Aufl., München

Sieck, M. (2011) Der strategische (Key) Account Plan, 2. Aufl., Norderstedt

Simon, H. (2000) Power Pricing, Frankfurt a. Main

Sommerlatte, T./Grimm, U. (2003) Kreativität besser managen, in: Harvard Business Manager, Heft
2, S. 49–55

Steward, D. W./Shamdasani, P. N./Rook, D. W. (2007) Focus Groups: Theory and Practice, 2. Aufl.,
London

v. Bischopink, Y./Ceyp, M. (2009) Suchmaschinen-Marketing: Konzepte, Umsetzung und Controlling
für SEO und SEM, 2. Aufl., Berlin

Von Hippel, E./Thonke, St./Sonnack, M.: Creating Breakthroughs at 3M, in: Harvard Business
Review on Innovation 9 (1999)

Weber, M., The methodology of the social sciences, The Free Press, New York, 1949. p. 76

Winkelmann, P. (2012) Integriertes und fachgestütztes CRM – Vortragsmanuskript

Winkelmann, P. (2010) Marketing und Vertrieb – Fundamente für die marktorientierte Unternehmensführung, 7. Aufl., München

Winkelmann, P. (2008), Vertriebskonzeption und Vertriebssteuerung, 4. Aufl., München

List of Figures

Index